DANIEL STONE is a member of the Department of History at the University of Winnipeg.

WILLIAM ROSE (1885-1968) learned the Polish language and became an enthusiast of Polish culture under unusual circumstances; at the outbreak of the First World War the young scholar from Minnedosa, Manitoba, found himself trapped in Europe behind enemy lines. He was restricted to the village of Ligotka in Silesia. In the last days of the war he made a dramatic escape to Paris and attended the Paris Peace Conference as a representative of nationalist groups in Poland. After the war he returned to Poland to help organize the YMCA movement and was very active in other social work. He took his doctorate in 1926 at Cracow University.

By 1928, when he returned to North America to teach, he was a well-known specialist on Poland. He began teaching at Dartmouth College, NH, and in 1935 was invited to the University of London's School of Slavonic Studies, which he headed from 1939 to 1950. On his retirement he returned to Canada, helped to establish the Department of Slavonic Studies at the University of British Columbia, and was elected the first honorary president of the Canadian Association of Slavists in 1955.

Professor Rose's recollections of those parts of his varied and interesting career which deal with Central Europe and Slavonic Studies are gathered together in this book. The memoirs are a unique record - of Central European life in the war and post-war years and of the development of Slavonic Studies in Britain and North America.

Portrait University of Winnipeg Library, photographed by Lorne Coulson

Edited by Daniel Stone

The Polish Memoirs of William John Rose

UNIVERSITY OF TORONTO PRESS
TORONTO AND BUFFALO

© University of Toronto Press 1975
Toronto and Buffalo
Printed in Canada
Reprinted in 2018
Library of Congress Cataloging in Publication Data

Rose, William John, 1885-1968.
The Polish memoirs of William John Rose.

Includes bibliographical references.
1. Rose, William John, 1885-1968. 2. Poland –
History – 20th century. I. Title.
DK418.95.R65A36 1975 943.8'007'2024 [B]74-79986
ISBN 0-8020-5306-8
ISBN 978-1-4875-8545-7 (paper)

Preface

Old cliches are occasionally true. William John Rose was a gentleman and a scholar. It is a pleasure, therefore, to bring his memoirs to public attention, particularly since Rose himself had failed to find a publisher for them despite acknowledgments of their value. He came to the conclusion that they were unpublishable as written and finally expressed the hope that sometime in the future some sympathetic editor would make the cuts that needed to be made but that he could not bear to make himself.

This editor has taken it upon himself to prepare an edition strictly limited to Polish affairs, since Rose's contributions to scholarship and human welfare lie principally in this area. Several unrelated chapters of the original memoir, 'Thirty Wander Years, 1905-1935,' have been omitted despite their considerable charm. Some material has been added, however, from another memoir fragment dealing with the School of Slavonic Studies in London. In preparing the final text, I have remained as faithful as possible to the original. Some minor polishing has been done, first names and other identifying details have been added on occasion, and an attempt has been made to regularize orthography by striking an uneasy balance among competing claimants: Rose's own predilections, national forms, and common English usage. The full text of 'Thirty Wander Years' and 'School of Slavonic Studies in London' can be found in the University of Winnipeg library. Copies of the former are also available in the YMCA Historical Library in New York and the library of the University of British Columbia, which holds most of Rose's papers.

I should like to thank Dr Arthur Rose for supplying the original texts used in preparing this edition and for his interest in the project and Professor Peter

Brock for his encouragement, assistance, and criticism. Mrs Rosemary Shipton, the manuscript editor, has also saved me from embarrassing errors. Those which remain are my responsibility, of course. The number of persons who expressed interest in the publication of the memoirs and submitted patiently to my questioning is a testament to Rose's continuing reputation; I regret that they are too numerous to mention. The University of Winnipeg assisted greatly in solving some legal issues connected with copyright as well as granting financial aid.

Preparation and publication of this volume have been made possible by generous financial support. The University of Winnipeg Research Fund assisted my research and manuscript preparation. The book is being published with the help of grants from the Social Science Research Council, using funds provided by the Canada Council, and from the University of Toronto Press Publications Fund.

Contents

PREFACE / v

INTRODUCTION / ix

1
Prologue / 3

2
Wartime in Silesia 1914-18 / 25

3
Amateur at Peace-making / 58

4
Liberated Poland 1 / 107

5
Liberated Poland 2 / 135

6
Liberated Poland 3 / 168

7
Silesian Research / 197

8
Epilogue: London & the Return Home / 217

INDEX / 233

Introduction

No one who met William John Rose in Winnipeg or Oxford before World War I would have suspected that he would become a leading authority on Poland, author of five books and numerous shorter pieces, director of the University of London's School of Slavonic Studies, and an influential pioneer of Slavic Studies in Canada.[1] Paradoxical as this may seem today, Slavic Europe was more exotic to Westerners at that time than China – where Rose expected to do missionary work after finishing his studies. When questioned before the House of Commons in 1919, David Lloyd George, the British prime minister, could not identify Teschen, an important town in Central Europe, and twenty years later Neville Chamberlain, another prime minister, publicly doubted that anyone was familiar with that area of the world. Canada, far more than Britain herself, lived in a state of 'splendid isolation,' far from European developments, let alone the East European literary and political scene.[2]

The influx of millions of Slavic immigrants at the end of the nineteenth century to the New World did nothing to stimulate awareness of the home countries. The newcomers appeared merely the 'wretched refuse of [Europe's] teeming shores,' poor, often illiterate, and generally unused to urban life. They took the worst-paying and hardest jobs, living in ugly slums in cities ill-prepared for rapid expansion. Their foreign looks and alien customs made the inevitable drunks or

---

1 See Victor Turek, 'A Bibliography of the Writings of William J. Rose,' *Canadian Slavonic Papers*, IV, 1959, 1-30.
2 V.J. Kaye, 'The Ten Years Leading to the Formation of the CAS,' *Canadian Slavonic Papers*, II, 1957, 3

misfits painfully visible. In Canada, many older inhabitants reacted in a hostile manner to these immigrants from Southern and Eastern Europe. Some proclaimed them genetically inferior and feared for the purity of the heretofore dominant 'Anglo-Saxon race.' Others merely objected to foreignisms which might disrupt prevailing political and social mores.

Thousands of Slavs came to Winnipeg, Manitoba, the scene of Ralph Connor's popular novel, *The Foreigner*, which was published in 1909. The author portrayed Slavic immigrants as essentially good, but ignorant and savage, living amidst debauchery and filth. Personal vengeance dominated their moral code instead of ethical principles. According to Connor, Canada's task was 'to grip these peoples to us with living hooks of justice and charity till all lines of national cleavage disappear [and] the blood strains of great races ... mingle in the blood of a race greater than the greatest of them all.'[3]

Similarly, Winnipeg journalist A.R. Ford admitted that in the popular imagination 'Poles and police courts seem to be invariably connected ... and it is difficult for us to think of this nationality other than in that vague class of undesirable citizens.'[4] Ford wished to create a more positive image and hastened to remind his readers of distinguished artists and scientists like Fryderyk Chopin, Henryk Sienkiewicz, Nicholas Copernicus, and Maria Skłodowska-Curie.

Despite the prevailing ignorance of Eastern Europe and disapproval of recent immigrants to North America, a handful of English-speaking scholars took an interest in Slavic studies. Important Russian and Polish novels appeared in English translation. At the turn of the century Harvard offered courses in 'Northeastern European History' (Poland and Russia) and Russian literature. A few years later the University of California began to teach Slavic literature. Across the Atlantic scholar-journalists like R.W. Seton-Watson, H. Wickham Steed, and Bernard Pares introduced the British public to the Slavic world.

Interest in Eastern Europe grew sharply as a result of World War I (which stemmed, after all, from 'obscure' national rivalries in a 'distant' part of Europe) and the creation of new, independent states in Central and Eastern Europe. The immigrant groups in North America also achieved greater respectability through the formation of self-help organizations and the sheer passage of time. While the numbers of students and faculty involved were still quite small, new programmes opened in American and British universities to investigate Slavic history and culture (Canada did not establish such courses until World War II[5]). Since these

---

3 Ralph Connor, *The Foreigner* (Winnipeg 1909), Preface. See also Carl Berger, *The Sense of Power: Studies in the Ideas of Canadian Imperialism* (Toronto 1970), 147-51.
4 A.R. Ford in J.S. Woodsworth, *Strangers within Our Gates* (Toronto 1909), 139
5 W. Kirkconnell, 'The Place of Slavonic Studies in Canada,' *Slavistica* (Winnipeg), XXXI, 1958, 6

Introduction

studies had not been part of the previous curriculum, the new courses were staffed by emigrés or by natives who had somehow come into contact with Slavic Europe.

William John Rose was born on a farm near the small Manitoba town of Minnedosa in 1885 to a poor country family of Scottish descent. The chance visit of the president of Wesley College led to Rose's enrolment in that church school in nearby Winnipeg. Between 1900 and 1905 he studied the classics with distinction, winning a Rhodes Scholarship to Oxford thanks to superior performance in Greek and Latin. After receiving both a Bachelor's and a Master's degree in classics from Oxford, and broadened by some travel on the Continent, Rose returned to Wesley College as a lecturer in classics and mathematics. Three years later he felt that he still needed further training, so returned to Europe to get his doctorate in Germany, where his wife wished to study music. While attending a summer conference of the Student Christian Movement, a branch of the YMCA which Rose had first joined in Winnipeg as an undergraduate, he agreed to cut short his studies in order to go to Prague as a 'student-secretary.' His duties consisted of forming study groups of young people interested in social problems and, if possible, moving them into the realm of practical solutions to these problems through volunteer work.

On arrival in Central Europe, Rose was very much the 'innocent abroad,' quite unaware of the nationalist problems afflicting the Austro-Hungarian empire. He unwittingly offended both Czechs and Germans on occasion, resulting in painful personal experiences and, subsequently, a new consciousness. In order to work more efficiently, he studied the Czech language, but the outbreak of World War I interrupted his linguistic progress and altered his life completely. Rose and his wife happened to be on a walking tour of the Carpathians during the summer of 1914. The war broke out while they were visiting friends in a Polish district of Silesia near Cieszyń (Teschen). Austrian authorities permitted them to live unhampered in the village of Ligotka, not wishing to subject Mrs Rose to the rigours of internment.

Rural life in Silesia reminded Rose of his own farm in Manitoba, and he felt deeply drawn to the Polish people. After a year, he switched from the study of Czech to Polish, which appeared more immediately useful. The well-stocked library of his host, Pastor Karol Kulisz, enabled him to familiarize himself with contemporary Polish literature as well as to fill in gaps in his general education. Sienkiewicz's *Quo Vadis* and the historiosophical writings of August Cieszkowski made the greatest impact on him.

The sudden collapse of the Austro-Hungarian monarchy in October 1918 brought an end to Rose's idyll and launched him, quite unexpectedly, into international diplomacy. The Polish National Council of Cieszyń asked him to undertake a mission to the Western Allies in order to gain their support. Rose was to report the desire of Silesian Poles to belong to a Polish state, to ask for the dispatch of a 'mission' which would lend moral authority to the council, and to inform the world of the good relations existing between local Poles and Czechs who had succeeded in finding a mutually acceptable demarcation line.

Provided with some sausage and black bread, Rose slipped through the window of a train bound for Vienna; he had not even time to inform his wife. Since no representatives of the Western Allies had yet appeared there, Rose went on to Ljubljana in search of them. The Polish Legation in Vienna commissioned him to contact General Józef Haller on their behalf, and he carried a message urging Haller to put his army at the disposal of General Piłsudski, to urge Western recognition for his Warsaw government rather than for the Polish Committee in Paris headed by Roman Dmowski, to claim representation at the Paris Conference for the Warsaw government, and to demand a share of the Austro-Hungarian fleet for Poland. No Allied representatives had reached Ljubljana either, so Rose continued on after accepting additional appeals for Western support from the Slovenian National Committee. In the company of a Polish army officer, he went to Trieste, which he reached on Armistice Day, and finally to Italy, where the American Red Cross aided his journey to Paris.

Rose's dramatic appearance in Paris made a sensation. He was the first resident of Central Europe to reach the west. Acquitting himself of his mission by presenting lengthy reports to American and British authorities, he undertook to educate the large numbers of British and Americans gathering in Paris about the nature of Central Europe. In public and private talks, he described the region as afflicted by chaos caused by four years of war, wandering demobilized soldiers, breakdown of the economy, collapse of civil government, and material privations. Nevertheless, Rose expressed confidence that the local populations possessed the political sense and moral force to cope with these problems. He called for prompt western recognition of local governments in Poland, Bohemia, and Slovenia coupled with the dispatch of small military missions (a corporal's guard or only a corporal) to Ljubljana, Zagreb, Sarajevo, Cieszyń, Cracow, Poznań, Warsaw, and Gdańsk, which would bolster the moral authority of the local forces. Further, he urged the immediate dispatch of Haller's army to Poland, the repatriation of demobilized soldiers, and the sending of food supplies wherever necessary, especially to Slovenia.

Rose believed that these measures would allow the nations of Central Europe to stand on their own feet in short order. He compared that region to a weak organism which must be exposed to light and air in order to effect a cure. Danger existed only from the onset of infection. In this case, the 'infection' of

Introduction   xiii

anarchy (coming from unstable local conditions) might produce the disease of Bolshevism with possibly fatal results. Applying these principles to Poland, Rose called for prompt recognition of the Piłsudski government (which appeared to many in Paris as Bolshevik itself) and the relaxation of visa restrictions which had kept Piłsudski's ambassador, Michał Sokolnicki, waiting in Geneva.

After the unification of Piłsudski-ite and Dmowski-ite delegations at the Paris Peace Conference, Rose became an outsider once again. While on salary from the Student Christian Movement, which was trying to arrange a relief mission to Poland, Rose met many leading figures. He renewed acquaintances with Eduard Beneš and Tomaš Masaryk, whom he had met in Prague before the war, and met such British and American Eastern experts as Robert H. Lord, Lewis Namier, and Wickham Steed, as well as T.E. Lawrence. Rose also made the acquaintance of many leading Poles. Finally, the long-awaited permission to return to Central Europe arrived, and he returned to Silesia for his wife, made a quick tour of Poland, and returned to Winnipeg for several months.

Between 1920 and 1927, Rose served the YMCA organization in Poland while generally deepening his knowledge about that country. His primary responsibility lay in Cracow and Łódź where he organized local committees composed of university professors, public figures, and successful businessmen. He received most pleasure, however, from those activities which allowed him to meet private citizens. In 1920 Rose helped organize extensive relief activities and later, in more settled times, he worked with young people. He also managed to find time to enrol in the Jagiellonian University. Avoiding the classics, in which he thought he could do only second-rate work, Rose looked for themes that would help him understand modern problems. Stanisław Kot received him into his seminar on the history of culture and permitted him to write a doctoral dissertation on an eighteenth-century educator, Stanisław Konarski. The degree was awarded in 1926, and publication of Rose's thesis in 1929 made a welcome contribution to English-language historical literature.

Shortly after receiving his doctorate, Rose decided to return to teaching. Growth of the YMCA organization forced him into increasing administrative work and restricted the personal contact with young people that he considered essential. Through acquaintances made in the YMCA, Rose received an invitation to teach at Dartmouth College, New Hampshire. As early as 1930, however, Sir Bernard Pares approached Rose to bring him to the University of London as Polish reader. Administrative arrangements luckily took five years to complete, allowing Rose to research and write his most original work, *The Drama of Upper Silesia*. In 1936 he became reader in Polish history and literature at the University of London. In 1938 he was appointed professor and, the following year, succeeded to the directorship of the School of Slavonic Studies after the senior candidate, R.W. Seton-Watson, disqualified himself as temperamentally unsuited for administrative work. During World War II Rose and his entire school worked for Arnold Toynbee at Chatham House collecting information about occupied Central and Eastern Europe. After the war he re-established the School of Slavonic Studies before retiring in 1950 at the age of sixty-five. In retirement he helped set up the Department of Slavonic Studies at the University of British Columbia, spent a year as teaching fellow at his *alma mater* in Winnipeg (United College, now the University of Winnipeg), during which time the Canadian Association of Slavists was organized in Winnipeg and elected him first honorary president. In 1956 Rose left the university world entirely. He settled at the Naramata Christian Leadership Training School in British Columbia, where he worked until his death in 1968 at the age of eighty-two.

Thus, after forty years' involvement with Central European affairs, Rose returned to missionary education. A Western Canadian farm boy from a religious background, Rose had studied classics at a small denominational college and prepared for missionary work in China. One wonders why his life swerved so far off its expected course. Why did Rose form so passionate an attachment to Poland, a Catholic country little known in North America? The answer seems to be that, in a peculiar fashion, the values instilled in him by his early education, particularly at Wesley College, predisposed him towards an appreciation of Poland and Polish values.

At the turn of the century, when William Rose sought his higher education, Wesley College had become the home of the social gospel and the fount of much of western Canadian radicalism. Like its contemporary Catholic counterpart, which Pope Leo XIII gave voice to in his encyclical *Rerum novarum*, the social gospel aimed at achieving the Kingdom of God on this earth through Christian love and brotherly co-operation. Social gospel clergymen aimed more at directing their parishioners' energies towards rooting out social evils than at saving their souls through introspection and prayer.[6]

Rose came under the influence of this movement. Two men made particularly strong impressions on him. J.S. Woodsworth, who had graduated from Wesley in 1896 and preached in Grace Church across Portage Avenue from the college, made himself unpopular by denouncing his flock's economic individualism. In the 1920s and 30s Woodsworth entered politics, won a seat in Parliament, and organized the CCF. Dr Salem Bland taught church history at Wesley until 1917, when the trustees dismissed him for doctrinal error and social radicalism. From

---

6 Richard Allen, *The Social Passion: Religion and Social Reform in Canada 1914-1928* (Toronto 1971), 4

Introduction   xv

Woodsworth, Bland, and others Rose learned of the need for social reform. He learned to respect men who acted with a high moral purpose and whose actions improved the spiritual values of human existence. To him religion consisted of realizing Christian values on this earth. Like Woodsworth, Rose was relatively indifferent to theology.[7]

Under Woodsworth's direction, Rose and other Wesley College men undertook practical social work in Winnipeg's North End slums. They dispensed medicine, gave reading classes and non-denominational moral lectures to East Europeans in the All Peoples' Mission. The immigrants, who were pouring into Winnipeg by the thousands, obviously did not impress Rose greatly except as objects of charity and he developed no special interest in Poland. Even when his younger brother, Arthur (Wesley College 1909), went to Poland for two years to learn the language in order to do more effective social work, he showed no reaction. The following year he left for Germany to continue his study of the classics.

Rose's interest in Slavic Europe arose fortuitously when the Student Christian Movement asked him to redeem his missionary pledge by going to Prague instead of China. Prague stimulated him, but the Czechs did not arouse his admiration. He found them abrasive in their self-confident assertiveness and opposed their self-righteous attitude towards other nationalities on their borders. Even in 1913 he noted with sorrow that Eduard Beneš spoke as if all Silesia were rightfully Czech. He strongly deplored the unilateral military intervention by Czechoslovakia in 1919 to secure Cieszyń. In general, however, there seemed no need for Rose to become involved with the Czechs since they had suffered little from World War I and appeared quite capable of taking care of themselves.

Poland, in contrast, made a deep impression on Rose, as he found in the nationalist movement moral values corresponding to his earlier training. Throughout his forced sojourn in Silesia, Rose remained a guest of Pastor Karol Kulisz, whose Protestant religiosity made him feel at home in this strange land. An ideal clergyman who fitted well into the Canadian vision of the social gospel, Kulisz had rejected honours from the Austro-Hungarian government and lived humbly in order to devote his life to the cares of his flock. He was also a Polish patriot, though still a loyal subject of the emperor, and he helped Rose gain an appreciation of Polish literature, language, and customs. In short, Rose received communion with Poland from the hands of a Lutheran pastor.

Rose's conversion to philo-Polonism can be dated to his decision to translate August Cieszkowski's historiosophical work, *Desire of All Nations*, a work which lies remarkably close to the spirit of the social gospel. Appropriately, the

---

7 Kenneth McNaught, *J.S. Woodsworth* (Toronto 1959), 48-9 ff

Student Christian Movement Press published the translation in 1920. Like Rose, Cieszkowski believed that religion aimed at the fullest participation of men in secular affairs in order to achieve social change. A Hegelian, he argued that two stages of world history had already occurred: first, the 'natural' period of amoral, worldly concerns, and second, the Christian era, dominated by the other-worldly Christian ethic. Through the dialectic, Cieszkowski predicted the imminent arrival of a third period in which worldliness and other-worldliness would merge to produce 'absolute heaven.' Through the activities of volunteer associations which worked in this world to spread Christ's love, liberty, equality, and fraternity would reign. In short, Cieszkowski considered religion the 'soul' animating politics, the 'body.' Incidentally, he expected that the triumph of the Christian spirit would also bring Polish independence.[8] Another book which made a profound impression on Rose was Henryk Sienkiewicz's *Quo Vadis*, which preached Polish nationalism in the guise of a study of early Christianity.

Polish nationalism appeared to Rose to stress moral regeneration and the rejection of materialism. During the Paris Peace Conference, Rose publicized his Christian view of Eastern European affairs as 'A New Idealism in Central Europe.' In an article by that title, he reported a conversation with a Silesian Polish friend who told him that, 'If we were out for our daily bread, we should never be so foolish as to hold to our Slav nationality. Nothing is easier than to become a renegade and be sure of a full stomach. But that would mean selling our birthright, a thing we cannot do. Better freedom, the right to develop along the lines God has meant us to follow, with want, than that sort of thing.' This idealism manifested itself in a liberal nationalist spirit, according to Rose's optimistic forecast of December 1918, which permitted free co-operation between newly liberated peoples.[9]

Rose enthusiastically embraced Polish 'Messianism' as a counterweight to Bolshevism, which he feared might engulf the Central European lands. For him Bolshevism was 'the logical reaction on the despotism of the ages ... carried to a logical extreme.' But he thought it 'an idealism gone wrong' which produced nothing but 'disruption, subversion, annihilation.' Nonetheless, Rose retained faith in the traditions of the Polish peasant and 'the Messianists from Mickiewicz to Szczepanowski' to prevent the spread of the Bolshevik disease. He confessed to having smiled when he heard claims of a 'resemblance between suffering Poland and the "suffering servant" or "suffering son"' and at conclusions 'that Poland was actually the Messiah among nations,' but he enthusiastically sup-

---

8 August Cieszkowski, *The Desire of All Nations* (London 1919), translated and abridged by William John Rose, 99, 111-12, 143, 200, 203
9 'A New Idealism in Central Europe,' *The New Europe*, 12 Dec. 1918, 197-201

Introduction xvii

ported the Polish position at the Paris Peace Conference. Rose emphatically rejected views of 'certain "unconverted" politicians, who persist in thinking that the bigger the land is the stronger it will be,' yet he gave special thanks to General Piłsudski for having moulded Poland into moral unity.[10]

According to Rose's analysis, Poland still suffered after the war from a deficiency of moral strength because of her loss of statehood in the nineteenth century, but he felt that Poland was improving rapidly. In an article entitled 'The Building of the Social Order,' he looked to Polish youth for a 'social consciousness' which would produce a 'healthy, self-supporting, confident, social fabric.' He expressed concern that adults, 'born under a *regime* where everything was done for them ... cannot be taught overnight what national and social service means, even with the best will in the world.'[11]

Therefore, Rose decided to participate in the process of rebuilding Poland which, he hoped, would ensure full development of Polish idealism. His attitude was not without Anglo-Saxon condescension. In a 1918 article, he expressed the opinion that the ending of German control created an intellectual vacuum in East-Central European universities which Anglo-Saxons would have to fill.[12] Nevertheless, Rose was entirely free of personal prejudice. He wholeheartedly embraced the YMCA philosophy of turning administration over to Poles as rapidly as possible.[13]

As a university professor, Rose's crude historical idealism yielded to far greater sophistication, but his scholarly writings still reflected the same concerns that led to his original involvement in Polish affairs. A religious upbringing led him to give primacy to moral and idealistic factors in history, a tendency which his studies in Polish Messianic thought strengthened. He evinced little interest in narrow political studies, preferring to take a broader cultural approach.

Studies at Oxford contributed to this breadth of view. British classical scholarship at the turn of the twentieth century concerned itself with history, sociology, and economics, and not only with linguistic and literary subjects. Students were pressed to see 'the study of Greece and Rome [as] a help to the unravelling of the twentieth century,' useful because ancient events could be viewed dispassionately. Even purely literary scholars like Gilbert Murray decried narrow specialization and proposed interdisciplinary lectures on 'archaeology, literature,

10 'Messianism versus Bolshevism,' ibid., 24 April 1919, 43-6
11 'Poland: Building the Social Order,' ibid., 25 March 1920, 257
12 'My Mission from Silesia,' *Polish Review* (London), II, 3, Dec. 1918, 224; also *Manitoba Free Press*, 1 Feb. 1919
13 Paul Super, *Twenty-Five Years with the Poles* (New Jersey nd [1947]), 47

anthropology and the like.'[14] One of Rose's tutors set him writing on ancient Roman bureaucracy, a subject which he came to understand (or so he notes in his *Memoirs*) only when he saw the Habsburg empire at work. He later abandoned the classics, but made good use of the linguistic training for his doctoral dissertation. He also retained the sense of historical importance of literature and moral example so characteristic of classical thinking. The actions of classically heroic individuals against an identifiable social and economic backdrop play a prominent part in his historical understanding.

Cultural subjects had long been studied in history, but World War I vastly accelerated their popularity and led directly to the institution of new undergraduate courses like the one Rose was hired to teach at Dartmouth when he left Poland in 1927. Even before the war, James Harvey Robinson and Charles Beard had collaborated on the formulation of a 'New History' which would explain the social, economic, intellectual, and political structures underlying current affairs. During World War I, the American government requested that courses be devised to instruct student-cadets in the background to the war. Columbia College introduced such a course and later prepared an 'Introduction to Contemporary Civilization' which aimed 'to present the features of our civilization, past and present, which are of significance for those who expect to take part in the solution of the problems which now confront us.'[15] The Dartmouth version which Rose taught between 1927 and 1934 was called 'The Development of Western Culture' and studied 'the geneology of occidental civilization, with special reference to formative influences in shaping the pattern of modern social and institutional life.'[16]

Rose's understanding of culture, however, derives more directly from his European teachers than from his American experience. He enrolled in the Jagiellonian University in Cracow at a time when new schools of cultural history were developing. He first attended lectures by Professor Ignacy Chrzanowski, whose *History of Polish Literature* he had studied in Silesia during the war. Chrzanowski's interpretation of literature was social and political as well as aesthetic, consequently even journalists and publicists found a place in his literary treatment. The fifth edition of his *History of the Literature of Independent Poland*, which Rose must have used in Cracow, concluded with a quote from Kazimierz Bro-

---

14 Gilbert Murray, *The Interpretation of Ancient Greek Literature: An Inaugural Lecture delivered before the University of Oxford, January 27th, 1909* (Oxford 1909), 7
15 Richard Hofstadter and Wilson Smith, eds. *American Higher Education* (Chicago 1961), II, 902
16 Dartmouth College, *Catalogue, 1928,* 10

Introduction   xix

dziński, that 'the literature of each nation is its moral existence [which], safe within its borders can never lose its independence.'[17]

Rose worked far more closely, however, with his doctoral adviser, Professor Stanisław Kot, who held the chair in history of culture at the Jagiellonian University. As his *History of Education* (1934) shows, Kot maintained that all aspects of cultural development were united in a common pattern. He explained that societies develop educational structures to fit their social, economic, and political needs; neither curricula nor pedagogical methods develop in isolation.[18] The impact of these ideas on Rose's selection of Stanisław Konarski, the eighteenth-century educator and political publicist, as a subject for his doctoral dissertation is obvious. A patriot, Konarski used education to further social change. He founded a *Collegium Nobilium* which provided the first modern curriculum in eighteenth-century Polish schools. His students received a secular education, though still permeated with religious spirit, which prepared them to take part in public affairs. After twenty years of academic preparation, he exposed his ideas to a wider public through the printing of his multi-volume study, *On Effective Government*, which set out clearly the faults in Poland's anarchic government. Konarski died in 1763, but his ideas affected Polish politics throughout the partition era.

As a mature scholar, Rose turned primarily to writing popularizations instead of original scholarly works. Administrative duties at the University of London prevented him from undertaking studies like *Stanisław Konarski* or his eloquent defence of Polish sovereignty in Silesia, *The Drama of Upper Silesia* (1935). His three London books, *Poland* (Penguin Special 1939), *The Rise of Polish Democracy* (1944), and *Poland, Old and New* (1948), were introductory works for the general public. Rose understood the sacrifice he was making, but 'could not be indifferent to the demands of a fast-growing reading public' which needed background information to comprehend current developments.[19] The onslaught of World War II strongly influenced his decision. Poland's future was once again in doubt and public opinion in the English-speaking world might help decide its fate.

Rose never seemed entirely comfortable with contemporary studies. The constant refrain runs through his work that it is 'too soon to know' what opinion to have on a given subject or individual. Regarding W.F. Reddaway's biography of

17 Ignacy Chrzanowski, *Historia literatury niepodlegley Polski*, fifth edition (Warsaw nd [1923]), 618
18 Marian Henryk Serejski, ed., *Historycy o historii* (Warsaw 1966), II, 331
19 *Poland, Old and New* (London 1948), v

Józef Piłsudski, he noted that, 'of course most of these [interpretations] can only be properly dealt with when time has mellowed things and given us a truer view of them.'[20] Similarly, his obituary for Wojciech Korfanty, leader of the Silesian uprising of 1920, ended with the remark that one should speak only good of the dead, a clear sign of disapproval, but left the reader with no clear impression of what Korfanty had done wrong.[21]

Rose's unwillingness to take a strong stand also stemmed from his reluctance to condemn any Poles in the eyes of the world. The only truly harsh criticism in the entire body of his works applies to two non-Poles who seemed to challenge the fundamental justice of the Polish cause. He attacked Frederick W. Kaltenbach as 'ignorantly pro-German' for accepting the decision of the 1921 League of Nations plebiscite awarding part of Silesia to Germany because it 'simply put a premium on the *kulturarbeit* of imperialism in the past.'[22] And the British historian, R.F. Leslie, was accused of anti-Polish bias for his view of class conflict in the insurrections of 1830 and 1863.[23]

The historiographical debate over responsibility for the partitions of Poland provides a significant example of Rose's historical approach. Most Polish historians before 1870 blamed the partitions on the greediness and immorality of the partitioning powers (Russia, Prussia, and Austria) as well as on a few Polish dupes or allies. Around 1870 a group of Polish historians living in Austrian Poland attacked this thesis, blaming, instead, the Polish nobility for tolerating constitutional weakness and social injustice in order to increase its own wealth and prestige. Not that the 'Cracow School' was any less patriotic than its rivals. To them patriotism required that harmful illusions be destroyed. Polish scholarship turned around again in the 1890s with the 'Warsaw School,' which stressed the recovery of Poland in the late eighteenth century from economic and social decline. These historiographical positions took on contemporary political significance. Those who blamed Polish weakness tended to favour 'realistic' political collaboration with the governments of the Austrian, German, and Russian empires and concentration on constructive 'organic' economic building, while their 'romantic' opponents, confident of Polish strength, preferred insurrection.

Rose's own work sought a median position between the extreme views of the 'romantics' and the 'realists' (or 'optimists' and 'pessimists' as these schools are sometimes called). He declared that blame must be shared by Poles and foreigners alike. The foreigners were selfish, but the Polish nobles had not developed

20 *Slavonic Review*, XVIII, 52, July 1939, 227
21 Ibid., XIX, 1940, 318
22 Ibid., XIX, 1940, 331
23 See below, 229.

Introduction

enough public spirit to put national interests ahead of their own.[24] He praised therefore both the 'realist' and the 'romantic' historians of the nineteenth century, supporting as well their contradictory political positions. Not unexpectedly, Rose did not produce a coherent interpretation of his own. In an article critical of both schools, he failed to find a label for his own approach.

Poland needed both the romantics and the realists to regain independence, and the historian must understand the practical cost of sacrifice no less than its heroism, Rose maintained. He must honour heroes, but he must 'honour no less than whose lives were spent, often unseen and unrewarded to create a world where heroism is rarely called for.'[25] Rose aimed at synthesizing mutually antagonistic historical views and transcending them in a manner reminiscent of Cieszkowski's dialectic in *The Desire of All Nations*. He commented that 'no one can appreciate Polish history who has only intellect at his disposal, but anyone who gives way to sentiment will be in hot water all the time.'[26]

Rose's view of the twentieth century was dominated by the thought that Marshal Józef Piłsudski embodied both realism and romanticism. Guided by a vision of Poland's future, Piłsudski was not blind to the realities of her condition. The movement which he led before World War I was filled with 'a mystical element in the hearts of all, rather than any thought for material profit,' while the means were reality itself: the careful organization of armed force. Piłsudski had other virtues as well. Reliance on 'the dynamic of the nation itself' struck Rose as essentially democratic, in contrast to Roman Dmowski's diplomatic dealings which seemed to him to show a lack of faith in the people.[27]

Unfortunately, many Poles lacked Piłsudski's hard-headed understanding of the need for further development before aspiring to the pinnacle of Western European political organization, Rose thought. In reaction to more than a century of despotism the constitution of 1921 laid too 'great stress on liberty, but not enough on discipline' which the Poles needed after their long statelessness. 'A strong and unbroken executive' was needed in a country where the majority of the deputies were political novices, and where no routine of government had been attained at all.'[28] Piłsudski had the wit to divine the problem and refused to submit himself to the new constitutional ways.

Rose supported Piłsudski's *coup d'état* of May 1926 as establishing a guided democracy necessary to jump 'from the eighteenth century to the twentieth

24 'Realism in Polish History,' *Journal of Central European Affairs*, II, 3, Oct. 1942, 246
25 *Slavonic Review*, XIV, 41
26 'Realism in Polish History,' 246
27 *Poland* (London 1939), 44, 58
28 *Poland*, 79

century.'²⁹ He accepted Piłsudski's lack of respect for the Polish parliaments of the 1920s whose deputies he lectured like 'naughty children, mostly, it must be admitted, with right on his side.' Convinced of the general correctness of Piłsudski's line, Rose tended to dismiss what he gently termed the 'railroading' of the opposition. He considered the imprisonment of opposition political leaders under harsh conditions before the 1930 elections unwise, but noted that 'the historian of the future may well decide that what was done as a *malum necessarium*.'³⁰ He discerned little change in Poland in the years after Piłsudski's death, since the regime had 'the mind and spirit of the Marshal [as] its guiding star' and the 'Colonels' had been chosen by Piłsudski himself. He found in Rydź-Śmigły an appropriate head of state endowed with the virtues of duty, charm, and patriotism.³¹

Rose was not ignorant of the authoritarian aspects of the regime both before and after Piłsudski's death, but he considered them an inevitable, if not a necessary, part of Poland's great experiment. Like many travellers to the Soviet Union in the 1930s, he had great faith in the future. He saw Poland involved in 'an effort to solve the vexed and vexing question of the relations between the government and the governed, so that the former would not be hampered at every turn and often for irrelevant reasons, while the latter would retain liberties of person and property, and so share in the handling of affairs.' He viewed the sharp increase of political activity by youth after Piłsudski's death as a healthy phenomenon, reflecting a natural process. He expressed no surprise that young people, the first generation born in an independent Poland, should seek change. Even political demonstrations, which sometimes degenerated into riots, seemed to him to display 'the new Poland [which] is seeking its way, and before long we shall know better where it is going.'³²

Rose's optimism extended to the Polish economy, which he considered essentially sound. He pointed with pride to economic achievements as repudiation of 'those people who think that Poles are constitutionally fitted [only] to be artists, philosophers or gamblers' and proof that the popular division between Czech realism and Polish romanticism did not exist.³³ He untiringly quoted statistics showing improvements in agriculture and industry, citing as well his own personal observations.

Similarly, Rose saw no threat to Poland's survival in the minority problem. He easily dismissed the large German minority as too dispersed to create pro-

29 See below, 102.
30 *Poland*, 90
31 Ibid., 102-3
32 *Poland*, 108
33 'National Minorities in Europe: IV, The Poles in Germany,' *Slavonic Review*, XV, 43, July 1936, 170; and ibid., XIV, 42, April 1936, 726

Introduction

blems for the Polish state and the Belorussian population as still too primitive. The Ukrainians formed a large, concentrated, and educated group capable of destructive agitation but Rose hoped to convince the outside world (or the Ukrainians themselves?) that their position in Poland was 'enviable,' and that good sense demanded co-operation with the Poles. He thought Ukrainians should continue to build up their economic and cultural strength before launching political programmes. He made no predictions about their eventual political demands nor what the Polish response might be.[34]

Only the Jews represented a definite liability for Poland. Rose harshly termed them 'the least desirable type whether physically or culturally' and complained that 'Poland, one of the poorest countries on the continent, has nearly one-quarter of all the Jews in the world.'[35] He recognized that Jews were subject to discrimination but considered actual anti-Semitism uncommon and of recent date, deriving from economic competition. The real problem was not Polish attitudes but the refusal of the Jews to assimilate. He strenuously opposed Zionism in so far as it led to a resurgence of Jewish nationalism in Eastern Europe. The best solution would be emigration, preferably to established countries where Jews would not be too 'arrogant' to assimilate.[36] Rose applauded those Jews who considered themselves Polish nationals whether they maintained the Hebrew faith or converted. In an obituary for the historian Szymon Askenazy, a practising Jew, Rose noted that 'ties of religion never stood in the way of his national affiliation.'[37] Nonetheless, assimilation could not offer a solution to the mass of Jews. History showed that 'the trend ... of things is not to be denied ... nine-tenths of any population are bound to get their way over one-tenth, cruel as that assertion may seem.'[38]

The rapid Polish defeat in World War II did nothing to alter his favourable opinion of the Polish system of the 1930s. He changed his assessment neither of the Polish-German Non-Aggression Pact of 1934 nor of Beck's attempts to assert Polish diplomatic independence in 1938-9. He seems to have maintained the pre-war government's illusions that Poland could play a major role in European affairs. He did not dismiss speculation that Poland was a 'great power' nor ridicule demands for Polish overseas colonies.[39]

Rose's attitude towards Poland as it emerged from World War II was similar to his approach after World War I. He praised the spirit of the Poles who repaired

---

34 *Poland*, 170-9
35 Ibid., 162
36 Ibid., 124, 163-8
37 *Slavonic Review*, XIV, 41, Jan. 1936, 428; see also ibid., XVI, 46, July 1936, 209.
38 *Poland*, 162
39 Ibid., 233-5

the ruins and started cultural life once again. Without involving himself in print in the disputes between the London government-in-exile and the Lublin communist-dominated regime or analyzing the near-civil war which continued in Poland until 1947, Rose passed on to happier subjects with the comment that 'politics is only one phase of modern life and by no means the most vital one.'[40] The harshness of the Communist revolution in 1947-8 took him unawares and he retreated into public silence. Despite advancing age, Rose remained active in universities until 1958 and personally active until his death ten years later. The eruption of the Polish spirit in October 1956 must have cheered his final retirement from the field of Slavic studies.

In his memoirs Rose portrays himself as an outsider discovering an unfamiliar land. He is not one of those sophisticated travellers who look down at the weaknesses of foreigners with a superior Anglo-Saxon eye. Rather, he describes himself as a 'tenderfoot' from the raw Canadian West whose education continues despite his mature years. Rose bows to the accidents of fate which push him far into his life's course and open up unexpected opportunities.

Rose's graceful yet strong writing style holds the attention of specialist and general reader alike, while providing both with useful information. The memoirs are valuable in two respects. First, they give a rare inside view of day-to-day developments during World War I in Silesia and of the 1920s in the newly-independent Polish state. Avoiding formal political, economic, and social analysis, Rose shows us everyday life during a crucial time in Polish history. He also describes the treatment of Central European problems at the Paris Peace Conference. Second, the memoirs expose to the scholars of the 1970s an earlier stage of Slavic studies.

Students of Eastern Europe may be struck by the changes in scholarship which have occurred since World War II. The number of scholars has increased dramatically, of course, along with greater professional training, but a change in attitude can also be observed. Present-day scholars seem mostly to examine the weaknesses of the states which emerged after World War I. They explore problems like political instability, the rise of anti-democratic ideologies on the left and right, the clash of nationality groups, and social unrest. This conception of Eastern Europe reflects World War II and the communist takeover. The nations which appeared so proudly on the maps in 1919 seemed to have failed. Rose's generation, on the whole, took a more positive approach.

William Rose was one of those pioneers of Slavic studies who believed deeply in the future of the Slavic countries. From his YMCA social-work experience he

40 *Poland, Old and New*, 385

Introduction   xxv

knew well the problems that faced Poland and considered them capable of solution. He thought Poland a vigorous country, striving energetically to overcome substantial obstacles and re-establish itself in the European mainstream. His memoirs introduce us to many idealists from all social classes and he scarcely seems to have met an undeserving person.

These memoirs provide a valuable, if partial, record of the interwar years. If, in the light of later developments, the author's rosy view of Polish history seems naïve, we should not lean to the opposite extreme and view those years as a series of unbroken failures. The strength with which Poles resisted the German occupation during World War II and rebuilt Poland after its end show that the qualities which Rose describes so eloquently did in fact exist.

THE POLISH MEMOIRS OF WILLIAM JOHN ROSE

1
Prologue

William John Rose, born in 1885 in Minnedosa, Manitoba, studied classics at Wesley College, Winnipeg, and Oxford. After teaching for three years at Wesley, he returned to Europe for further study, but a surprise invitation by a representative of the Student Christian Movement (with which Rose had been previously affiliated) to assume the position of 'student secretary' at the Charles University in Prague brought him to East-Central Europe in 1913.

If Rose had come to Prague a century earlier he would have found it a pleasant, if sleepy, provincial city dominated by German-speaking aristocrats and merchants. After all, Bohemia had been ruled by the Habsburgs for several hundred years and only the peasants still spoke Czech. But profound changes occurred in the course of the nineteenth century. The industrial revolution brought streams of Czech-speaking peasants to work in the factories while a nationalist current revived the scholarly and artistic use of the Czech language. Nationally conscious musicians like Antonín Dvořák spread the fame of the Czech Renaissance to the outside world. As early as the 1860s a National Theatre was erected by popular subscription and promptly rebuilt after accidental destruction by fire. By 1910 Czech-speakers far outnumbered Germans, although they still lagged behind politically and economically.

Political activism followed closely behind cultural revival. Spokesmen for the Czech national cause arose to demand concessions from the imperial government in Vienna. Some required full national autonomy. Others were willing to accept piecemeal reforms in education and the civil service while the nation gathered its strength for further political action. No one before World War I advocated full national independence.

Rose came to Prague with no foreknowledge of the complicated situation awaiting him. As he went about his Christian mission, the nationality problem of the Austro-Hungarian empire began to impinge on his consciousness and he came to see it as one of the pressing moral issues of the modern age. He adapted to circumstances. His willingness to come to grips with this new force changed his life and precipitated a note-worthy career. [DS]

It is not too much to say that from this hour I was launched on a complete re-education. As will transpire, a second phase was to commence in the fall of 1927; but I can see in retrospect that everything now was to build itself into the situation that called me in the high summer of 1935 to the School of Slavonic and East European Studies in the University of London. At the time no one could have had the slightest inkling of the tricks fate was to play with us; to all intents and purposes I thought I was leaving academic work for good.

The first half of this re-education was truly revolutionary. I was now committed to a field of study quite different from anything attempted before. The years 1914-19 completely altered my outlook on European civilization, whether the culture of the individual or of the group. It amounted to an introduction to the 'submerged' half of Europe, in particular to people and peoples numbering nearly 100,000,000 souls who had been living in a state of arrested development for centuries and whose lives had been violently interrupted more than once through the ages while the West had been going on in relatively undisturbed fashion. I was to discover that they were human beings not different from ourselves.

True, this part of the continent, while belonging quite definitely to the same tradition as ours – that of the Old and New Testament on the one hand and of Greece and Rome on the other, had as yet attained little of the urbanised, industrial pattern familiar in the west. It had remained almost totally a rural, agricultural society, and so was looked down on as 'backward.' To me personally this did not mean much at the time, as I had never lived or worked in the shadow of business or industry and so knew little of its mind and tone; but the time came when I did realise what was at stake, and this enriched the whole experience. What none of us realised in 1914 was, of course, that this contrast between the Atlantic seaboard countries and the heart of the continent was soon to be ended. The relatively idyllic, if still primitive, world of the Slavs was to be drawn swiftly into the vortex of modern life; thirty years later Russia was to emerge as one of the three Great Powers – not the Imperial Russia we knew, since all the empires were to come down in ruins, but a new and dynamic structure fraught with untold possibilities both for good and evil.

Prologue

Nothing of all this could be in our minds during those winter months of 1914 in our new surroundings. Even in Germany we had been 'innocents abroad'; now the picture was even worse. We were among friends, yet everything was strange. The city of Prague itself was ancient and respectable; it had served as the capital of a kingdom and then as one of the capitals of the Holy Roman empire. It possessed the first university in Europe east of the Rhine. A hundred years before Luther nailed his theses to the door of the church in Wittenberg, Czech reformers, led by the redoubtable and learned Jan Hus (whose name we have wrongly come to spell 'Huss'), had made a brave stand for precisely the same things; a stand that might well have won through had those making it possessed the printing-press. In 1618 the city had been the scene of the somewhat irregular proceedings which launched the Thirty Years' War. In 1848 it welcomed the delegates of the first Congress of Delegates of the Slav Peoples, whose purpose was to demand an end of servitude to outsiders and the right to be themselves.

As we got to know the place, we found visible evidences of this historic past on all sides. Chief among them were the Cathedral of St Vitus, as noble as any in France, and the vast castle-palace that envelops it, known as the Hradčany, whose site above the river and the city has few equals in Christendom. There was also the stately Charles Bridge, one of the oldest on the continent outside the frontiers of ancient Roman rule; and there was a wealth of churches (mostly in the baroque style, which I happen not to admire) not to be surpassed anywhere north of the Alps. Outside the city itself the same story prevailed; all the earmarks of Latin Christian culture were to be found – castles, country-houses, monasteries and convents, and of course much of industry and business in addition to a level of soil exploitation second to none. In time I discovered that the traditions of the arts-and-crafts guilds were continuous since the end of the Middle Ages. As for music and drama, dancing, the fine arts, folk-lore and legend, Bohemia was not set at the heart of the continent in order to slumber while others toiled.

From the outset two barriers lay across our path. In the first place the Czech people did not like to use German when they could avoid it, and we could not hope really to become friends unless and until we had learned their speech. This meant years of patient and concentrated effort. In the second, as we soon came to realize, they were not masters in their own house. This proud people had seen three hundred years of complete subjection to hated Habsburg imperialism, with which was linked the power of the Roman church. During the last years of the old century they had begun to win back some of the 'lost positions'; their own university in 1882, and virtual control of the municipal government in Prague some ten years later. This no doubt explained why, before leaving Leipzig, we had heard of the way 'those Czechs are thrusting themselves in and separating

Vienna from Berlin.' Now we were to hear the other side of the story. For the Czechs, not only Prague but the whole, or nearly the whole, of Bohemia had been their 'home' (as their national anthem so well says) for a thousand years. That there was also a sizeable minority of Germans no one could deny, or even that in places they were in a majority; but this did not alter the main picture.

Neither these facts – common knowledge now to every student of modern history – nor their significance was known to me in the first days of 1914. In any case we had more mundane things to think about, chief of them being quarters to live in – no easy matter to handle in the overcrowded conditions obtaining. For the first time in our lives we were in a city where, apart from the well-to-do, every room in the house was used as a bedroom. It was difficult, at first, to get used to seeing a bed in the dining-room; disguised, it is true, by coloured bedspreads but not used as a sofa because it was piled high with the soft feather ticks under which most people slept. All this meant extra work for the housewife; and things were even harder because of the vast amounts of brown coal used in the big tile stoves, which filled the air with a special brand of 'smog' and made the washing of curtains a monthly necessity. With the help of friends we did find two rooms with a young couple on the castle side of the Vltava (German Moldau) not far from the big stadium and the Sokol parade-ground, where the big gymnastic ceremonies were staged every year.

We took some of the money that had been meant to keep us in Berlin and bought a piano, so that E[1] might get on with her music. Breakfasts we prepared ourselves, our other meals we took outside. Things looked good until we discovered that the good woman (there were no children) was not the wife of her 'husband' and that, though he did not ill-treat her, she was far from happy. We reported this state of things to our friends, to be met with a shrug and these words, 'You are getting very soon to know our conditions!'

How often I wished in these days that I had learned French in school! In the long run, however, it was perhaps better that we had no choice save to work hard at Czech – the first Slav tongue I had come directly to hear all around me. On commissioning us in Berlin, Dr Mott[2] had used words like these: 'Go down there, live with those people, get to understand them; then you will be friends!' How wise that counsel was, we were in time to discover. In retrospect I can see that it would have been better for us to hide away somewhere in the country for six months for intensive study, before showing ourselves at all to a wider public. Had we done this, I should have avoided not a few mistakes. As things were, never during our half-year of residence could I even begin to discuss intelligently with

1 Emily Cuthbert Rose, WJR's wife.
2 John R. Mott, important official of the Student Christian Movement and YMCA.

those about me the things they held most vital, or even the things to be seen in the daily paper. There are those who will say that this does not matter, but I cannot agree. Not to be able to do this (though one should not waste time at it) means that one is an object of compassion, and this means a bad start.

Take the issue of national independence. It was a shock to me at the time to discover that not only those men and women who were active in public life but many others, indeed all save the people who were after money only, put the recovery of their one-time freedom in the forefront of their living and thinking. They were courteous but firm in saying that even the cause of the Kingdom of God, including their personal faith, had to wait for the settlement of this issue. At the time I felt strongly that they were wrong, but ten years later, and since then even more, I have not been so sure. Some of the reasons for this change will appear in the sequel.

We did meet in Prague a few Germans (not Austrian officials) who were concerned for something broader and higher than what existed. From them we heard two kinds of complaints. One was that many of the 'Germans' in the city were in reality Jews,[3] that they were interested only in mammon, and that this hurt the German cause. The other was that they felt their Czech neighbours made themselves tiresome by always harking back to ancient things, in particular to the work and traditions of Jan Hus. Why drag in the past when, forgetting the things that are behind, we should all press on toward the goal? These folk seemed not to be aware of the use constantly made by their own kind of the name of Luther; nor did they realise that people tend everywhere to think of the past when they are deprived of elementary rights in the present. In actual practice the 15 per cent of the population that spoke German as a mother-tongue had little or no contact, save in business, with the Czech majority. Even church life was divided on national lines, joint meetings being rare. The American minister-missionary of the Baptist church, whose name was Porter, told us that the synod of that denomination was his 'annual German bath.'

The re-emergence of the Czech national as a vital and active force in Bohemia and Moravia during the nineteenth century had been a serious shock to the Germans of the Dual Monarchy.[4] A couple of years later I was to hear a cultured Viennese lady say (apropos of anti-Austrian currents abroad in the armed forces), 'Why their grandfathers were all Germans!' This remark shed a lot of light on the schooling the children received all over the Danube lands. It revealed a strange lack of understanding of what had been going on since the days of Napoleon.

3 The old and influential Jewish community was largely German-speaking, but it made up only a small fraction of the German population.
4 Austria-Hungary. The Czech lands, Bohemia and Moravia, lay in the Austrian half of the empire.

Again, a year later, I noted the surprise with which another lady from Vienna discovered, when on a visit to the Duchy of Teschen, that more people around her spoke Polish than German: 'We were taught that Silesia was all German!'

There existed already in Prague a 'Circle of Friends of the Student Movement.' Called into being largely on the strength of Wilder's[5] visit of the previous year, it had just published a small but neatly bound book about its plans, which became one of my first 'readers' in Czech. Mostly informational, it contained news of the Student Christian Movement in various countries, some pages on Bible study, a chapter on Social Christianity, and a register of addresses of national leaders from all continents. It was introduced by 'Greetings' from well-known workers from European lands, including Russia.

A Steering Committee, composed for the most part of professional men and women, was charged with the guidance of activities, and among them we found our best friends. The chairman was a respected medical man, Dr Adolf Lukl; the secretary was an engineer, Karel Bohać, who had attended a summer conference of the infant Russian SCM in Finland; the treasurer was Dr Anton Frinta, a rising young philologist, whose elegant French was the envy of us all. Among the most helpful was a lawyer, Dr Anton Šum, who held office in the City Hall. But the most active of the 'graduate' members of the group was the younger daughter of Professor T.G. Masaryk,[6] whose proficiency in her studies was only equalled by her skill as a skater and as a champion at lawn-tennis. The influence of Wilder's visit on her life had made things look different to her than before, and her charm as a group-leader was unquestioned. Sympathetic to what was going on, but too busy to help much, was her older sister, Dr Alice, who had been for some time a resident in Chicago in Mary Macdowell's Settlement.

So far as I know E and I were among the first British visitors to enjoy the hospitality of the Masaryk home, and we got to know a family that was soon to be famous the world over. This was due chiefly to the combination of qualities that made Thomas Masaryk the intellectual leader of his nation and in due course the first president of the free republic; but it was also the work of the courageous and gracious lady from Brooklyn, of Huguenot extraction, whom Masaryk had met as a student in Leipzig and who became his life partner in all that followed. During the closing years of the old century this professor of philosophy in Prague was making himself the conscience of the Dual Monarchy – something that cost him much but was to bring rich returns. Because of his unequivocal devotion to truth and justice, he was for a long time as unpopular with many of his own com-

---

5 Robert Wilder, SCM leader.
6 Thomas (Tomaš) Garrigue Masaryk, first president of Czechoslovakia. In 1913 he was a professor of philosophy and a well-known political figure of markedly independent views.

patriots as with outsiders, but he never flinched. His motto was and remained: *Magna est Veritae et prevalebit!* When we first met him he had just seen through the press his two volumes, *Russland und Europa*, which were to appear ten years later in English as *The Spirit of Russia*.

After long waiting, the family had at last secured a pleasant flat, not far from the castle, and Mrs Masaryk was 'at home' there at least one day each week to all kinds of people. She was one of the few women we got to know in Central Europe who could have guests in, serve them a cup (or cups) of tea with a sandwich or a biscuit, and leave things at that – no elaborate reception, no rich foods. For one thing she could not afford it; for another she didn't want the kind of people who came because of the loaves and fishes. Only one rule was enforced – no smoking! Few of us who enjoyed those happy hours had any idea of what that rather frail woman was to put up with in the immediate years ahead at the hands of the Austrian authorities.

Dr Alice was too busy to give much time to social hours, but we did see her at the Seminar on Social Problems, conducted at the university by a young *Dozent* named Eduard Beneš,[7] to which we had a standing invitation even though we understood nothing of what was going on. It was my first 'bath' in Czech. The second son, whose name was Jan, returned in February from a stay of some years in the United States – just in time, as he would remark later, 'to start the World War.' He brought with him the richest store of good (and bad) American slang I ever encountered. E would go into fits of laughter at it, with which was mingled at times a modicum of home-sickness.

I knew that Phildius[8] had been honoured by the professor a year previously with a long interview in which the whole matter of a Student Christian Movement had been discussed, including methods of action. The older man had his doubts as to whether we could hope to make any headway with the gospel message, and reminded his visitor that when Jesus came to earth he addressed himself not to the learned people of his time but to the working-men – in this case, to fishers. That he was in sympathy with our aims could not be questioned. When he spoke to a great meeting in Mandel Hall in Chicago in the late summer of 1918 he put the case for the small nations of Europe and declared that the future lay between two things – Christ or chaos!

Feeling that it would not be fair to a busy man to ask him for counsel until I had become better acquainted with the nature of the field and of my task, I did not approach Masaryk before the long vacation; my plan was to seek his guidance

---

7 Eduard Beneš, nationalist and politician; foreign minister (1918-35), premier (1921-2), president (1935-8 and 1940-8).
8 Eberhard Phildius, a Swiss national, head of the SCM bureau in Vienna.

and help in the autumn. As things turned out, I next saw him in London in December 1918, when peace had returned. We had a long talk about what had happened, chiefly about his own great responsibility as president-elect of the now constituted Czechoslovakia. I have felt the irony of this turn of things, for I could have learned much more during the war years if I had been better prepared. In the meantime Masaryk had become a world figure, thanks to the accomplishment of deeds – after he was sixty-five – which might have daunted a man of forty. The story of all this is told in his memorable book, *The Making of a State.*

It was, nevertheless, my good fortune to get to know Masaryk's younger colleague, Professor František Drtina, on whom the burden of university work had fallen in view of the other's absorption with public affairs; and it was my plan to do some serious work under him in the coming year. Among other teachers I met Dr Jan Foustka, whose championing of the cause of anti-alcoholism had won him wide recognition. In view of my ignorance of Czech, I asked one of our group members, Basil Skrach, to take me with him to the lectures on philosophy he was attending in the German University – the subject being the then fashionable *Philosophie des Als Ob*, the title of the notable book by Vaihinger. This was the continental brand of pragmatism, of which I had made an acquaintance in Oxford. Skrach was to survive the war and become librarian to the president in the Hradčany, where I had the pleasure of a fine visit with him in 1934.

But we must get back to our story. Having settled in and launched on daily study of Czech, we wrote at once to our home-folk asking them to send on some of our belongings – including E's wedding presents. One box of these arrived duly, but another (filled for the most part with a selection of my books) got caught in Antwerp by the outbreak of war and was held there for the next five years. I finally got it, safe and sound, in the summer of 1919 – a sign of the way private property was respected by the belligerents of those days, in contrast to what happened a generation later.

One of our first concerns was that the circle had no place of its own, either for formal or other meetings. To find 'quarters' of any kind in the middle of the town was far from easy, and the cost of equipping such a 'centre' – the term in use was *foyer* (fireside) after the Swiss example – would be considerable. But the decision was taken and, after a month's search, three rooms with kitchen were found. By an all-out effort, including the making-over of packing boxes into supports for cushioned seats all around the main room, we got together the needed furnishings, and a woman with a daughter in school agreed to take care of the place in return for lodging. She also cooked lunches each weekday for some of us who were glad to avail ourselves of them. The formal opening was set for the Universal Day of Prayer for Students, which fell towards the end of February.

Prologue

Among the first presents made to the new *foyer* was a framed portrait in black-and-white of a man with a high brow and a long beard, which was given a place in the large room. The face was new to me, and I had to ask whose it was. 'Oh, that is Dostoevsky!' was the somewhat surprised reply. The fact of my ignorance gave me much to think about. In time, as will appear, I got to know the work of that remarkable man and I then knew why Czech students rated him so highly. I was also to discover something that is even now not generally realized – that Masaryk regarded his two great volumes on Russia as an introduction to a proper study of Dostoevsky as the chief opponent of Nihilism in his own land and elsewhere. The outbreak of war interrupted this work, and it was never completed.

Another 'jolt' was to come my way a few weeks later. When we got back to Prague after the Easter break, during which a spring conference was held in Silesia, I thought it well to let people know that I would be in the *foyer* at certain times during the week and should be glad to talk with anyone who cared to come in. The committee accepted the suggestion, but no one ever came! At the time I was nonplussed, but looking back after five years I had to ask myself: Why should they? What had I to give them?

However, it would be wrong to think that I did not have many a 'session' about life issues with both younger and older people. These came often when least expected, and two of them stand out in memory. One was with a young woman teacher who came regularly to our gatherings, though she was not a university student. She had read a good deal and had become rather a disciple of Tolstoy. But she found him strangely unsatisfying and was looking for a better teacher. I suggested that there was one called the Great Teacher who had never failed any willing pupil. Why not turn to Him? She did not query this, but she was afraid. It would mean committing herself – a venture of faith she was not prepared to make. As I knew her devotion to music, I asked her why she had no fears about 'committing herself' to this affection. To this she could not find any proper answer.

The other 'interview,' which was in fact a series of discussions about the Good Life, involved a senior student who afterwards did fine service for his nation. Each of us learned from the other, as we tried to analyze the secret of the happy and useful personality – whether the one centred on God was happier and more useful or that not thus anchored. A little book had just appeared from the pen of our own committee member, Dr Frinta, *The Fight for a View of the World*, and more than once we came back to the German phrase *Weltanschaung*. We could not reach complete agreement, but my friend summed up the whole in words like these: 'You are fortunate in coming from the New World, where the air is freer than with us. With you the student of life can take his time, follow St

Paul's counsel to prove all things and hold fast to the good. With us it is different. On your way one can avoid mistakes better than we can. With us it is a matter of necessity to settle one's view of things as soon as we can; and to hold to this strictly, even though we go down and out.' The last phrase of that summing-up stuck in my mind, and gave me much to think about. The more I pondered it, the more I was compelled to accept its validity, for the following reasons.

Officially Southeast Europe was overwhelming Roman Catholic, at least as far as the Iron Gates. Children were 'born into the Church,' and their confirmation at fourteen was more of a formality than anything else. The easiest thing for all was to accept what the church had to say, with as little thought about it as possible. (Let it be said that this was also the case with the average 'run' of Protestants.)

To compound the mischief, though nominally Christian, the atmosphere of the schools was secular, if not pagan. Many teachers openly scoffed at all faith, and still more at institutional expressions of it; how things looked in the classroom where the teacher was an agnostic or a free-thinker can be easily imagined.

Finally, the fact that through the centuries Roman Catholicism had been closely identified with the Habsburg regime, that the Throne and the Altar had for so long been allied to deny national freedom to other than the 'ruler-people,' made the task of the church and its leaders doubly difficult among non-Germans. This was especially the case with the Czechs, who could not forget what happened in 1415 at Constance or in 1621 on the town square of Prague. The consequence was that, although six-sevenths of the nation belonged nominally to the Mother Church of the west, the formative thinking and planning of the nation has been the tradition of Hus, Comenius, Palacký, and in our day Thomas Masaryk.[9]

Matters of conduct were quite as much at stake as those of belief or dogma. Experience with actual cases showed me the extent to which the schools and universities were beset with sexual promiscuity and perversion, and along with this went flabbiness of attitude to life both private and public. Both medical men and 'shepherds of souls' (even in Protestant circles) revealed ignorance and cowardice

---

9 In 1415, Jan Hus, rector of the Charles University and well-known Czech preacher, was burned at the stake after condemnation by the Council of Constance for heretical views;
 In 1621, on the town square of Prague, thirty leaders of the unsuccessful Bohemian movement for independence were executed;
 Jan Amos Comenius (Komeńský), seventeenth-century Moravian educational reformer, was forced to leave Bohemia because of his Protestant religious views, settled in Poland and other areas;
 Frantisek Palacký, nineteenth-century historian and political leader of Protestant background.

Prologue 13

in dealing with adolescence – in what has been called 'biological urges.' Too often the brothel was recommended to young men as the 'solution' of their problems. This I found in Vienna rather than Prague; but it could be assumed of any larger city and university, and was due in part to the complete disregard of physical education (sports, games, and physical training) in the school curriculum. Such things were frowned on as a waste of time, or even as harmful, for the growing boy. It was a rare thing to find a school with a playground, and the double vacuum thus created worked no end of mischief. It should be said that all this was changed in startling fashion in Central Europe after the First World War. This transformation brought back the Greek ideal of a sound mind in a sound body and is one of the greatest things that has come to that part of the world in our time.

The formal opening of our *foyer* in Prague was an undoubted success, with upwards of eighty people present at the morning dedication service, and fully as many at the informal reception in the afternoon. I was absent, owing to the fact that I had been asked to help in Vienna during Wilder's second visit to the Austrian universities. I felt justified in asking leave of my committee, for the chance to look on while a master was at work was not to be neglected. Apart from this, no centre of university life in Europe was more diversified before 1914 than Vienna; and the fact that Slavs from half-a-dozen countries met there on common ground made it of peculiar importance for me. Merely to be present for ten days of meetings would be of value; but to live for that time in the hostel in Lenaugasse, sleeping on a camp-bed and having meals with the students, would do something for me I badly needed. Some 400 were present on the first night, and the number on the fourth and last was certainly 300.

Good advance work had been done, notably by Phildius' German assistant, Herbert Petrick, who was preparing to enter the Baptist ministry. The permission of the Rector Magnificus (the vice chancellor or president) had been obtained, and one of the formalities in which I took part was in Wilder's brief visit to his office to thank him for his courtesy. These were still the formal days *ante bellum*, when the rector was 'somebody,' and one had to appear in a dark suit and with a pair of gloves. Only the gloves were carried, not worn! His Excellency stood high in the galaxy of notables that characterized the 'imperial and royal' order of things, and etiquette was strict.

From the side of the teaching staff we enjoyed complete neutrality; their business was 'science' – things of the mind – and what we did did not interest them. Only one man of professorial standing showed his support of the enterprise, Friedrich W. Foerster.[10] Had he not been transferred to the University of

---

10 Friedrich Wilhelm Foerster, professor at Zürich and Munich universities, author of several books on pedagogy, ethics, and pacifism.

Munich a few weeks later we should have had a firm friend and helper in the years ahead. In time E got hold of all his handbooks of pedagogy, and we learned a great deal from them. It was from Foerster that I got my first notions of Slav Messianism; he was one of the few German thinkers who saw anything of value in the thinking and writing of Poles, Russians, or other Slav peoples.

It was clear from this and other signs that the founding of a student association in Vienna was meeting a real need. Trouble arose only in getting a suitable name for it. The word 'Christian' had long since been appropriated by people with political aspirations, and in any case it could hardly be used in a city where in the minds of all it had just one meaning - that one was not a Jew! Hence the decision taken by our groups to call their association 'Christocratic' - a term that was etymologically sound and had the merits of treading on nobody's toes.

On the way to Vienna I had stopped over for a few hours at the 'capital' of Moravia, Brno (German Brünn), to have a look at the Czech School of Engineering. A month later, when plans were maturing for an Easter conference at the villa in Ligotka, I made a second visit here, during which a new discovery came my way. Having secured a room for two nights at a modest hotel, I asked two young engineers interested in our work to join me in the lobby for a cup of coffee. They came as far as the door, but nothing would induce them to enter. Wondering at this, I made enquiries and found that the hotel was owned and run by a German! The men took no offense, however, and both of them came to our conference. This was only one of the mistakes I made in those months - innocently enough, but calculated to endanger my good relations with the people around me.

To avoid this was by no means easy in Europe of 1913. In a report-letter to Dr Mott I wrote: 'The first question you must put to any new acquaintance is about his nationality; otherwise you may come a cropper the next minute. You dare not say anything about religion that could offend a Protestant (of any sort), a Catholic, a Greek Orthodox, a Jew or a Muslim. Vienna gave Wilder meetings at which at least as many peoples were represented as were at Pentecost.' Speaking about my own talks with students I wrote of a Russian (it is almost certain that he was a Little-Russian, that is a Ukrainian) who said to me: 'I have lately become a Christian, but I am absolutely at a loss. I belong here to a union which has the strongest sort of national prejudices, and whose members cannot practise or even believe in the brotherhood of man. How am I to reconcile these two things?' I told of a Croat from Trieste, who knew the Gospels but had difficulties over some of the sayings of Jesus, and who gave me money so that I could have a copy of Mark sent him in the Century Bible Series. His English was good enough for him to use it.

At our meetings were many unhappy Jews. One of them told me that he was kept from taking his own life only by the fact of the trouble it would make for

Prologue

his family. Some were open doubters, having no anchor in their faith and being skeptical of there being anything better. Of our relations with students of the Mosaic faith I shall have more to say in these pages. Even those of us who regard Zionism as no solution of their problem have to admit that their lot in Central Europe was little short of tragic.

Much of my time was now given to preparations for an Easter conference to be held in Silesia, in particular for the bringing of a good Czech delegation. I recall only one of our *foyer* meetings of these weeks, at which the American consul and his lady were our guests. He made a fine speech, in which two things about the American way of life were stressed: the high place held by the Bible in the Anglo-Saxon tradition, and the chivalrous attitude of men toward the fair sex. Even if he overstated the case, it was worth while to draw the attention of our people to these facts. They were the subject of much subsequent discussion.

The Easter conference was to fall into two parts: a general meeting of students, and a three-day session for local leaders. The gathering was truly international. There were Germans from Vienna and elsewhere, Czechs from Prague and Brno, Poles from Teschen and Cracow – our own constituency; the Hungarians were to send a fine group of leaders; guests were coming from Switzerland and Holland, and – as chief speakers – Robert Wilder from London and Baron Paul Nicolay (his good friend) from Russia. The last named could be called the founder of the Russian SCM, which had been formally admitted to the federation in the previous year. The theme of the meeting was to be 'Rebirth,' and it was to be presented by three men of standing: Professor Hans Haberl of Vienna was to speak on the Rebirth of the Nation, Dr Beneš of Prague on the Rebirth of Society, and the eminent Polish scholar, Professor Marian Zdziechowski of Cracow, on the Rebirth of the Individual. At the last moment Zdziechowski was prevented from coming, so Wilder took his place. It was a regret to all of us that we could not have the Catholic point of view on this matter properly explained to us.

When I suggested to my committee that we have the draft-programme printed in Czech as it was being printed in German in Vienna, our secretary, Mr Bohać, objected on the grounds of economy. For the first time I sensed a certain coolness toward me which could do the cause real harm. In part, as I have reflected on the matter, it seems to have been due to some feeling that I was his rival, in part to a conviction that no outsider was needed in Prague for the work at all. He would only say that at the Russian conference they had used mimeographed programmes, and he felt that this was good enough for us. The printing went through, and most people were glad of this; but Bohać did not travel with the delegation; he preferred to come on two days later. All this put me on my guard, since the last thing we wanted was any rift in our ranks.

At Phildius' request I went on to Teschen a few days ahead to help with certain preparations. A drawing of the villa in Ligotka against the forest background had been made, and I was to have a few hundred postcards made of this for the use of the delegates. A rush job was done, and the cards came out well, but on the address side was put (quite innocently) the German word *Korrespondenzkarte*. Not a single card was bought or used by the members of the Czech delegation! What is more, the error was mine, but I could never be rid of the feeling that it was blamed on my Vienna colleague. Here again was a sample of the firmness with which Czechs boycotted whatever looked like German (Austrian) overlordship; and it deserves to be recorded in view of what, years later, has been thought by many to be a policy of compromise. The Poles, however, seemed to go along with the Habsburg hegemony, in sharp contrast to the national policy that emerged in 1919.

A rather lyrical, but quite sincere, call was put out by the Vienna student group:

A torn and confused Christendom stands today in the same relation to the Man whose name it bears, as does a field overrun with weeds to the husbandman who has sown it with wheat. One could not know from appearances that Jesus has come to cast a fire on the earth, designed to sweep all lands and to destroy among the nations whatever is unprofitable. But the signs are multiplying that even through our countries a burning brand will soon go; and since all new movements begin among students, the Christocratic Student Movement in Austria announces the coming of a new time ... The aim and end of all history is the renewing of making. This is the final goal of our Easter Conference.

Some who read this were probably disturbed by the 'eschatology' of its ideas; some were doubtless annoyed by the confidence with which it announced 'something new'; few, if any, who saw and read it had the slightest notion of how true it was to prove as prophesy!

Our Czech 'message' was more matter-of-fact, but it did suggest the need, and the prospect, of something different from what existed. Nearly thirty students and teachers from Bohemia and Moravia responded, and the conference as a whole numbered close to a hundred. Most of those who came, whether from far or near, saw a corner of Europe that was new to them. Yeomen help in getting them settled (only half could be accommodated in any fashion in the villa) was given by the Teschen Boy Scout troop, the first of its kind to be organized in this part of the continent. Members of the local Lutheran congregation responded to their pastor's call, and some kind of 'shake-down' was provided for everyone. To our great regret one-third of the delegates had to get their meals in the local inn.

Prologue 17

One-fourth of those present were women, and for them beds were available in the conference house.

The daily programme was more or less that familiar to 'student-movers' the world over, and no account need be given here. The important thing was that we did come to grips with realities, even of politics, and for the most part there was harmony of views. Only in one thing was there a forthright difference of opinion – the form of state organization envisaged in a reborn world. One group favoured the *status quo* – something like empire; but the other, with the Czechs leading, came out for the right of self-government for all nations. 'I am an Austrian through and through' had been the declaration of one of the senior Poles; to which the spokesman for the Czechs replied promptly, 'I am a Czech through and through.' (It will be evident, on reflection, that the two men were using the terms 'Austrian' and 'Czech' in different senses.) The chairman put it to all that an SCM conference was not the place to pursue the matter further, but a good deal of private discussion followed – all of it friendly, though firm. The discussions were held for the most part in German, though both French and English were heard. Dr Beneš treated his theme from the point of view of the sociologist, and showed already some of the understanding that was to make him five years later foreign minister of his restored motherland.

Both on this occasion and on others where guidance was needed, Baron Nicolay proved to be a tower of strength. Not even the Czechs could question his wisdom or sincerity when he pleaded for the larger view – now in French, now in German, now in Russian. What astonished some of the Prague delegation was that he was quite ready to use German where necessary; he had no antagonism to the language because it was the instrument of imperial designs in the hands of Habsburgs or others. When he came to give the closing address of the general conference he spoke in French, and those who did not follow in that tongue sat apart, hearing the gist of the whole thing through an interpreter. But there was one point of tension of which only a few initiated knew at the time; even I did not hear of it until later. In his address Dr Beneš said a few introductory words about the eagerness with which those from Prague were seeing for the first time a corner of the 'Bohemian crownlands' few knew anything about.[11] Those lands did include Silesia, and this reference caused anxiety to the Poles of the duchy, who were in a two-thirds majority. They took him aside afterwards and expressed their concern. Five years later the dispute between the two neighbour countries

---

11 At its height under the Luxemburgs in the fourteenth century, Bohemia controlled Lusatia, Silesia, and much of Brandenburg. These comments by Beneš are significant in view of his proposals to the Paris Peace Conference for special status for Lusatia as well as the issue of Silesia, which Rose discusses.

over this 'border area' became a serious cause of conflict – again something that few could have dreamed of at Easter 1914.

On many grounds we could consider this first South East European conference a success. The very fact that Germans and Slavs and Magyars could meet together in an atmosphere of friendship was significant, but when one adds that among those present were Protestants, Catholics, and Jews, with at least some *confessionslos* (what we should call 'free-thinkers') as well, the gathering was historic. Our hopes that it would be the first of a series were to be dashed to the ground, but there were no regrets in our minds as we turned homeward. Only one thing happened shortly afterwards that sobered our spirits. One of the finest of the Vienna delegation, a young Roumanian law student from the Bukovina, took his life in the basement of the university. So far as we could learn the cause was worry about lack of money to complete his year. His pride had kept this hidden, but all of us wondered whether we were not in some part to blame for not having discovered his need.

Back in Prague we found plenty to do – work at Czech, study in general, meetings, the making of new friends. The *foyer* was being used for four study-groups weekly; it was being loaned twice a month for meetings of the Total Abstinence Society; it was the scene of regular social gatherings; it was becoming a place where members and friends would meet for informal chats. On Sundays at eleven-thirty a short leaders' meeting took place for prayer and counsel – all of it still in the experimental stage. But there were 'doubters.' In one of my report letters I wrote: 'People here are sensitive, and many are quite convinced of the superiority of their nation in intellectual things. More than once I have been told "Religion may be all right for your nations, but we have got farther than that!" Some pity our earnestness, thinking we shall get over it; others fear it. A lady begged my wife yesterday that we should not pursue a friendship with a prominent Roman Catholic, saying, "I know you are good, but please do not try to win her over to your doctrines!" To this we replied that we have no doctrines save the New Testament, only to hear this: "That's just what I'm afraid of: you do not value enough traditions."'

At times, being from the New World, we tended to expect results sooner than was proper; but we had behind us the wise counsel (rooted in calm faith) of senior committee members, as well as the even older wisdom of men like the 'grand old man' of Czech evangelicanism, Dr Jan Karafiat. To him I would go from time to time, seeing in him the rare combination of scholar and saint. Had we been fated to continue our work in Bohemia, I should have learned much from him. Men and women of this calibre were to be found in the most unlikely places, and I made it my business to seek them out. Officialdom and the 'traditions' referred to above kept them from ever coming together – a great misfor-

Prologue

tune for the whole country. In different ways they treasured one thing above all – the hope of what de Maistre called 'A new explosion of Christianity.'

Much of my time was given to preparation for the three-week summer school planned for late July and early August in Ligotka. I was to provide a competent leader for a course on the Book of Acts, and with the help of others to enlist at least a dozen participants. This latter task was not easy, for few students could meet even the charge set for board; and when school assembled we had more seniors than undergraduates. I made the mistake of letting some people enrol who were not students; something I never did again. There was nothing for it but to confine our attention to one type of person, otherwise we should have been in conflict with the churches and destroyed the peculiar atmosphere of our associations.

Before the end of June, and with the academic year well behind us, we were ready for what was to prove an adventure. We had signed the lease of a flat in the middle of town, so as to set up a home of our own, and arranged for the storing of our few possessions. Then we left for Vienna, on our way to attend the summer conference of the Hungarian SCM – by way of responding to the visit of their leaders in Ligotka at Easter. With one German student from Vienna, we took the express from Vienna to Budapest, meaning to spend Sunday in the Hungarian capital and go north with the students from there to the conference site in the foothills of the Carpathians, at Losonc (in Slovak, Lučenec), inside the borders of what was later to be part of the Czechoslovak republic.

We made the Saturday journey in lovely weather, but it was memorable to me because of a conversation carried on by three businessmen in our compartment, which soon turned to the theme of 'peace or war.' Much of it was academical but one fragment of it stuck in my mind – particularly in view of what happened the next day. The three agreed that war came, as a rule, over the question of bread and butter (*die Brotfrage*); if people had enough to eat there would be no wars! I felt at the time that this was too simple an analysis, and not true to history. But when I realized later on that Europe, by far the smallest of the six continents, had inside its borders one quarter of all the people in the world, I had to reconsider things.

On this quiet Saturday, with the fertile plains about us, our thoughts were of quite other things. We were to be met by student friends in Budapest, and looked forward to seeing that celebrated city. Everything turned out as planned; we were taken to a quiet hotel, and the next day, after resting in the morning, we were shown some of the things most worth a visit. In the middle of the afternoon we were sitting in the open-air cafe on the slopes of the Buda Hill, looking eastwards across the river at the main part of the capital, without a care in the world, when all at once there appeared flags flying at half-mast on the public buildings below us. Half an hour later we heard that the successor to the Habsburg throne, the Archduke Franz Ferdinand (nephew of the old Emperor Franz Josef), and his consort had been shot by an assassin in a place we had never heard of, Sarajevo in Bosnia, while representing the dynasty at the summer manoeuvres of the imperial army. Then the news came that the shots had been fired by a Serb, and it was said that trouble would follow.

The whole affair meant nothing to us, but we did wonder why our Hungarian friends showed no trace of sorrow. They did not like Serb assassins, but they did not like the archduke either; partly because he had married a Czech countess (Sophie Chotek) but still more because he was known to be critical of the Dual System existing since 1867, which gave the Magyar people so favoured a position. In short, his death caused satisfaction rather than regret, and no one shed any tears for him. Only later were we to discover that the 28th June was St Vitus's Day, sacred in the memory of the South Slav peoples because of the destruction of their armies by the Turks on that day in 1389 on the field of Kosovo. It was, therefore, in the eyes of the people of Bosnia, an insult for an alien power to be parading its military might under their eyes on this special day.

Early on Monday we all boarded the train for Losonc – a company of at least forty men and women. For the first time I was to take part in an open-air conference on the continent. Those attending were lodged in tents, although older guests like ourselves had rooms in the town more than a mile away. The walk took time, but things went well until the third evening, when a heavy thunderstorm with accompanying cloud-burst broke over the district. Virtually the whole camp was washed out, and it took most of the next day to get things straight again. Along with the students were some Boy Scout troops. They knew how to get things done, and evening meetings could go on as before.

Knowing not a word of Hungarian, we were provided with an interpreter, who kept us posted as to what was going on. With the help of German (or even English) we had quite a few talks with fellow-campers, and the 'innocent abroad' in me was soon to get into trouble. On the Saturday afternoon there was a sort of 'open house' to which friends from the town and neighbourhood were invited. While standing listening to some music, I heard a man and his wife next to me speaking Slovak – which is very close to Czech. So I spoke to them in my faltering Czech, and we chatted about what was going on. Scarcely had I taken leave of these folk when my interpreter came up, plucked me by the sleeve, and told me that it would be better for all concerned if I was not heard talking with anyone in a Slav language! I took the hint, though far from pleased at the discovery. It was my first glimpse behind the curtains of Magyar rule in prewar days. Our SCM friends expressed their regret at this kind of thing, but they could do nothing about it.

Prologue

A pleasant episode that week was a Sunday afternoon visit to a nearby chateau-castle – the property of a nobleman who had an English wife. It involved for the men and boys a longish walk, and everyone arrived hungry. To make matters worse the numbers were larger than were expected, and something of a riot followed. The ladies were at once taken to smaller rooms and served with tea and all sorts of good things. For us men a long table was set out in a huge dining-room, loaded with food of all kinds, and it was a case of every man for himself. Those who did not feel like elbowing their way came off rather badly, and it was only after half-an-hour of waiting that we older men were found, and taken to join the ladies. When I saw that table some time later it was a sorry sight – only the bones of fish and fowl, and a mess of dirty dishes. Even so, many of the men went home with half-empty stomachs. This was no reflection on Hungarian hospitality, but simply the consequence of faulty planning. Our hostess was kindness itself, but I doubt whether she would want an invasion of that sort every week.

The spirit and tone of the conference meetings were high. I recall one address by a YMCA secretary on 'Clean Living' which was a model of frankness and good taste. Our congratulations went to Victor Janos (we should call him John Victor) and his helpers on what was done, as well as our thanks for the reception we enjoyed at their hands. We knew that a number of those present were to join us ten days later in Silesia for summer school, so it was a case not of farewells, but of *Auf Wiedersehn*.

E and I and our Vienna colleague planned to see something of the lovely Slovak country – the southern Carpathian range known as the Tatras – before making our way northward through the Jablunkow Pass into Silesia. Having three full days to spare we decided on some hiking. Sending on our suitcases to Teschen, we took with us only haversacks and the clothes we had on. After an hour on the train, we left the railway at a point where it turns west, meaning to follow northwards a beautiful valley, cross a 'summit' (nothing very high) the next morning, and then descend westward, joining the railway again north of Kremnitz. Unfortunately our companion was taken with severe stomach cramps before we got far, so he had to turn back and come on by rail. E and I pursued our way, and toward evening reached a charming Slovak village close to the 'saddle' where the kindly school teacher agreed to put us up for the night. The surroundings were superb, the evening perfect. In every direction, particularly to the north, there rose wooded mountain slopes, with the range of the Tatras towering above the rest. Our host proved to be one of nature's gentlemen. He spoke fairly good German, so we could ask him many questions. Thus we discovered the extent of his task – the care of 119 school children, only part of whom could be accommodated at one time!

After a good night's rest, for which our host could only with difficulty be brought to accept payment, we set out on our second day's walk. From the first hour it was downhill, and we found it easier to make full time. Well before evening we reached the railway point, to find our companion had arrived at noon and had made arrangements for us to sleep at the local inn. But at supper he told us that for some reason he did not like the feel of the place. While wandering about he had heard scraps of conversation that revealed unrest, and he made the suggestion that, if there was an evening train, we take it and get over the border into Silesia (part of Austria) for the night. What bothered him was that I had surrendered my passport to the Jewish inn-keeper. 'I have two identification documents,' he said, 'and the one I handed him is my university card, which is the less important.' At first I objected that he was seeing troubles behind every tree, but in time I swung around to agree with him; so I suggested that he slip over to the station and ask about trains. He was soon back to say that there would be one about nine – just at dark. By now he was even more restless, so I said to E, 'Let's pack up and go!'

While she saw to this, I went to see the inn-keeper. I told him he should have his money for the rooms, but that we had changed our minds and would not use them. Taking the change from my pocket, I asked for our documents. At once he began to oppose this; he could not let us go, he would have to report to the police; 'after what had happened at Sarajevo everyone had to be careful,' etc, etc. That clinched the matter for me. I stepped up to him, put my hand on his shoulder, and told him in plain language that he should get our passports inside of two minutes or take the consequences. That did it; he wilted, and in a short time we were clear. From what I came to know later of the role inn-keepers used to play in Slovakia, I can see that we were well rid of what might have meant unpleasant delay.

One should not generalise from single incidents, but there was something else E and I noted when talking afterwards about this walking tour. Wherever we passed children on the road we greeted them; on the Hungarian side of the frontier it was a rare thing to get any response, while the moment we were in Silesia our greeting was at once returned with a smile. That sort of thing does not happen without reason!

Our arrival in Ligotka was expected, but we found friends plunged in grief. The professor of music in the Normal School in Teschen had been shot on the street the day before by a half-crazy student whom he had not allowed to pass in his yearly examinations. He had been at our Easter conference, was a man highly respected by all, and the father of five sons. For years he had been organist in the huge Lutheran church, and the throng seen at his funeral attested to the sense of loss felt by the community. His oldest son became his successor; at first 'acting,' but when he had passed the tests required, a regular member of the school staff.

Prologue

In spite of this sad event, our summer courses got off to a good start. As leaders of groups we had Haberl from Vienna, Pastor Urbanek from Prague, and Miss Elizabeth Clark (New England) who had done some years of *foyer* work in Switzerland. In addition, Phildius had prevailed on the veteran American missionary worker in Albania, Pastor Erickson, to give us two weeks of his vacation period. He proved to be a really good lawn-tennis player, and helped us to initiate our rather rugged court. Victor Janos was with us, and we could always call on Pastor Kulisz in case of need. Thirty undergraduates were present, coming from five national backgrounds.

The weather man was kinder to us than he had been in April, and with harvesting in full swing the countryside presented a picture of peace and industry. The plainland of the Upper Oder basin, just outside the Moravian Gate, could be seen from the terrace of the villa, with at night a reflection of the big furnaces for smelting that mark the beginning of the huge industrial region. This was the scene as one looked north. Behind us, rising directly above the few acres that surrounded the house, were the forest-clad slopes of the Western Carpathians (here called the Beskids), which reached in a broad belt close on a hundred miles before they looked out on the plain of Hungary. Each week we took a day off for a longer hike into the uplands - rising to 3500 feet at some points; otherwise we confined ourselves to outdoor games on the spot. Each week a musical evening of some quality was arranged, in which E was to play a leading part.

In a letter to my mother, dated early in August, which managed to reach her before the frontiers were closed for four years, I said: 'The sudden breaking of the war-cloud put an end five days too soon to our school. It was a sad parting, since not a few left to take up arms. No one knows whether we shall ever see them again, but we hope for the best. Our School was a time of real help and blessing to all, and we may expect to see some permanent results if circumstances permit.'

To us, occupied with our work and unable to glean much from the reading of the daily papers, the declaration of war by Austria-Hungary on Serbia came as a bolt from the blue. I recall, as if it were yesterday, how one morning a Vienna student, who had gone down to the post-office early, came into the dining-hall while we were at breakfast to say in a voice that all could hear, 'War is at the door!' He had the morning paper in his hand to confirm this. It is safe to say that not a soul of those present had any idea of how acute the tension had been, and only afterwards did the world learn of the efforts made in more than one capital to relieve it. Even the ultimatum to Belgrade had not been turned down by Serbia; but the big question disturbing all was, 'What would Russia do?' We were soon to have the answer.

Within twenty-four hours the villa was empty save for the Haberls - father and mother and three children - and ourselves. All travel was now forbidden to civilians for fourteen days in order to make the mobilisation of the armies easier. Phildius knew that he was liable for service in Switzerland. The Kings wanted to be safe in Vienna, though they knew that as Americans they were immune from any involvement. As for the Roses – there were no indications that Britain would have any part in the war, so why worry? Had we known that the Asquith government would take its momentous decision on August 4th, we should probably have gone to Vienna with the others. And had we done this, what follows would never have been written.

2
Wartime in Silesia 1914-18

THE FIRST SHOCKS

Hostilities between Austria-Hungary and Serbia, with Russia coming in as the traditional friend of the Balkan Slavs, were already five days old when Britain declared war on Germany. All this seems a complicated business, as indeed it was. It concerns the present story only because we, as British subjects, could have no idea during those days that we should be personally affected by what was going on. And right here the rest of the tale of our political relationships may as well be told.

Three months later, when I ventured to go to the County Office in Teschen, with Pastor Kulisz as a guide, to enquire whether we could get permission to move to Vienna with a view to taking up some kind of Red Cross work, I discovered that the officials in charge thought of Canada as belonging to the United States! The answer I got was, 'Why, of course; Americans are free to go where they like.' When, however, I explained the error, the prefect (who was a fine example of aristocratic Pole attached to the Austrian Civil Service) made a long face. His final advice was that we stay quietly where we were, not attract unnecessary attention to ourselves, and not think about getting back to our home in Prague, where anti-Austrian feeling was running high.[1] When the imperial anthem was being played in the cafés, the Czech people refused to take their hats off or to stand up. The pastor and a retired school principal were named as our sponsors and I was directed to keep clear of political discussions or issues.

1 Czech resistance to World War I, while real, has sometimes been exaggerated.

Had we been aware of all this at the end of July, we should have almost certainly taken the train with Phildius to Vienna. I had got to know the American ambassador there, during Wilder's visit, and we might well have got ourselves 'evacuated' safely to Switzerland in due course. It is easy to be wise after the event. Actually, we had no cause for anxiety, except the fact that our families in Canada would be imagining all sorts of things about us for some time to come. As it turned out, the letter to my mother quoted above reached its destination, and I take from it the following further paragraph:

Everything looks darker from day to day. It may be that we are foolish to stay here, but now it is too late since no one is allowed to travel except the soldiers, and this condition may last some time. At first there was no notion in anybody's head that Germany would declare war on Russia, but now that this has happened there is no telling what the end may be. One thing is certain, that she is going to work in a business-like way, so there is no danger of anything happening to us on Austrian soil. We are as safe here as we should be anywhere outside Canada. We decided to stay because there is a chance of Teschen being made a sort of hospital base, so there will be work to be done. In the meantime we can only wait and suffer; as all those are doing who remain behind, knowing that many friends are in the field and that some may already have fallen. It is hard even to pray because one has the feeling that no power can stop things. If, as today's paper reports, the problem of Belgium leads to strife between Germany and England we may see times such as have not been seen since Napoleon's days ... I should like just to advise the following of all reports, so that you may know how things stand. You will see on a map that the Russian frontier is less than 50 miles from us, but that is only a corner of Russian Poland, which is by no means friendly to Tsardom. The border has already been crossed and two cities taken by the Germans, so that the advance will be towards the East and not towards Vienna or Berlin. Things are so quiet here as we look out over the plain from our balcony, that we find it hard to believe what is going on within a hundred miles. We shall stay here for some time, but are totally at a loss about giving any address ... I have written to Dr Mott for advice, but it will be some time before a reply can reach us. Fortunately we have enough money for immediate needs and more is due from London if we can only get it ...

Already the tragedies of the war situation have been forced upon us from all sides. There is scarcely a family in the village without father or son or even three or four members taken. Saturday and Sunday were days of tears and sorrow. The road to the station at Gnojnik was lined with men on foot, each with a small pack on his back on the way to Teschen to enlist. One man in poor circumstances leaves a wife and ten children behind. The farmer who has been sending us milk leaves a smaller family, but it is the same with all. Kulisz is nearly beside himself. The other day he saw in Teschen the huge Lutheran church, requisitioned as a barracks, in an unspeakable state - the floor covered with straw, everything in disorder, packed with soldiers, no regard for decency and certainly no reverence for a sacred building ... If, as rumour has it, a large body of German troops is placed near us as a reserve, there will soon enough be a shortage of all means of subsistence, and if the war lasts till the snow flies the suffering will be indescribable ...

A few comments on this letter will save space and time later on. Few people imagined that any war could last over the winter. For us it was fortunate that, for a time at least, we thought of our confinement in terms of weeks or at most months. Had this not been so, an almost intolerable prospect of enforced idleness would have been faced by two people always used to work. Only when the news came through of Kitchener's statement that it would take three years to beat the Germans - a remark that was treated by all around us with high scorn and amusement - did we begin to realize what was ahead. By this time we had learned to take things as they came, though (as will appear) during the whole of the first year we were in a constant state of uncertainty.

Thanks to the good offices of Miss Clark, arrangements were soon made in Berne for the treasurer of the federation (Dr Walter Seton) to send from London a regular allowance through Swiss intermediaries; and only once during the war did we find ourselves short of funds. It was arranged that, for the duration, I was to draw half my salary, and this promised to meet our needs. Before the winter came, we were able to get our personal effects sent on from Prague, including our piano, so that for the time being the villa in Ligotka was to become our home. Dr Mott left the entire decision as to our movements to me; at least until we should have a clearer idea how things would shape up.

Our plans for being of some use in or around Teschen, for instance in Red Cross work, were soon to be disappointed. A Russian victory east of Lwów forced a withdrawal in September of the whole Austro-Hungarian front; and the famous fortress on the San River with the unpronounceable name of Przemysl was soon surrounded. This forced a withdrawal of the Austro-Hungarian GHQ westward - to Teschen, right under our noses. From now on, until the collapse of the Russian threat and the transfer of the army to the new front facing Italy, the little world in which we lived was 'war territory' and was provided with a special police cordon. This made it quite impossible for any outsider to move about, and it is still a mystery to me how we managed to stay put. Had I been single, my fate would certainly have been sealed - an internment camp in the west of Austria! However, so far as I know, the authorities had no plan for interning women and they would not have known what to do with E. Apart from this, witness must be borne to the decency of the officials and the sense of humanity towards strangers for which Austria is celebrated. One may even say that the people of Vienna never felt that they were at war with Britain; once the authorities had agreed to leave us in peace they seemed to regard the matter as settled.

Two things in the course of time did threaten to alter this policy. Some of the local zealots, particularly when news came of British successes, kept bothering the authorities to get rid of 'this Englishman' who was 'on free footing' in the neighbourhood. Further, until it became clear that they would lead nowhere, special efforts were being made by Dr Mott to get permission for us to be interned in Switzerland, where I could be of some use in humanitarian work. We afterwards learned that he had tried two channels of approach: that of the Vatican, to which Vienna was likely to be sensitive; and that of the Swedish Royal Family, which had always been interested in our work. The only consequence was the piling up over many months of a huge dossier of material about us, both in Vienna and Teschen. I have always regretted not filing a request with the Polish authorities, when they took over in the latter city in November 1918, with a view to securing these papers for my own satisfaction. They were seen by friends, but later disappeared.

And now for the desolation brought in the community by the calling up of all able-bodied men. This sort of thing is no longer a novelty in the modern world; but nothing of the kind had happened in Central Europe for a century, and for us outsiders the very principles on which it worked were strange. Not only was every man between twenty and forty-five ordered to report at once to his regiment, but every peasant who had two horses had to give up one (later on even the second was taken); and very soon the same kind of rule was extended to cattle in order to provide meat for the troops. Larger farms and estates escaped with less severe treatment, and at times personal influence secured favours about which a lot of grumbling followed. Of course, all live-stock was subjected to valuation and written receipts were given to the owners which in due course were honoured by the banks. The peasant got his price for his cattle, but he was poorer not richer. The time came when he had turned nearly everything he owned into money; but he could not buy anything with the money, and, of course, he could not eat it! The end result was inflation, and people learned the hard way the lesson taught long ago by Aristotle that money is only a token, a means of exchange – but nothing more.

For the most part the men joined up willingly enough. There was real patriotism for the monarchy, especially where Russia was the enemy. In the case of the younger men the chance of getting away for a time from the farm or the mine or the factory, and thus of seeing a bit of the world, counted for much. No one had any doubts as to who would win the war. On all sides one heard the greeting, as neighbours took leave of one another, 'Auf Wiedersehn in Moskau!' True, the harvest was still unfinished, and they knew that a heavy burden devolved on the older men – and on the women; but they made the best of a bad job, and more tears were shed by those left behind than by those going out to fight.

Within a few months all this was reversed. The advance of the imperial armies into Serbia, proclaimed with much sounding of trumpets, met with a rude check; and after six weeks of severe fighting those armies were back where they started. On the northeastern front, against Russia, things were even worse. Lwów had been taken, the line of the San was lost, and the Russians were threatening the passes into Hungary and the ancient city of Cracow. Only the sending of emergency help by the Reich saved the situation at the end of October; the Tsar's armies were beaten at Limanowa, and a new front on the river Dunajec became stabilized for the winter. A supreme effort had stopped the Russians from reaching the big industrial area of German Silesia, from which the way would have been open through the Moravian Gate into the heart of the monarchy.

There was, as already hinted, one notable exception to this readiness for war. From the outset Czech recruits had balked at the idea of fighting their fellow-Slavs, and some regiments openly mutinied. The shooting of every tenth man in some disaffected units sobered everyone, but it did not make for good-will. A humourous anecdote told up and down the country reflected the feelings of the Czech people in general, and indeed of many others:

A peasant, with his one ox hitched to a wagon, was crossing the Wenceslas Square in Prague, when the beast suddenly lay down on the tramline and refused to move. Traffic was blocked, a crowd soon gathered, and the traffic police could not restore order. A higher official was promptly sent for to deal with the situation; but while they waited for him an old villager stepped up to the peasant and offered to get the ox up. He was referred to the policeman who told him politely to mind his own business; however he persisted and was finally given permission to try his luck. He went up to the ox, stroked its back and neck, and then leaned over and whispered something in his ear. At once the ox got up and began to move off – cheers from the crowd! The old fellow wanted to slip away, but was stopped by the officer who said (taking out his notebook), 'Excuse me, but we must get a record of all this. Tell me your name and address! And I must also know what you said to the ox.' With the usual fear of all officials on the part of simple people, as well as of anything set down in writing, the villager objected to giving these details; but he was threatened with arrest unless he submitted. Finally he told who he was, but got the officer's word that no record would be made of what he had said. 'You see,' he went on, 'I just announced to the ox that the band was going to play the Austrian national anthem; and when that is to be played every ox stands up.'

Among the better informed, the seriousness of the whole situation was felt from the day when the news came that England, as they all called the British empire, had entered the struggle. I recall two quiet remarks made by Professor Haberl when that word arrived: 'The time will come when every last man has to go,' and 'Now we shall really find out what it means to pray 'Give us this day our daily bread.' As things turned out, he was right on both counts.

A rather different expression of the same seriousness came my way from a quite different corner. Shortly after the outbreak of the war we had a letter from a devout lady in Berlin who had been much interested in Christian work among students. It contained a warm invitation to make her house our home, if this seemed desirable, for as long as we liked. To this kind gesture I had given an evasive answer; but a second letter came late in September repeating the offer, and including this startling paragraph: 'We must all get accustomed to the following; that this terrible war will last a long time, even though things go as well as possible. Paris must first be taken, England completely brought to her knees, and Russia totally defeated. If we can achieve this in one year, and then in another year create a new order of things, God will have wrought a great miracle.' I copied this pronouncement in my diary and added the comment: 'So say we, all of us!'

Oddly enough, by the same post there came a letter from Haberl, who was long since back at his work in Vienna. One of his friends, a pastor in Carinthia, was ready to take us into his home if I would become the warden of a hostel for high school boys in Klagenfurt. This would have been an interesting experience, but was not to be entertained as long as the federation regarded me as one of its workers. In any case the thing became unworkable when a second letter arrived two days later – this time from the pastor himself. In it I was told that I should definitely have to pass myself off as an American, and to take the German rather than the Allied side in the great struggle.

According to notes made at the time, I was twice in Teschen in the winter and spring of 1915 to enquire again whether we might have permission to move our residence. In one case the suggestion came from our friends in Prague; in the other it was made by Phildius, who by the end of November had got release from his duties as a Swiss soldier and was back in Vienna. He felt that I could be of use in the capital. Each time I was given a polite but firm refusal, so we had to resign ourselves at last to the prospect of what seemed idleness, but was in fact to prove something quite different. As will appear in the sequel, we soon found plenty to do which had a bearing on our whole future.

One rather odd episode of this time deserves recalling, since it may have had something to do with why we were left in peace in Ligotka. In the spring of 1915

E began to have trouble with her hair. When she combed it the hair would come out - no pleasant experience for a young woman; so after some deliberation we decided that I should cut it short and then shave her head, with a view to trying a massage cure and getting a new growth. This operation was performed, not too successfully since my razor was dull, and for a week she stayed in the house. The hair soon began to grow and she appeared then in the village wearing a skull-cap. When he saw her, Pastor Kulisz greeted her with the words 'Blessed St Francis of Assisi!' and there was a good deal of merriment. Within a month's time a rich growth of new hair was achieved such as E could not remember, and a complete cure was affected. I tell this story only because, as we heard later, the authorities had been told by the local gendarme of how this 'foreigner' treated his wife badly, even to the point of cutting her hair off! Word got about that he was a 'poor fool' who probably was not all there and, in any case, quite harmless. There are few better ways of getting by with something than to encourage in people the notion that you are half-witted.

OUR HABITAT

Lloyd George was not the only person of distinction in the world who could say in 1919 that he had never heard of Teschen. The small, almost square territory known as the duchy of that name, though it lay precisely at the centre of the continent and was inhabited (according to the census of 1910) by over 400,000 souls, was the kind of area visitors from the outside world passed by, but rarely stayed in. This was a pity, for the landscape is pleasing and places of historic interest are numerous. What is more, the people were worth knowing and tourists could live comfortably at small cost. In more ways than one the duchy was a *piccolo mondo* of its own, set between the open plain of Moravia and the almost unknown Galicia to the east, with the industrial area of Prussian Silesia on the north, and the broad belt of the western Carpathians stretching to the Hungarian plain in the south.

As a separate political unit it dates from the year 1742, when Frederick of Prussia helped himself to the whole Oder region, but left two small duchies, that of Teschen and that of Troppau, to the Empress Maria Theresa. Its indigenous population was Polish, and roughly one-third of these people belonged to the Lutheran faith, which they had never lost since Reformation days. But virtually the whole of the country of Frydek on the west was long since Czech in speech and sentiments. Let it be said that in using the terms 'German' or 'Polish' in this connection one must be wary. The duchy was no part of Germany, having only Austro-German affinities - a very different thing. But it was also no part of Poland since there was no Poland on the map. What is more, the simple people had been taught for generations to despise everything Polish - something which was easier in the case of the 90,000 Lutherans because Poland traditionally was thought of as a solidly Catholic nation.

The big estates in the duchy and the big interests (mines, factories, and foundries), which had developed notably since 1870, were almost all German-owned. Moreover, an important factor in this country town of the duchy was the privately-owned railway line, built in the seventies, running from Oderberg (*Bohumín*) on the northern border southward through Teschen and the Jablunkov Pass into Hungary (strictly speaking Slovakia), where it turned eastward as far as the city of Kaschau (*Košice*). For half of its distance this railway served as a link in the trunk line from Berlin through Břeclav to Budapest and the Dardanelles – a thing of continental significance, as the war was soon to show. Jobs on this railway were much sought after; but the condition of holding one, or still more of promotion, was that you bring up your children as loyal Austrians!

Teschen had been an important centre of religious life in this part of Europe from the year 1707, when Charles XII of Sweden, acting as champion of the Protestant minority, secured from the Habsburg overlords the privilege of building a 'Church of Grace' with guaranteed freedom of worship. Alongside this church there soon grew up a private high school to which the sons of Protestant gentry came from nearly all of the Danube lands. The parish of Ligotka belonged to this group of favoured Protestant communities; and was indeed the border parish, since a mile-and-a-half away to the west of the village lay the line which separated the Czech-speaking Catholics of Frydek from the Polish-speaking Lutherans of the rest of the duchy.

A region of this kind, lying at the crossroads of the continent, was bound to have a mixed population. I say 'crossroads' because the north-south railway just mentioned was traversed at Oderberg by the main railway coming from Trieste and Vienna and going eastwards, on the one hand to Kiev and Odessa or in turn to Warsaw and Moscow. Small wonder then that, in addition to the nationalities mentioned already, there were Slovak and Hungarian elements, and, of course, a sprinkling of Jews. The officials were mostly German, as were many of the business people. In industry the Czech element was strong, as managers and foremen; but most of the labour, especially unskilled, was provided by the Polish peasant communities. Of course the government was Austro-German, and it was part of public policy to disguise as far as possible the existence of non-German elements.

Self-appointed representatives from the duchy had attended the famous Congress of Slavs held in Prague in 1848 and declared themselves Polish in speech and loyalty, though their homeland had been separated from Poland since the fourteenth century. Yet they would have been the first to admit that the masses of still illiterate peasants had little notion of any national affinity. At best they had a sense of regional attachment – they were Silesians; and in many cases they regarded the emperor in Vienna as a sort of divinity – a left-over from ancient days. Decades of education were needed before their grandchildren began to realize where they really belonged; and even in 1914 most of them were still concerned for their daily bread more than anything else. We shall see how this kind of thing made the task of drawing new frontiers after the war exceedingly difficult.

Looking back forty years, there are those today who argue that these people were pretty well off under the benevolent despotism from Vienna; that by comparison with what they have been through since then their life was almost an idyll. Of course that kind of argument proves too much. It is only acceptable to people who hold that the visible things of life, like the amount of butter you can have every day on your bread, are all that count. But that leaves out so much that it must be rejected. Of course, the sociologists may well hold that 'adjustment' is the law of progress; that the fewer the tensions to be found in any community the better; and that therefore governments are justified in using a variety of means to reduce divergencies to a minimum. Against this it should not be forgotten that nature loves diversity and that the truest riches, cultural or other, are to be found in the cherishing of variety rather than its extinction.

Years passed before I discovered the significance of all this, or before I realized that in the parish of Ligotka we had in microcosm a picture of the whole babel of tongues and creeds presented by the Dual Monarchy. Pastor Karol Kulisz, a remarkable shepherd of souls, was native-born, of peasant stock, and was easily the most influential man in the place. By conviction he was a Pole, though his elder brother (also a minister) had married a German lady and long since became a German. From his tenth year he had been educated in German schools and universities, but this in no way altered his outlook on life. In contrast to his position, though they had Polish names, both the village mayor and the school principal were German in sympathy. To their Polish neighbours they counted as 'renegades.' The owner of the little summer hotel was an Austrian German of the old type, whom everyone respected. The keeper of the village 'pub' would call himself a Czech; in reality he was nothing at all but a money-maker. The village gendarme also had a Polish name, but he was a zealous servant of the emperor and of the Austrian regime. The forester, who had charge of huge stands of timber covering the lower regions of the Carpathians, belonging to the Archduke Frederick would say that he was Hungarian; but his name was Czech, and he would tell of how his mother was a German.

To the church services which, except on the emperor's birthday, were always in Polish, people came from surrounding villages to the north and east – some of them walking two hours and the poorer ones carrying their shoes, to put them on before entering church. I got to know many of these simple people in the last two years of the war, and found them to be a healthy and forward-looking element. All the village school teachers were Poles by conviction, and their influence was notable on the younger generation; nevertheless the pull of material well-being was strong.

The landscape was overwhelmed by the mountains on the south, behind which the sun went so low in winter that the days were very short. There were patches of forest in this rolling country; but rye, wheat, oats, and barley, as well as clover and roots of all kinds, were grown on every farm or farmlet, since many of the holdings were less than five acres. All the fruits known in the temperate zone were produced, and the sight of the cherry, apple, and plum orchards in bloom was one never to be forgotten. Scarcely less memorable was 'the murmuring of innumerable bees' in the lime-tree blossoms in June, the honey of which was lighter in colour and daintier of flavour even than that taken from clover. A marked contrast was the darker honey gathered earlier from the buckwheat blossoms. True, much of the fruit grown was of poor quality, since only people who took care of their trees got good results.

The toughest combination of brawn and brains was needed to wrest even a meagre living from the none-too-fertile soil. In places stony, it was also heavy to till; and especially the peasants whose holdings lay on the slopes (with their northern prospect) paid dearly in labour for all they got. Every acre of land had to be renewed yearly by manure or fertilizer to keep the balance. This made mixed farming a first-rate necessity, and every cartload of good manure was 'worth a king's ransom.' As the demands of war depleted the livestock of the duchy, the soil deteriorated, and fallowing was the only resort. But how could people allow themselves this luxury, when every square rod of land was needed every year to grow food? Small wonder that even here the condition which was general farther east could be found – during the pre-harvest month (*przednówek* in Polish) when there was no more bread and the potatoes were still small, one tightened one's belt every day!

Many of these small holdings were worked by the women and children by hand. On some of them there was not enough level ground in the whole place to lay out a tennis court. It was interesting to speculate who were luckier; those whose farm buildings were near the lower boundary of the holding, or the reverse. In the former case all manure, seed, and tools had to be dragged or carried or pushed uphill; but then the reward came in harvest time, when all the crops could be brought much more easily downhill to winter's shelter. Hay, clover, and straw were mostly carried in a huge linen sheet (home-spun of course), held firmly by the four corners and swung onto one's back. The knack of carrying this kind of load was no easy one. The worst task of all was ploughing and for this some sort of shift was made for mutual help between neighbours. Where horses could not be had, the milk-cows would be hitched to the plough – at times again with neighbourly co-operation. Toward the end of 1917 a Russian prisoner-of-war who came from the black-loam lands of the Ukraine was assigned to the village as a farm helper. When he saw how hard people had to work and how little they got in return he made a long face. Measuring on his finger and then on his arm, he would say: 'With us we work so much (showing six inches) and we get so much in return (showing two feet); but here you work so much and you get only this' (with the gestures reversed).

What made it possible for these people to live at all was the earnings brought home, by the father or a grown-up son, from his week's work in industry or in the mines twenty miles away to the north. Before daylight on Monday morning these men would be off, and they would not be home till the following Saturday afternoon. Then, however, they had real money in their pockets – except in the case of those who spent it on vodka; and bills could be paid which could not be met from the soil. I used to wonder how their fathers lived before these chances of extra earnings were available. To questions I asked no good answer was given. Pastor Kulisz's father was still alive in 1915, ninety-one. He told me once of how as a young man he had walked out thirty-five miles to see the new wonder of the world – the railway that had just come through from Vienna on its way to Warsaw. Of course, his memory went even further back, to the days of serfdom before the liberation of 1848.

The changes that had come during his life raised a ticklish question, which I once put to the pastor: were the people of his generation really the better for the material advantages that had come to them by contrast with their fathers? He pondered this for a moment and then answered: 'Nothing of blessedness (he used an old Polish word) has come to my fellows from the opportunities they have won of higher earnings. I cannot say that they are really happier.'

HOW WE LIVED

When the village was depleted of its manpower in the first days of August 1914, it seemed to many as though the end of the world had come. Two things caused serious inconvenience at once: small change was hardly to be had and the purchasing of everyday necessities was interrupted; secondly, important articles of everyday use disappeared from the shops, and those who had no reserves at home were caught helpless. Both of these dislocations were due to one or another kind of hoarding, but the authorities had too many other cares to be able to deal with them. Of course, gold coins were never seen again, and though silver did still circulate it was not for long. We had soon one- and two-crown paper notes that became a nuisance as they got worn and dirty. Even copper and nickel were replaced in 1915 by small change in iron; both the other metals were called in for war use. A year later orders went out for the surrender of all utensils of copper or brass, and iron ones were provided in their place. Even door knobs and copper wiring were taken. The worst shock of all followed when the churches were bidden surrender their bells. I still have a photograph taken when those from the Lutheran church in Ligotka were loaded on a lorry, to be sent off and melted down for ammunition.

But all this was still hidden mercifully from our sight in the first war-months. For the time being the scare was that of the rising prices, which meant serious hardship for many. In due course, however, many people began to make fortunes and too much money was in circulation. Everyone who produced goods for war use prospered – even the farmers. By 1915 they were getting unheard of prices for everything they had to sell and the proverbial 'stocking' began to swell. Inflation remained controlled till the end of the war; but with the opening of the frontier local currency had to compete with 'real money' coming in from outside and the wild and terrible conditions of after-war years will never be forgotten by those who went through them.

Tea soon cost ten crowns a kilogram (a crown was a gold franc) and in a few months was virtually unobtainable. Coffee went the same way. For the latter, substitutes were soon on the market, some of them quite palatable. E and I followed the practice of the village folk and learned to grind in a hand-mill roasted rye or wheat or barley, which took the place of the real coffee. Before Christmas flour was dearer than sugar, owing to the fact that Central Europe had always been a great producer of sugar beets. By April 1915 the long expected breadcards appeared, and for a time things were rather better.

Both then and later, though we were foreigners, we received exactly the same treatment as all others, and I never heard that there was any resentment in the community on that account. But from 1916 on the quality of the bread became so bad that it was uneatable; worse still, it threatened to poison the system. The first 'alloy' to be used was maize, which made a dryer loaf that crumbled and no knife could cut. A variant of this was barley flour, from which the loaves were so heavy that one could have used them for bricks. Then, so rumour had it, chaff and chopped straw began to be mixed with the flour. Some other source had to be found than the official one, if we were to have bread at all.

Even in the crowded countryside of the duchy, which imported much of its food, this was a much easier business than it could be in the towns. The poorest farmer, if he was well disposed, would share in some way what he had. The farmer's wife was even more generous, provided the door of friendship was opened. E and I were fortunate in this regard. First of all we were known to have the firm goodwill of the pastor and his wife. Had this not been the case, we should have fared badly indeed. The Central European peasant of those days would never sell produce to a stranger, even though offered a high price. The enquirer would be told 'there is nothing,' especially at the great festival seasons such as Christmas or Easter. Once the way of friendship opened, however, everything changed. But we had also another asset, the fact that both of us had grown up on a farm, and so were in a position to do useful service to hard-pressed husbandmen. I could turn to in the rush of harvest and help both outside and indoors. True, my efforts at using the scythe to mow wheat or rye (what is called 'cradling') were extremely clumsy, though I had learned as a boy the rudiments from my father. But when you have no beech you must use basswood; and I did manage to learn as time went on. It should be realized that in the harvest field it was a man's job to mow and a woman's to bind; but there were times when I took part also in binding and stooking, at which I was more competent.

In season there was also much work with the potatoes, the picking of fruit, and the saving of garden stuff. Not that I hired myself out; but I did lend a hand when news came of a labour shortage, and always I was told to bring along my haversack, which never came home empty. One time I would find half-a-loaf of rye bread (whole loaves would weigh up to 15 pounds each); another time there would be a half-a-gallon of rye or wheat, or a slab of bacon or a half-pound of fresh butter – the most precious thing of all. The grain I soon learned to grind in a hand-mill in a cottage nearby; and by sifting this coarse meal E got 'grits' for porridge on the one hand and fine flour for bread or biscuits on the other. In time she became an expert in making the best of both worlds, and we never went hungry.

The trouble was that, often enough, we were without the things needed to produce a balanced meal, such as one could set before guests. There was plenty of sugar, and we were able to preserve fruit in quantity for the winter. So too salt was never lacking, though later on there were parts of Central Europe where it became very scarce indeed. Spices, which were imported articles, soon disappeared, and people who had hoarded some pepper were the object of envy. A large box of succulent prunes was sent to us in the winter of 1915 by a young officer posted in Sarajevo, and that was a great treat. I should add that two parcels of good things were sent through the Red Cross from London by Sir George Parkin in the first year of the war, of which the first arrived safely, but the second was half plundered. I got word out to him not to send any more. Not being a smoker I had no use for the tobacco coupons that could be claimed by all: but from 1917 on I realized that they were extremely valuable as a means of exchange, so I secured my package of tobacco (terrible stuff!) every week, and many a farmer was glad to have it in return for some article of food. After the war, American cigarettes came in, and almost anything could be procured for them which no money could buy.

I mentioned the difficulty of serving a meal to unexpected guests. Hospitality is the 'middle name' of the simple people of Europe; the Polish proverb says, 'A guest in the house is God in the house!' We soon came to realize this, and the problem was what to do in case of emergency. One afternoon in the late summer of 1917 I happened to notice a light farm-wagon coming up the road from the village, drawn by two ponies; and I recognized it as that of very good farmer friends from four miles away. It was about three o'clock and Mr and Mrs C were coming to see us. When I told E she said, 'But I have nothing in the house to give them!' What was to be done? For once courage failed us, so we slipped out the back way, locking the door, and went off along the path through the woods up the slopes of the Kiczera. An hour later we came back – to find that our friends had settled down in the yard and were having a picnic of their own. Of course we joined them. Water was soon hot, and tea of sorts was provided. There was food enough from the farm for a score of people, and a whole basketful remained for us to enjoy in the coming days.

Toward the end of the war the problem of fuel for the coming winter became acute. Even in the fall of 1916 coal was simply not to be had, unless in driblets, so we were compelled to turn to wood. This we had used in part from the outset, at least for kindling fires in the white-tile stoves of German type which heated the living rooms. Even wood, however, could not be bought; so we took council with the pastor and with our old caretaker, Ulrich, and decided to take out some of the less valuable trees standing on the few acres of ground that surrounded the villa. Ulrich had been employed for years on the Habsburg estates and was quite at home in this kind of work. We had to borrow a cross-cut saw for cutting the logs into stove-wood length, but otherwise the tools needed were available.

Never have I known a more orderly craftsman than Ulrich. Each year he chose, from the wood purchased, finer sticks for making kindling, and the pile of this finely-split that stood in part of the one-time stable across the yard was so neatly arranged that it was a joy to look at. What is more, he knew the value of a good tool, and how easily it can be spoiled. So his axe and his 'buck-saw' were handled as carefully as he would handle a razor. Personally, I preferred to work with an axe, but together we got the wood out and cut into stove-wood length, after which the task of splitting and piling fell to me.

From time to time, during the summer, I had volunteer helpers – some of them students and all of them without experience. They were summer visitors, and one of them deserves mentioning. He was the son of a prosperous Jewish merchant in Ostrava, and was living for a month with his mother at the summer hotel. He had finished high school, but had never done any work with his hands in his life. He was a bright boy, interested in and ready to discuss everything from poetry to metaphysics or international relations. After watching me at work on different occasions he wanted to try his hand at splitting wood, so I got hold of a lighter axe and showed him what not to do if he was to avoid cutting his feet. Needless to say he soon had blisters on both his hands.

But what sticks in my memory has to do with a subject we got into one day on the real values of living. I pulled him up short with this straight question: If you were tomorrow suddenly to find yourself set down on the docks of New York or Montreal, what is the first thing that you would look for? He had no answer to give to this question, but after some reflection he suggested, though without conviction, 'a friend.' This did not suit my book and I was at a loss how to proceed when, just at that moment, a Polish student, the son of a miner, who was staying with us while preparing himself for examinations in Vienna, happened to come out of the house to go for a walk. I called to him, introduced him to the other lad, and then put the same question to him in the same terms. Without a moment's hesitation he replied, 'a job.' That saved the day, and I think it was a useful lesson to the young philosopher.

But I should like to return for a moment to Ulrich. An Austro-German of the old order, he had been a gunner at the age of nineteen in the Austrian army on the Russian frontier in 1859 when the Habsburg monarchy was engaged in defending its patrimony in Italy, and was threatened with war on two fronts. More than once I have heard him tell of the simple business war was in the days when the artillery man could see the target he was shooting at and aim his guns accordingly. His daughter was married to a sergeant who took part in the first battles against Russia in August 1914 in the Lublin area; was in fact a machine-gunner, working under totally new conditions from those his father had known.

Our own domestic arrangements had to be of the simplest, and devolved chiefly on 'the lady of the house.' We had only oil lamps and these were much in use from October to April. Frau Ulrich helped in the kitchen, and would light the fires in winter in the big living-room stoves. But after doing for two years without a maid – a mistake as I can see in retrospect – we took a middle-aged 'girl' from a remote corner of the parish who proved a most faithful helper. E was thus relieved of many routine duties. One consequence of this was the begging of a small strip of field from a nearby neighbour, on which we grew in the last war-year at least a ton of potatoes, cabbages, carrots, and other things. With this source of fodder, our 'girl' resolved to rear a pig, and she was soon able to get hold of one in her home village. She insisted on giving it the name of 'Canada' – heaven only knows why! By November it had grown to a respectable size, and provided some needed ham and bacon in a critical time. As will appear in the sequel, I was called away, so I never tasted it.

Having a piano, E had been going steadily on with her music. She was giving lessons to the odd girl from the village, and after the departure of the GHQ from Teschen she would go there fortnightly for a piano lesson herself. But her real business was singing and in the summer of 1917 she arranged an informal recital in the large room of the villa, in which she was helped by a gifted young violinist from the coal-mining area twenty miles away, who had been a student of Hubay in Budapest during the previous winter. She sang folk-songs in six languages – English, German, French, Czech, Polish, and Italian, to a small invited audience, partly of summer visitors from other places. Among those present were a few who did not like her including in her programme the Czech national anthem 'Where is my home?' Later on she was to add Ukrainian and even Russian folk-songs to her repertory; but the arias of the great masters and operatic works in general were not neglected.

As for me, it would be idle to pretend that I made the best possible use of those early years of inactivity. I should have kept on with my study of Virgil. I should have set about learning to play a musical instrument, or at least taken to collecting Central European stamps – anything to take my mind off what was going on. Under such conditions the first thing needed was to preserve one's balance, not to let events 'get one down.' There were times when this alone seemed to tax all my powers, and it was a blessing that I found myself charged, particularly after the sweeping victories of 1915 put the whole of Poland in German hands, with the task of acting as a nursemaid to despairing Polish friends. I would spend hours telling them all sorts of things to cheer them up; nor did I dare to let myself be discouraged by the remark one of them once made on leaving: 'It's grand to hear you say all this about the strength and prospect of the Allies, but of course we dare not believe a word of it!' Only years afterwards did I learn of the comment with which Joseph Conrad took leave of his friends in Cracow in the early winter of 1914-15. During the summer he had been detained as an enemy, but was finally allowed to leave because he was over the age-limit for military service. The words were these: 'As long as there is one Englishman alive, the Germans will not win this war.'

SOME OUTINGS

People in our situation did well not to move about, if only to avoid attracting attention. In consequence of this there was only one direction in which we could wander from the house – into the woods and highlands of the Western Carpathians. Across these one could roam for days without meeting half-a-dozen people, but they were closed in winter unless for the hunter or ski-master, and I was neither. In summer, however, we did make many brief excursions, and I once got away alone with some bread and cheese in my haversack, drank from the springs, and slept for two nights under the trees. I'll admit that this satisfied my *Wanderlust* and I did not repeat the experiment.

Even such outings were only possible from the fall of 1916, when the GHQ was moved to Vienna, and police regulations were everywhere relaxed. Four shorter or longer outings remain in memory, one of them made with the Kulisz family to the chalet on White Mountain, from which an extended panorama could be viewed in all directions; another made by road with Mr C and his wife to visit relatives twenty miles to the east; a third, made with Pastor Kulisz, gave me a chance to see the ancient Moravian shrine of Radhost; while a fourth was a rather amusing local hunting expedition in a neighbouring parish.

On the first of these, Pastor Kulisz with two of his children went along, and we were taken by horses-and-carriage three-quarters of our way up one of the deep valleys which front Silesia and Moravia. Five hours of driving on tolerable macadam roads brought us to within an hour's climb of the shelter where we planned to spend the night. On arrival, we still had two full hours of daylight during which we had supper and enjoyed the vast stretches of evergreen forestland reaching out north, south, east, and west - a sight never to be forgotten. Immediately to the south of us was the old Hungarian border - properly Slovakian. We visited a couple of rude huts in which shepherd-folk lived, the most primitive I ever saw in Central Europe. In one of them, the door of which was standing open, though there was no one at home, there was not only a mud floor, but under the rude table, where various kinds of refuse had collected, a spindly potato plant was growing. What the place must have looked like in winter one cannot imagine! It was, alas, only an extreme sample of the kind of thing the authorities in Budapest cared nothing about along their whole northern frontier.

On such an evening one wanted only to sit down on a comfortable boulder and drink in the scene - a clear sky overhead, the calm and beauty of nature all about, with here and there the smoke of a cottage chimney rising in the distance. But one thing on the horizon drew our attention above all others. Seventy miles or more to the east, and clearly to be seen, since the sun was setting in the west, towered above the forest area the Alps of the Carpathians - the high Tatras. We saw them from the end of the range, so they rose as a cluster of towering rocky structures, seeming in the light of evening to be much closer and, their tops being covered with snow, resembling a bouquet of flowers against the sky. None of us had seen the Tatras before, though in later years we got to know them very well; but I would not have missed this first sight of them for anything.

We all slept well, and on the following morning made the three-hour gentle descent on foot, westward to Althammer, as it was then called. Here we had a hasty lunch from our basket, while we waited for the daily train that came out of the mountain valley to take us to Frydek. While changing at this station we had a narrow escape from trouble. The police were searching for a run-away, and everybody had to show his identity card. This E and I did not possess, and for a moment the pastor was dismayed. However, he kept us out of sight, went alone to the ticket office and, when asked about his party, simply said that 'everything was in order.' This, of course, was true, though the sergeant was deceived in respect of ourselves. We were not held up and got safely home. This incident taught us to be careful – at least to avoid railway travel.

On the second journey I was alone. Our good friends Mr and Mrs C asked me to come on foot in the evening to their home, from which we started out with the ponies the next morning. We followed a primitive road eastward around the slopes of the Carpathians, crossing the little Olsa River and going on past the ruins of the fifteenth-century castle marking the village where Pastor Kulisz was born. Before evening we reached Ustron on the Upper Vistula, and an hour later we were at our destination.

I remember little about what we discussed that evening, but we had a real farm supper. When bedtime came I discovered that the big family-bed – the best the house could offer – was to be put at the disposal of the visitors, three of us. This was a bit of a surprise, but my one thought was *Honi soit qui mal y pense*. I asked no questions, and all I need say is that I slept well at the back of the bed while Madame had the front, and said that she slept well also. But it was my only experience of this kind, and not one that commends itself to general practice.

On the third excursion, again made at the suggestion of the pastor, we were four in number – all men. It came in the summer of 1918, when the prospect of peace was already looming up. We went by train westward through Frydek to the shrine of the ancient God of Hospitality – Radhost, meaning more or less the Happy Host. A small chapel stands on the site of an older pagan temple, at the top of one of the last shoulders of the Carpathians before that range turns abruptly southward toward the Danube. The day was fine and the view of the Moravian Plain, with its rolling wheatfields, well tilled in spite of war conditions (it was always the granary of Austria), was imposing. But the shrine itself was closed, and the place for the time being quite deserted. All this was to be changed with the liberation that came a few months later.

And now a word about two rather futile hunting escapades. During the harvest months, in fact from the middle of June onward, much damage would be done to fields lying close to the forest-belt of the mountain by deer or even wild boar, and the losses were resented by the small-holders. Actually, I never saw any of these animals, though their marks were often to be found in winter in fresh snow. No one was allowed to go in chase of them without a licence, but angry farmers paid little attention to such rules. So, when I was asked by the son of an older teacher in one of the parish communities, who had a licence to hunt, whether I would join him one night on an 'errand of good will' well up the slopes of the larger forest reaches east of Ligotka, I agreed with pleasure. We slept a few hours at the school, and then set off well before morning for an hour-and-a-half tramp to the edge of the wood. We had only taken up our position, each equipped with a fowling-piece, when 'the mother of dawn, rosy-fingered morning' appeared in the east.

My guide had placed me in a tree at the lower end of a narrow meadow-field, while he himself went some distance higher up. There we waited while the whole forest burst into life and song. No deer appeared, however, and it soon became clear that we had come in vain. Then, all at once, I heard a shout, 'Look out, a fox!' and I stiffened to attention. Like a streak of light a fine big fellow crossed the hundred yards of open space, but I only got my gun into line when his tail swung high and he was gone. So that was that, and we returned empty-handed for breakfast. A few days afterwards my companion went back to his military service in Dalmatia, to be killed in action before winter and buried not far from the Bocca di Cattaro – fallen in an alien cause.

About a month later one of the farmers from the same village, whom I had got to know well, told me that he had heard of our bad luck and asked me to go again with him to try for the buck which was still harrying the crops. I consented, and this time we set off in the evening, spending the night in the cottage of the annoyed farmer. A few sheaves of last year's straw were brought in and thrown on the floor of the living room, and here we got four or five hours sleep. By four o'clock we were at our post, not far from the scene of my previous visit. Again I was placed in the fork of a stout tree at the edge of the field, while my guide took up a position at the other end of the clearing.

It was still dark, and one could barely distinguish the form of things. Complete silence had to be maintained, and we had waited half-an-hour when, with the first hint of dawn, I heard a foot-fall and then the munching of oat-straw. Looking cautiously around I could just see the form of a stag not twenty yards from me on my right, but almost behind me. Out of caution I had not cocked my piece, so I proceeded to do this as quietly as possible. But the buck jumped a rod when he heard the click, and only after looking all around him did he again begin to feed.

I was now to fall a prey to inexperience, which spoiled all the fun. In taking up my position I had to set back to the tree trunk, of course for comfort; but with the result that I could get my gun to my shoulder and shoot only in one direction. Had the buck been on my left all would have been well; but as things were I did not dare to move a leg or an arm, for he would have been gone in a trice. By now there was a good deal of light, and my partner saw the intruder and was wondering why I did not shoot. He was tempted himself to risk a long shot, but did not want to invade my preserve. For ten minutes I debated what should be done. In retrospect I know the only thing to do was to get my gun to the left shoulder and take chances. The target was as big as a barn door, and I could hardly have missed. Instead of this I tried silently to change my 'perch' in order to get my sights on him; but in so doing I touched a branch, and with three jumps the buck was gone. Needless to say I took a lot of teasing about that failure.

But that is not the end of the story. On our way home someone must have seen me carrying a gun, and reported the fact to the game-warden forester in Ligotka. Three days later I was asked by the village mayor to come and see him. I went at once, much wondering what he wanted. He was very polite, but came straight to the point: 'Had I been seen in such a place on such a morning, carrying a gun? Had I been shooting and had I a licence?'

This was a poser. Of course, I had to admit that I had been carrying a gun in the company of another man on that morning. At his invitation I had joined him for the expedition, but had not shot anything! All this was carefully written down, and I had to sign it. The penalty was ten crowns, paid into the Poor Fund of the parish. Needless to say I did not tell the worthy mayor of my intention, or of the kind Providence that did not let me break the rather strict game laws of the imperial and royal domain. But the fun was worth the fine.

STUDENTS

From all this the reader might get the impression that during four years I did nothing for the cause I was paid to serve, unless by way of preparing myself against the future. Marooned as we were far from university centres, and with the vast minority of students scattered to the four winds on military service, this might have been expected. Nevertheless, there were two things I could do, one of them being to keep in touch by correspondence with as many as possible, and the other to bring a few to Ligotka for part of their furloughs.

Those serving were glad of letters, but they also appreciated parcels of any kind - with biscuits or socks or fresh handkerchiefs; and in this field E did more for our friends than I did. In view of the political situation we were safer to keep in touch with students from Vienna than with our own friends from Prague. The latter were all watched, their mail was censored, and it was risky for them to correspond with a foreigner. I do, however, recall receiving a card from one of them, written in German in 1916, in which things were said that could have got the writer into trouble: 'The struggle must go on for some time yet. The Proud One must come down, otherwise there will be neither justice nor peace.' I knew what he meant, and he knew that I knew - that was enough.

Wartime in Silesia

From the start all university men were regarded as raw material for officers; and most of our people were detailed to training camps. This training they found to be very distasteful both for the company around them and for the kinds of things they had to do. Ted, who had been with us at the Hungarian summer conference, wrote pathetically of the ordeals, physical and moral; but he stuck them out bravely and after the New Year found himself in charge of a company deep in the snows of the Slovakian mountains, facing the Russian armies that were trying to get through the passes. Here there were times when the service of supplies was blocked by snow and the men killed and ate anything wild they could find. Even the pet dogs of officers disappeared. The next winter he was in the deep south, not far from Sarajevo; and he wrote of having seen the peasants of the village threshing out their wheat by driving oxen around a post to trample the sheaves, just as it was done in the days of Abraham.

But of more interest to us was what he told, especially when he came on furlough, about the attitudes prevailing in the mess and among his men. One year of service, in which more than one defeat had been suffered, had sufficed to change the whole outlook of the rank and file on life, and in particular on war. What had looked to many in August 1914 to be a grand adventure was now become something quite different. Men who had taken with them in their haversacks volumes of modern German poetry no longer read them. Even Goethe was being discarded, oddly enough in favour of Dante - of course in translation. Occasionally men were found who had their prayer-books or even New Testaments with them; and the joy of some of his own privates at finding that their leader (he was a second lieutenant) read his Bible every day was endless.

One of the keenest Vienna colleagues had been dismissed at the call-up as quite unfit for active service, and was, therefore, able to continue his law studies. He was of Jewish blood, but a loyal Lutheran. He had a good mind, and was well aware of the issues at stake. When he came to Ligotka in the summer of 1916 to spend ten days with us we had many a spirited discussion about politics. By now I had come to understand the situation fairly well, and I did not hesitate to tell him that the only solution for the Danubian basin was a proper united states of Southeast Europe. To this he was prepared to agree, but on one condition - the hegemony would remain in German hands! Of course, he knew that the Slavs would never accept this, but he would not give in. Poor L! He set up after the war a practice in Western Austria, married, and was living a useful life when we visited him in 1932. But the Nazis got him a few years later and he ended his days in one of the 'annihilation camps' in Poland - all because he was born a Jew. I recall his saying to me one time: 'No one can know what it means to a man in Central Europe to have Semitic features!'

But we had, of course, not a few students right at our door. One of them, of Polish origin, who called himself a 'loyal Austrian,' had heard Wilder in Vienna and had been at our Easter conference. I lost sight of him until the spring of 1915, but suddenly we met on the square in Teschen while he was home on furlough. The experiences of eight months had sickened him of the whole business. He seized me by the hand and broke out, quite seriously: 'Can't you write at once to Dr Mott in New York and ask him to come over to Europe and stop the war?' I persuaded him that the thing was not as simple as all that. Little did any of us imagine that Henry Ford was going to try two-and-a-half years later to achieve that very result.

This brings to mind a bit of real evidence which was to come later into my hands of the power of our federation to transcend frontiers lying between nations. From Corfu, whither the battered but unbeaten remnants of the Serbian army had found their way across almost impassable mountains, there reached our Vienna office a picture-postcard. Written in fair German by an ex-student from Belgrade who belonged to our group there, it brought fraternal greetings. But there was also this request: 'When you enter Belgrade as victors, remember that there also Christians can be found, who will give you the hand of friendship.' I have that postcard still.

This message was only one of many encouragements that reached Phildius, who was carrying on what could be done in Vienna with the help of a few students. We learned much about conditions in the capital from two visits he was able to make in Ligotka, the first of them in the spring of 1915. It was only then that we heard the facts about the battle of the Marne, as well as countless other things from the outside world. One useful bit of warning had indeed been conveyed to us long since by Miss Clark, and in a clever way. Knowing well the sort of thing we were being told by the German press, she put this sentence on a card from Geneva: 'You remember Longfellow's "Psalm of Life." Well, bear in mind the last line of the first verse.'[2]

It was important that the work in Vienna should not be wholly interrupted; above all that contact should be maintained with former students serving on many fronts (if they were still alive); and that there should always be a 'home' for them on leave and/or when passing through the capital. To help in maintaining these contacts the committee began to publish in German a small monthly *'Unter die Fahne'* (Beneath the Flag), which reached students through the post and brought them greetings and scraps of news as well as brief homilies on life. For this monthly I wrote two or three short sketches over my own name. The

---

2 'Let us then be up and doing,
　With a heart for any fate;
　Still achieving, still pursuing,
　Learn to labor and to wait.'

work on the spot was done mostly by theological students, who by Austrian law were exempted from war service. One of them was Jan Szeruda, who came from Teschen, and later became professor of New Testament and dean at the Protestant Faculty of Warsaw University. Another most useful helper, already a graduate, was Dr Josef Eberle.

The success accruing from this venture, which opened the way for much correspondence with despairing soldiers, suggested to us in Silesia the doing of something similar in Polish. A sizeable list of addresses of students-in-arms was not hard to compile, and six numbers were subsequently published of a small journal, *Amid the Fray*. For this too I wrote sketches which, of course, were given in translation. By these means at least some continuity from the past was preserved into the new world that was to come in 1918.

THE PASTOR

The Lutheran church in Ligotka, standing amid fine old chestnuts and slightly back from the main street, dominated the village with its high roof and tiny belltower. Though built for use rather than appearance, its classical style made a pleasing impression. Inside, facing two tiers of galleries, one got the impression of being somewhat crowded, especially when nearly a thousand people would gather for the long Sunday morning service. I used to say to Pastor Kulisz that these services were rather drawn out; but his reply was that many of the people had walked a long way, and they wanted to get their money's worth.

Kulisz had come to Ligotka early in the century as 'curate' to an older man – straight out of college. Long before the war he had attracted the attention both of the people of the duchy and of the authorities in Vienna, and for different reasons. Village-born, he had attended the German high school in Teschen (there was no Polish), taking with him from home on Monday morning one of those large peasant loaves of rye-bread as his chief sustenance till he came back on Friday night. From high school he went on to the universities of Vienna and Erlangen for theology. These he managed to survive without losing 'the common touch' and without becoming a traitor to home and country. At the same time, both then and later, he refused to be drawn into the national political controversy in which not a few of his colleagues were involved. He held the conviction that his one business was to serve the cause of the Kingdom of God. Of fine physique and a good preacher, he devoted himself heart and soul to his work; and the Austrian authorities tried for years to win him over to collaborate with them. Because he would not be thus bribed or bullied, he had been refused the position vacant for some years in the big Church of Jesus in Teschen – the prized 'living' of the duchy. On this account he was still in 1914 the shepherd of a village flock.

But there was more to it than that. From his student days he saw clearly that every established church, into which people were born and by whose offices they were wedded and then buried, needed an inner core of actively spiritual members - what the Pietist leaders of the seventeenth century had called 'ecclesiola in ecclesia.' Otherwise such a church would remain at best a very useful institution, serving social and political ends, but without furthering the Kingdom of God on earth. Knowing that there existed in the German churches what was called *die Gemeinschaft Bewegung* - a Fellowship Movement - he set about building up in the duchy groups of devoted men and women, some of them peasants, others teachers, who would hold some sort of a yearly conference to discuss their aims and aspirations. It goes without saying that this kind of thing was not welcomed by the Supreme Council in Vienna; it threatened a kind of ferment - something over which they could not exercise adequate control. In taking this line they were, of course, true to the old imperial tradition, coming down from Roman days (if not Egyptian), whose one desire was that the common people should be kept quiet. Warnings were given from Vienna and when these were unheeded, Kulisz was served with a notice, shortly before the war, that he was not to address any meetings of any kind outside his own parish!

His interest in wider horizons was not dampened by this injunction. On the advice of an older colleague, who spoke English and had been in England, he had got away for a holiday in 1907 and crossed the Channel with two ends in view: he wanted to be present at one of the Keswick meetings and he wanted to visit the George Muller Orphanages in Bristol. Though knowing no English, he did carry out his plan and came home strengthened in his resolve not to surrender to the powers that be. More than once he would tell me how he coveted for Polish Protestantism the kind of contacts with the Anglo-Saxon world enjoyed by the Reformed Church of Hungary, some of whose ministers had been trained in Edinburgh.

It will therefore not surprise the reader that Kulisz welcomed the unexpected arrival of our two young students from Winnipeg in 1909 and 1910;[3] and still more the first visit of Phildius, representing the World Student Christian Federation. Mention has already been made of the way the empty villa just above Ligotka had become a meeting place for students from 1913.

But nothing of this could be foreseen in the early years of his ministry. With the loyal help of his wife, a Teschen girl, he went about the humdrum duties of his parish, holding up the Word of Life to a congregation of which a good part had little sympathy with it all. The grounds for this indifference were partly per-

---

3 One of the two was Arthur Rose, younger brother of William, later a practicing physician in western Canada. The second, Edmund Chambers, appears briefly in Chapter 4.

Wartime in Silesia

sonal and partly political. The village dignitaries took the same view of the church as did the imperial government. The business of the pastor, to use the words of Clause One of the Church Statute, was 'to maintain the dignity of his office'; which meant, as Kulisz would say, to drive a carriage and pair, to maintain a good table, and even a good cellar; in general, to fulfil the functions of a state official. Apart from this he baptized the babies, married the young couples, visited the sick and infirm, and buried the dead. Of course he preached the gospel from the pulpit and administered the sacraments; but he was not free to go beyond this without running the risk of trouble. Above all, he was not supposed to raise his voice in regard to social evils of any kind or to take a stand in the cause of social justice. The care of the morals of the community was, in effect, the business of the police!

In every village, as the old proverb has it, 'wherever God builds a church, the devil puts a tavern next door.' Sometimes there were two. So then, if people who had come a long way to church on Sunday morning wanted to stay on for a social time and a series of drinks in the afternoon, or - in the case of the younger ones - to make merry with dancing late into the night, they had every opportunity to do so. The average village minister was content to turn an indulgent eye on such foibles, even though he knew full well what the risks were. He consoled himself with the thought that his business was to prepare people for the world to come.

This is no overstatement, but it meant for a man like Kulisz much worry. An example or two will explain what I mean. Conditions in Ligotka were a good deal better than in many other villages, but there were cottages holding more than one family in which no one could be sure of the parentage of the numerous children. There were also cases where most of the earnings of the husband and father went for fire-water, while the children were ragged. The village mayor was one of the problems. He was not a bad man, and he was a good farmer. He tilled over fifty acres, the largest holding in the community. A good part of this was under potatoes, most of which went to 'feed' his distillery. In this were produced three grades of *Schnapps* or vodka - the most vicious kind of spirit known to man. The finest grade would go for the traffic, being served over the counter in a dozen 'pubs' far and near. The second grade was given out daily by the farmer to his workers, men and women who worked hard for less than ten crowns (francs) a week, but with two meals of sorts thrown in. The poorest was mixed with chopped grain and roots, to feed his pigs and steers for the market. As Kulisz once said to me: 'For what that man and his kind do, they will be damned in the next world; but those who drink the stuff (he had in mind the workers in particular) are damned in this world already.' Nevertheless, it was at the peril of losing his position that he dared to speak out from the pulpit about the mischief of the whole business, especially that of thrusting the stuff under the noses of untaught people, who had not the courage to refuse.

In general he preferred another approach, that of building from the ground up. Hence the time and care he gave to the task of instruction each winter and spring for his class of young people coming up for confirmation. What this meant to him and the community was brought home to me quite clearly in the summer of 1916. One of the best of our Vienna students was spending ten days of his furlough with us, and we had some long talks about the future of society. Karl belonged to one of the 'patrician' families of the Capitol; but the emptiness of 'the social round' could not satisfy him, and together we were trying to discover *why* something else was necessary. He remembered Kulisz from the immediate prewar days, so I took him to the manse for a chat. It was harvest time and the pastor was busy helping to get in the precious crop from his three acres of ground. We waited for a few minutes in the little garden-house, where he soon joined us.

I told Karl that, in order to bring things to a head, I was going to put to our host a leading question: 'Why was it that, as a village parson, he was not content quietly to fulfil his duties as a servant of the community, but went out of his way to provoke thought and even dissension among those about him?' After a few minutes' chat about everything and nothing, I told Kulisz that we had come to him with a definite problem, which I then put. To point up the whole thing I went on: 'Why is it that you went to so much pains to leave some lasting impression on the lives of these eighty teenage youngsters who were confirmed a few weeks ago?'

His answer came at once. I should call it a sort of longing. 'It haunts me day and night, whenever I think of those young lives thrust out in the world we face to-day.' This was, in effect, the same thing as Lady Astor was to say some years later, when faced by the same kind of question: 'Because I care.' Kulisz cared. He was interested deeply in the saving of souls, in the ordinary sense of that term; but he was not indifferent to the lot of his fellows in the present world, even for those who were sick and helpless. On his way back from England he had stopped at Bickefeld, in the Rhineland, to visit the great 'Homes for Incurables' associated for all times with the noble name of Bodelschwingh. Before leaving this institution he expressed to Dr Bodelschwingh his sense of sorrow at so much misery and suffering, and received this enigmatic reply: 'We need it all!' From that time he was resolved to see something of the kind in Silesia, be it ever so modest. There were two ends to be gained: the older and helpless folk would get some kind of care; and the general public would have before them something concrete to work for, which would rouse in their hearts the spirit of the Good Samaritan.

From thought to action was not far. Just before the war he secured a small cottage in the heart of the village, opposite the post-office, and here the beginning was made of what was called Bethesda. Later, when money became more plentiful, he bought a lot nearby; and before the end of the war had erected two wings of a modest Home, one for the aged and the other for war-orphans. In and around this institution he was hoping to create a Training School for deaconess nurses - a project which was interrupted by the complications that arose at the end of the hostilities, but was taken up afresh in another place.

One notable war-time event, in the realisation of which Kulisz played the chief role, was the celebration in the high summer of 1917 by the Protestants of the duchy of the 400th anniversary by Luther's Reformation. So far as I know, the great gathering held in the grounds of our villa, to which not fewer than 3000 people came, was the only thing of its kind attempted in the empire at that time. He got the support of fellow pastors, and official permission was secured - though with difficulty.

Fortunately, the heavens were kind and we had a fine day. From early morning people began to arrive either on foot or by train at the station of Gnojnik, and by eleven o'clock they were all assembled in the open air for a solemn service of celebration. Seats for 1500 had been arranged on planks, and the rest stood round about - all of them armed with their hymn-books. Our piano was brought out, a sort of choir was gathered to lead the singing, and the throng joined with one accord in Luther's great hymn: 'A safe stronghold our God is still.' Suitable prayers were offered and a really fine sermon delivered by Pastor Mamica from one of the industrial communities in the north. Kulisz gave a short address on the meaning of the ceremony, and one or two poems were recited. More hymns concluded this memorable meeting, and luncheon in picnic style went on into the afternoon.

My own part in the whole enterprise was slight, but the moment came when I had to act quickly to save a nasty situation. The sun had got steadily fiercer, and even before the service was over hundreds of people were slipping away to the well, equipped with a good pump, which stood under the trees at the back of our grounds. Each one had a cup or a glass, and in getting water they wasted far more than was caught. The moment the service was over this stream of people became a mob, and I foresaw catastrophe if the water ran out. I hurried to the kitchen, got hold of all the clean pails I could find, and then insisted on taking charge of the pump, filling the pails, setting them out in order with the help of others, and mounting guard over the well for the next two hours. At first there was some murmuring, but people soon saw that with almost no waste five times as many people could be served in this way as were milling around before. Thanks partly to the perfect weather everyone enjoyed to the full the outing and the fellowship.

With one exception - the village gendarme was very unhappy! Rarely in his life had he such a chance to show his importance as on this day. As a Catholic he did not like the whole idea. As a good Austrian he was a bit nervous about a huge Polish meeting held in war-time. Perhaps under instruction from above, he strutted about in a hot uniform for at least five hours, rifle and bayonet over his shoulder, keeping an eye on everyone and, where possible, noting what people were saying. More than once I caught him standing near me to discover what was being discussed with 'the foreigner.' We had always been on terms of courtesy, but he certainly resented my presence in the village, and, of course, had been faithfully reporting my doings for nearly three years. Long before this day Wilson's famous pronouncement as to the need for restoring an independent Poland had become known to all, and loyal 'Austrians' as a rule did not like it. For my part I refused to discuss current affairs on this particular day with anyone, and took the trouble to offer the gendarme a glass of cold water more than once before he left the grounds. He certainly was a very tired man when he got home.

During the last year of the war, especially in the autumn of 1918, I was busy doing various things to help Kulisz with plans for the extension of his work in the parish, and even outside it. With the liberation that seemed to be in the offing, people were daring to hope for an awakening of spiritual forces. In the previous winter I had carried on fortnightly cottage meetings in two of the villages; and E had taken the initiative in forming a youth choir, which was soon able to sing many *chorales* quite acceptably. But I was also busy meeting some of the educated laymen in the duchy, and discussing a sort of Forward Movement with businessmen which would involve the expenditure of much money. We even started a fund, to which farmers and others were ready to contribute generously. I recall that on one occasion I got back to the manse, where Kulisz was in bed with a cold, with the promise of a large sum and with a first instalment in my pocket. When I handed it to him, telling him from whom it came, he was so surprised that he sat up at once and said: 'Though I were dead, yet would I rise again!' We were in the midst of this work at the end of October when, as a result of the break-up of the Austro-Hungarian armies on the Piave River in Italy, the Czechs took over control of Bohemia and Moravia on a single morning and the end of the Habsburg regime was at hand. As will appear below, I was suddenly called away and never returned to complete this work.

FURTHER EDUCATION

Two main tasks had to be attempted during what soon promised to be a long period of confinement while the rest of the world was trying to destroy itself. It would be difficult to say which of them was more important: to get some sort of understanding of the great issues involved in the war, or to improve my fitness for the work with the students undertaken from New Year's 1914. As soon as it was possible to settle down and do any serious work, in particular from the time when it was clear that the war-front was not likely to reach us, I began to engage in studies in both these fields.

The Vienna papers came regularly, and throughout the war I found *Die Zeit* a sober and useful guide to what was going on. True, the military censorship was absolute, and one had to read between the lines to get at the truth. As best I could, though without opportunity for daily conversation, I went on with my study of Czech and by spring had reached the point where I could enjoy Božena Nemcová's famous story *Granny*. At the same time I was getting some knowledge of general conditions from the remarkable book by Wickham Steed, *The Habsburg Monarchy*, for which I thank Phildius. In its pages, for the first time in my life, history came alive; the play of forces and the panorama of events meant something in a way no reading of books had ever done before. Even our Vienna friends had to admit the truth of its analysis, though some of them echoed the objections raised by Otto Weber that, even if everything was true, the publication was not expedient! From this reading I went on to a study of Danubian history from German textbooks, though this was far from systematic.

Not less helpful, but for quite a different reason, was a copy of Buckle's *History of Civilization*, which I was able to get from Leipzig. Only later did I realize Buckle's place in the writing of history; but some fundamentals did dawn on my immature mind, chiefest perhaps the fact of a constant war through the ages between the active mind of man and the entrenched authority of Throne and Altar, handed down from the past and often blocking the way of progress. Finally, a new and uncharted field opened up when I was able to procure Professor Masaryk's two volumes, *Russland und Europa*. This remarkable work, the fruit of a generation of study, was an eye-opener to those of us who knew nothing about the Russian empire and very little about the mind of the author. Some chapters in the second volume were beyond me and I never got to know them well; but the historical sketch to be found in Part One introduced me to the thousand-year-old development of state and church in a great area outside the traditional stream of Western civilization. There are still people who refuse to recognise the value of this great book, but the future may decide in Masaryk's favour rather than in theirs.

For lighter reading we did not need to leave the house in which we lived. The former owner had left behind a large number of pocket-size bound volumes in German, including most of the great continental novelists – masterpieces like George Sand's *Consuelo*, Hugo's *Les Misérables*, Freytag's *Soll und Haben*, and Eötvös's *The Village Notary*. Having devoured these with great profit, I took in

1916 a chance to buy, in a new edition (in German), five large volumes of Dostoevsky. At first they were only good stories to me, but I profited from a chapter in one of F.W. Foerster's works in which he explained the inner meaning of great novels – their purpose in expounding a doctrine or preaching a sermon. Thanks to him I realised that *Crime and Punishment* was an indictment of Nihilism, while in the same way *The Brothers Karamazov* set out on a great canvas the three Russias – the older official one, the contemporary free-thinking one, and the Russia to come, of which the author dreamed but which he was never to see. I came to love Alyosha, and told my friends that he would have been an ideal SCM secretary!

I was not much impressed by *The Idiot*, but the book was at least more satisfying than the similar work of Gerhard Hauptmann, *The Fool in Christ, Emmanuel Quint*. Both of these were trying to do in a different way what Wagner aimed at with the figure of 'The Pure Fool' in *Parsifal*. Let me add that, to redress the balance, I read for the first time Turgenev's *Fathers and Sons*, with its portrayal of the nihilist Bazarov.

As for German novels, the reading of *Debit and Credit* was followed by that of Fritz Keller's *Der Grüne Heinrich* – quite a different type of story; and then I got hold of what is surely a masterpiece of its kind, Gustav Frenssen's *Jorn Uhl*. This picture of the hard life of the Frisian peasant left a deep impression, and prepared the way for an understanding of Reymont's *The Polish Peasants* a decade later.

While this was going on, I was also engaged in finding my way into church history. With the help of Pastor Kulisz, and using his books, I got to know for the first time something worth while about the work of Luther and Calvin, and went on to a study of the Counter Reformation – in particular the life and work of Ignatius Loyola. All of this was of first-rate importance, if I was in any way to put myself in the place of students from Central European countries, whose traditional upbringing was so different from my own.

Of course, much of this reading followed on the decision taken in August 1915 to abandon the Czech language and turn to Polish. This was not of my choosing, but arose from the fact that we were in a completely Polish milieu, and it would have meant flying in the face of Providence to do anything else. My fair knowledge of Czech grammar was a help, but the acquiring of facility in speech was no easy matter. Inside of a year I could make myself understood on simple issues, and by 1917 I was reading some of the Polish classics. The reader would not be greatly helped by another account of how a grown man learns a foreign language. Suffice to say that, as with German so with Polish, I could learn with the help of the ear much better than from books. Of course, Slav tongues are remoter from our own in belonging to another branch of the Indo-European family, and their mastery takes more time. Fortunately, I had plenty of people around me who did not mind having their ears offended by my awkwardness and blunders, but even rejoiced in being able to help a complete outsider with something very few strangers had ever attempted.

One of many amusing incidents from these years is worth recording. A neighbouring pastor had come to the manse on a visit, bringing his small boy with him, and E and I were invited to supper. The lad was old enough to enjoy my grim efforts at speaking his mother tongue, but he was perplexed at some of the things he heard. In the middle of supper he pulled his father's sleeve and whispered in his ear: 'What a curious mug that Englishman has!' Small wonder if the whole party dissolved itself in laughter, with the victim of the joke joining in.

But the most fruitful single experience of that winter was the privilege furnished me by the pastor of attending from January on a two-hour session weekly, held for instructing his teenage boys and girls with a view to confirmation. They came from the village schools, and I saw that they could stand up to some solid stuff both in respect to the story of the church and in the fields of doctrine and conduct. Kulisz handled this with masterly simplicity, basing many of the hours on the Gospel parables and drawing plain lessons for the young in regard to both personal and social issues. Even had this been in English, I should have profited a good deal; but the fact of thinking it through in the tongue I was trying to learn enhanced the gain. One thing the teacher kept constantly before his audience: 'Whatsoever a man soweth, that shall he also reap!' Both in their daily lives and in the larger world around them, those boys and girls already had plenty of chance to verify the truth of that momentous pronouncement.

On the advice of friends I got hold of the single tale by Henryk Sienkiewicz (a master of Polish diction) that has gone around the world – *Quo Vadis*? Remembering the story from the English version, I was saved much dictionary work and could get along fast. Then I made this discovery: the graphic picture of the days of Nero was an allegory of the struggle being waged by the subject peoples of Central Europe against German and Russian imperialism. Later on I was to learn of the part the author had played ten years earlier as the spokesman of his people in Poznania, in the years of the school strikes.[4]

Thanks to the kindness of the retired school principal who was one of my sponsors (Jan Kubisz who lived near the station at Gnojnik, author of a volume of verse, and, after the war, of most interesting memoirs), I got hold of a most useful collection of essays by an unusual man – an oil engineer who had spent as a young man a number of years in London. These *Reflections on National Education*, both for the clarity of their style and the courage of their thinking, can

---

4 Strikes against Germanization of the schools.

be considered a landmark in Polish letters. Stanisław Szczepanowski was an enemy of the positivist cosmopolitanism which had swept over Poland after the failure of the rising of 1863-4. In this he saw recognition of failure, as well as appeasement of both Russian and Prussian imperialism which he could not accept. As a cure, he offered the soundest return to an enlightened patriotism, with the maintenance of all that was best in the national tradition and the exclusion of both cowardice and sham.

This book proved the best kind of introduction to the thinking and aspirations of the earlier nineteenth-century Polish poets and philosophers. Growing out of the Romantic movement in literature and rendered more poignant by the fact of the Partition, a group of men, with Adam Mickiewicz as their master, had proclaimed to the world a brand of Messianism, which many who understand it only in part regard as foolishness. For the time being I did not get to know the poets, but was drawn in a curious way to study the prose writing of the social and political philosopher, August Cieszkowski (1814-1894). The son of a landowner, he was a pupil of Karl Ludwig Michelet in Berlin and was trained in the Hegelian dialectic of history; but his Catholic piety revolted against much in all these speculations, and he turned to an ambitious plan for a series of volumes setting out the economic, political, social, and religious meaning of the Lord's Prayer. A study of 'Our Father' had been published early in the war years in a Cracow review – the work of Professor Ignacy Chrzanowski, already known everywhere as an historian of literature.

I got hold of this essay, translated it into English, and then (encouraged by Pastor Kulisz) decided to tackle the original masterpiece. I even wrote to the professor in Cracow about my plan, and had a cordial invitation to come and see him. This was out of the question, but Kulisz gladly made the journey in my place. The meeting must have been a strange one – between a Lutheran pastor and liberal Catholic layman, whose education had been totally different; but they were soon on the best of terms and Kulisz brought back for my use not only the four volumes of *Our Father* (all that had appeared up to this time), but also a copy of the professor's *History of Polish Literature*. This latter was to become my textbook and guide in exploring a new world; just as it had been the handbook of many generations of Polish students and indeed still is. The author, as will appear, was one of my best friends later in Cracow, and then met a terrible end in 1940 in a Nazi concentration camp.

While this study was in progress, we had a pleasant surprise. Out of the blue, in the high summer of 1917, an elderly gentleman arrived at the manse in Ligotka who announced himself as August Cieszkowski. He was the son of the philosopher and had been sent on from Cracow by Chrzanowski to have a look at the 'foreigner' who was interested in his father's work. Needless to say, we gave him

Wartime in Silesia

as warm a welcome as circumstances permitted and he spent two nights in our home. Caught by the outbreak of war in Eastern Poland, he had been able to slip through the battle-line in the summer of 1915 and get back to his ancestral estate near Poznań. This made it possible for him to visit his Cracow friends, and indeed to carry on some of his own cultural studies. His English was fair, though he had forgotten a great deal: 'I had to say "Good morning" to my father in English before I learned to say it in Polish,' was one of the first things he told us. His interest in what I was doing was keen, and on his return home he sent me some of his father's smaller works, as well as copies of French and German translations of the first volume of *Our Father*.

This unexpected visit, and conversations arising out of it with Kulisz and others, decided me on a matter of some importance. I resolved to attempt an English version, much shortened from the original, of these four volumes of exalted, almost Biblical prose, whose message to a troubled world (though written nearly a century earlier) seemed relevant today. This task was to occupy me for the next year, and it was nearly finished when the war ended. My plan was to take each Part of the original, and pick out the essential thought of each chapter, retaining the sequence of ideas and the exact words of the author. The result was a sizeable volume, more coherent than might seem in advance, because the author was given to many elaborations which enriched the argument but were not wholly essential to it. When in the spring of 1919 I showed the manuscript to Tissington Tatlow, general secretary of the SCM in London, he agreed to look it through and finally accepted it for publication. In doing this one mistake was made. We chose the title *The Desire of All Nations* – one which threw into relief the central purpose of the author, although he would have preferred another, 'The Religion of Action.' With the appearing of this book, which provided the outside world with a worthy glimpse of Christian thinking from the Slav world of the nineteenth century, I could feel that a small beginning was made with the task of interpretation that has been engaging me ever since.

So much for our work and play during nearly five difficult years which changed the face of a continent. Much more could have been done, but at least one thing was achieved: an 'innocent abroad' had been transformed into a person who at least knew his way about in Central Europe. He was no longer the helpless beginner of 1914! In addition, it all helped to convince the native-born that there was another outsider, willing to make a serious effort to understand them – their chequered past, their dynamic present, and their aspirations for the future. With the coming of peace in November a new era was begun.

3
Amateur at Peace-making

THE MISSION

Rose left his peaceful Silesian refuge in November 1918 to embark on a diplomatic mission concerning the collapse of the Austro-Hungarian empire. Following military defeat on the Italian front, an armistice was signed on November 3. Minority nationalities throughout the empire, encouraged by Woodrow Wilson's hazy promises of national freedom, set up local 'national councils' to replace the imperial government. Habsburg Emperor Charles, who had succeeded Franz Josef in 1916, acknowledged defeat. He made no attempt to rally his troops to the defence of the empire but tried instead to appease the nationalities with promises of major reform. Anxious to curry favour with Wilson, Austrian authorities even assisted would-be 'governments-in-exile' in Paris and London in making contact with national councils at home. [DS]

It all began about noon on 5 November 1918. I had come into Teschen from Ligotka, and was walking up Deep Street to the Town Square, when I chanced on Mr Górniak, owner of a brick kiln in the part of town west of the Olsa River. We had met more than once before, and his eyes lighted up at sight of me.

'You're just the man we need!' was his sudden greeting. He took me by the arm, and began to tell me that news had reached the newly-formed Polish National Council in Teschen of the presence in Vienna of agents of the Allies. They might even be in Prague. It was important for the future of Poland, indeed for peace in general, that someone who knew the highly complicated situation in

Amateur at peace-making   59

this crossroads of Europe should establish contact with them as soon as possible. Help might be needed and, in any case, counsel. Would I consider undertaking this journey?

Before long he had led me to the provisional quarters of the council, and I was being introduced to two members, Dr Jan Michejda and Professor Szczurek. On hearing of what happened, they added their requests to those of Górniak. In particular, an official plea should be got out to Paris for the releasing of the Polish troops in France, known to be under the command of General Haller.[1] Their presence in Poland might make all the difference between order and anarchy. These men were prepared to use my services to whatever limit I was willing to go.

The reasons for some action of this kind were obvious. After weeks of preparation, the National Council had taken over the government of the duchy, and Polish officials had taken the place of the former Austrian ones. This included the control of some forty miles of railway from Oderberg to the boundary of Hungary at the Jablunkov Pass — a segment of the famous trunk-line connecting the Reich with the Balkans. In the very nature of things this step was a daring one, since German armies were still in control both to the north and to the south, and they would not long tolerate a break in their precious communications. Deep in the lower Danube lands lay the huge army of General Mackensen, who had overrun Roumania; his line of connection with the homeland was vital for the further prosecution of the war.

All this enterprise had been made possible by the remarkable achievement of the Czechs of 29th October. At a set hour that morning they had simply taken over from the Austrians the civil and military administration of Bohemia and Moravia, without shedding a drop of blood. This action had cut off the Duchy of Teschen entirely from Vienna, and with it the whole province of Galicia to the east. The decision of the Poles to follow suit was not long delayed; and I learned that on that very day, 5th November, delegates of the two Slav neighbour peoples of the duchy were meeting in Ostrava Moravska to arrange the details of the new boundary between them. What for a week had looked to be a possible ground of dispute was now to be worked out in conference and without hostilities. Of this, too, it was desirable that the Allied Powers should have first-hand information.

It was far from easy for me to come to a decision. Shut off from the world, I had been given an unique opportunity to get to know the mind and spirit of this

1 General Józef Haller commanded the Polish army formed in France in 1917. Dispatch of the troops to Poland, demanded by Polish and French authorities, was blocked for several months by Great Britain, which supported German pretensions to certain border regions.

simple, mostly peasant folk; and with the collapse of the Austro-Hungarian armies on the Piave it seemed likely that the end of the war was in sight. Everyone was waiting, everyone expectant. Only a few days previously I had listened to a masterly talk given by Kulisz to a group of villagers, in which he tried to explain to them just what was in progress; how a great manor house, with all that belonged to it, was being taken from its former masters and handed over to those who had hitherto done all the hard work; with the consequence that they were, and for some time would be, at a loss as to how to behave, whether at table, in the drawing-room, or in the library. Therefore they ought to move with due regard to all the values thus inherited; seeking the best guidance so that as little as possible might be lost or destroyed.

Two things were uppermost in people's minds: Would their men get home safely from the fronts or from far-away prison camps? Would peace come, and what sort would it be? Wilson's great challenge had been thrown down – that of the right of nations to determine their own way of living. Did this mean that each little world, such as the duchy, could be held responsible for its future? Did it mean that Poland, so long in bondage to others, would at last again be really free? Everybody was talking; most people seemed to feel that they knew best what ought to be done. The wise word of an old peasant woman, spoken with a note of impatience, has stuck in my memory: 'Not many people nowadays are willing to admit that they are stupid.'

Had the time now come when a man who had never given a thought to such a possibility was to be driven by circumstances to put a hand to peace-making? I was in Teschen for quite other purposes. For months I had been helping Pastor Kulisz develop plans for a Forward Movement among the Protestants of the duchy, and we had got together thousands of crowns as a fund to make active work possible. The suggestion had even been made that I should give up my work among students and become a lay worker among the nearly half-million Protestants in the new Poland. To this I could never agree, but it did seem right for me to help wherever possible until the way cleared for me to get back to my own job. Now, however, something wholly different loomed up; was it to be regarded as a dispensation of Providence, or rather as a temptation?

I had nothing with me save the clothes on my back. Inside my waistcoat I carried my old English passport from the year 1912, but I had only a few crowns in my pocket. E was expecting me home before night. What was I to do? For the first time in my life, other people, perhaps one should say the force of events, settled the matter for me. I was not a free agent any longer. The die was cast.

'We shall give you a special passport, making you our plenipotentiary,' said the secretary. 'We shall also provide you with money. Your Polish is good enough, so that no German will know any difference. Speak Polish when and where you can, use German where Polish will not do. The moment you establish contact with the Allies, wherever possible, you will not need either.' To my doubts as to whether a civilian could travel safely, the answer was simple. 'There is no longer any military control. The trains are running, and those travel who want to. No harm will come to you for every one is sick of violence, and you can take advantage of this fact. Better that you should go, than for one of us. We have no one who can speak fluent English, and it is our particular hope that you can get through somewhere to the Americans. They will understand us!'

I went off to dinner with friends, saying nothing about it all. In general, secrecy was desirable for the moment. Two hours later I was back in the rooms of the council, to find that everything was nearly ready. The news from the conference in Ostrava was good. In effect the Czechs would get the county of Frydek, and the Poles the rest of the duchy. This part had a fairly large German minority, notably the solidly German 'colony' around Bielitz (Bielsko) on the Galician border. Something like mutual good-will on the part of neighbour Slav peoples was asserting itself; the still grave threat of German domination was over both. In the German press there was no talk of surrender. Their armies had taken grave defeats in the West, but they declared themselves still unbeaten. 'Wir werden siegen, weil wir siegen mussen' [We shall win, because we must win!] was still the slogan. Cut off from the possibility of knowing just what had happened in France, we had no means of knowing whether this was true or not. In any case something could and should be done to let the Allies know that in the heart of Europe the Slavs were praying for their victory, and were straining every nerve to help it along.

My new passport was a single sheet of paper, but it was sufficient. On the one side in Polish, on the other in English, it said as follows: 'The National Council of the Duchy of Teschen in Silesia, being the accepted representative of the Polish government in Warsaw, has prepared for its confidential agent, the bearer, W.J. Rose, Esq., sometimes lecturer at the University of Manitoba, Canada, this passport.[2] It invests him with full authority to present the will and wishes of the said Council to the proper civil and military authorities of the Entente and of the United States of America; and warmly recommends what he has to report to their consideration.' It bore the signatures of two veteran leaders of the Teschen people, Dr Jan Michejda and Father Józef Londziń.

Money was handed me, for which I gave a receipt. A no less important matter was food. No one could count on getting anything on the way, for the nearer one got to Vienna the scarcer it was. But the matter was at bottom not too diffi-

---

2 Wesley College, where Rose taught from 1909 to 1912, was a wholly autonomous part of the University of Manitoba. It has since evolved into the University of Winnipeg.

cult. A loaf of black bread, wartime brand, some sugar, and a pound or two of sausage (Wurst) were soon found. At eight o'clock there would be a train for Oderberg, and before midnight I should catch there the through express coming from Lwów and Cracow for Prague and Vienna. Once on my way I should have to fend for myself.

Returning to my friends I told them that I was leaving on a mission and that they were to ask no questions. One thing they would provide - a messenger who would go out to Ligotka at once and let Pastor Kulisz know that I would not be home for a day or two. He would then send word at once to the villa. It was an extraordinary thing to do, but the times were not ordinary, and there was no turning back. Shortly after nine I found myself in Oderberg.

From the start fortune smiled on my efforts. The young lieutenant, who with forty men had charge of one of the biggest railway junctions of Central Europe, had been a Boy Scout when the war broke out and remembered meeting me at that time. He at once engaged to put me on the train, and even provided me with a most useful help for travel - a haversack. There were scores of them lying in the store-room, since part of his duty was to disarm all privates of whatever nation and send them on their way. Rifles, side-arms, equipment of various kinds, and the oddest assortment of the things soldiers accumulate were to be seen. Somewhere I got hold of a towel and a bit of soap. The last-named was a scarce thing in those days, and it was to prove very useful as time passed.

About midnight the train from the east came in. I had provided myself with a second-class ticket, but, as it turned out, this was unnecessary. No official appeared to ask for it. The matter of getting a seat, however, was far more difficult. For a time I thought I should not get on the train at all. It was packed with passengers, chiefly military people returning home from the eastern front - Austrian Germans, Czechs, and even Croatians and others, both officers and men. The former had seats in the compartments, some of them with their wives; the latter were in the passages, on the platforms, even on the tops of the coaches. A few people got out at Oderberg, but there were many standing, who took their places. A good many like myself wanted to get in. Most of the windows in the coaches were gone. The young lieutenant said to me at once, pointing to a window in the middle of the coach: 'Tumble in there! No ceremony, otherwise you will not get away at all.' He gave me a leg up, and I literally fell through the window, to land on men sleeping in the corridor. Thus began my journey.

Through Ostrava, and on to Přerov. Here, as I knew, part of the train would be cut off to go to Prague. As luck had it, two people got out from the compartment opposite where I was standing, and I had a comfortable seat for the rest of the night. Beside me was an Austrian major, a gentleman of the old school, with his wife. From him I learned much of what had been going on in the east, and regret

Amateur at peace-making

I could not write it all down. In particular it confirmed the impression gained during the day, that everyone wanted only one thing – to get home. The war had been lost, Austria-Hungary was gone; but life was still dear, and home a place to hurry to after such miseries. Nobody wanted to think or talk about what had been – it was too bitter a nightmare. So, too, very few people cared to talk about the future. They were too exhausted; they wanted simply to rest and recover.

It was nearly noon when we arrived at the North Station in Vienna. I had friends enough in the capital, but decided not to trouble them. My first object was to find a young student from Teschen, and in this I had no difficulty. He gave me two good bits of news. First, that there was a spare bed in the place where he lived; and second, that there existed in Vienna an official Polish Legation. I therefore left my 'luggage' in his room, and accepted his guidance to the Polish offices. The secretary received me without delay, and made an appointment for me with the 'minister' for the late afternoon. So far as he knew, there were no representatives of the Allies either in Vienna or in Prague. This rumour, then, had proved to be false.

At the appointed time I returned, and was soon admitted to the minister's room. I found there a man of whom I had never heard, whose English was better than my Polish, Tytus Filipowicz, later ambassador to the United States. He listened with close interest to my story, looked for a moment at my papers, smiled at the old English passport – long since invalid, and said with a gesture of goodwill: 'Your credentials are wholly satisfactory. What is more, you have come at a time when you can serve a bigger cause than the Teschen one. Any day now, Commander Piłsudski will be set free from Magdeburg and return to Warsaw. For us Poles the question of organizing our own military forces is of vital importance. But our people are all in the armies of the three empires that have lost the war. We are more concerned to save them than about anything else. You know what disruptive influences are at work, and how hard it will be to counteract them. At this very moment we are preparing to send an officer to Laibach (Ljubljana) to see what can be done to rescue our men who are flooding back from the Italian front, and who will be completely demoralised unless something is done for them. Will you go with him? If so, we will give you additional documents, and it is possible that you may find someone there, representing the Allies. It is clear that we can trust you, and you know many things that the West ought to learn as soon as possible.'

Again I was faced with a decision, and I asked for one night to think it over. This was agreed to, for the officer was not to leave till the evening of 7th November. The next morning I had settled the matter. To come so far and then turn back would be foolish. There seemed to be something of value to be done, and it would be cowardice not to attempt it. That evening I was introduced to Lieutenant Bułowski, and furnished with a more adequate passport. On the first page in Polish, inside in French and German, it said this: 'The bearer, Mr W.J. Rose, is proceeding to Ljubljana as a correspondent of the Press Bureau of the Polish Legation in Vienna. The Polish Legation respectfully asks the civil and military authorities of the South Slav State to give him every aid and support in case of need.'

Mr Filipowicz told me ten years later in Washington that this 'visa' was probably the first one given to a non-Pole by the newly restored Polish administration. The date was 7th November, and the signatures were those of Mr Filipowicz and of his first secretary, Dr Szarota. The stamp of the legation made the document look very imposing. Late that night we left for the south.

The journey was a slow one. Every hour or so we met trains going toward Vienna, and all the next day I watched them on the long curves. They were jammed with troops, or rather the wreckage of troops. The sight of them recalled something I had seen the summer before – the dead body of a snake lying on the grass, and literally crawling with ants from end to end. The roofs of the coaches swarmed with men clinging to their knapsacks. We learned from the trainmen that a lot had been swept off the night before in one of the many tunnels, and lost their lives. To live through the war, and be killed on the way home!

We arrived late in the evening in Ljubljana, and I should have spent the night under a lamp-post had not my companion known what was to be done. Nowhere a bed in any hotel, nowhere the hope of quarters. The Town Command was very courteous, but threw up their hands. What could they do? The whole Austro-Hungarian army was flooding homewards, and Ljubljana was the railhead. At last one of the caretakers of the Town Hall said he would take me home with him, and I had a real bed after all. His good wife was willing to wash out a few things for me, and I gave them to her the next morning. I had no time to go back for them so I presume she kept them. In Vienna I had provided myself with handkerchiefs, collars, and cuffs made of paper. These served me during my journey, and were an object of natural curiosity to those who saw them later in Paris and London.

The next morning I joined Lieut Bułowski for 'coffee' at the officers' mess, and learned that he had already arranged for us to be received by the Council of the Provisional Government of Slovenia. Also, that I was to make a speech, and refer to him as my *Attaché Militaire*! We were to bring the felicitations of the government of a now free Poland to a brother-Slav people, now also free! How I got through that ordeal I do not remember. We were in a large room, with a big table, around which were seated the members of the government. I remember the minister in charge of transport, with whom I had a long conference afterward. There was at least one churchman, a bishop. There was also a younger man,

Amateur at peace-making

the minister of public works, who had trained with the General Electric Works in Schenectady, New York, and who spoke English. We at once found common ground, and I had the pleasure of dining with him and his wife that evening. My short speech was followed by a longer one, on a practical theme, by Lieut Bułowski. He told briefly of the anxiety of the Poles as to their own fellow-countrymen, and asked for the co-operation of the Slovenian authorities, with the view to collecting all Polish soldiers who could be located and taking them back across five hundred miles of Europe in some sort of disciplined order, instead of 'bolshevized.'

In a most interesting private conference, carried on in German, I learned afterwards from the minister of transport, a man with a patriarchal beard, something of the problems the Slovenes were facing as a result of the disaster on the Piave. Of a 'demobilisation' of the Austro-Hungarian armies, there could be no talking. They were returning headlong from wild mountain terrain as fast as they could, strictly controlled at a certain point by Italian officers. In time they arrived, mostly on foot and almost starving, in Ljubljana. 'We can do only one thing with them,' said the minister, 'Hurry them on, as fast as we can, homewards. We cannot even feed them for they would eat us out of house and home in three days. Our gravest need at the moment is for rolling-stock. The Italians do not make things easier for us when they seize a train, as they did the other day at Trieste. Only the men are allowed to be entrained; so that you would find today, wandering about the countryside, near the city, 40,000 army horses, asking for anyone to help himself to them. There are more arriving every day, but we cannot give them space on the railway.'

Of course the council had responded most kindly to our greetings, and Lieut B learned that quarters had already been assigned in the fortress on the magnificent hill that crowns the city for all troops of Polish origin. They furnished him with a guide, and by noon he had made his contacts with those in charge. So far, so good. In a way his task was done; but what about mine? Again we found that there were no representatives of the Allies in Ljubljana; and the Slovenes were as anxious as the Teschen people to establish contact with the West. They felt it keenly that the only Allied Power with whom they were in touch was Italy, whose advances they had quite as much reason to fear as those of Austria itself. A curious situation had indeed arisen. Their people were being 'set free' by forces whom they mistrusted, and with good reason. Nothing was more natural, then, than for the Slovene ministers to urge me to accept a commission from them also, and to continue the journey 'to the sea.' They had an interesting bit of news. The first train-load of Italian prisoners-of-war, who had been shut up in Hungary, would be leaving for Trieste the next day after lunch. Would I consider going with them and seeing who could be found in Trieste?

Again a difficult decision, but easier than the Vienna one. Bułowski had introduced me to a colleague, Lieut Sarnek, whom he had found at work getting together strayed Polish soldiers, and who now felt that he was free, since his colleague had come to take over. He had done his engineering studies in Nancy, and spoke very good French. He declared himself willing to go with me, if I would go on; and so it was settled. One of the ministers added a few words in Slovene and in French on page three of my passport, to say that I enjoyed the confidence of the authorities of Slovenia and had a free-passage anywhere on the railways of the country. The next day we set off for Trieste.

But not in a second-class compartment, as heretofore. The coaches were simple box-cars, made for 'forty men or ten horses,' as the French have it; and it was a fortunate thing for all that the nights were not very cold. Late in the evening the train reached the point where the Italian control was going on, and was stopped there till morning. The prisoners-of-war had been cheerful all the way, treating us to their soldiers' songs and sharing their simple fare. Lieut Sarnek and I at once made our way to the Italian headquarters to report. We were received courteously but our requests for beds brought only smiles. I spent the night on a billiard table in the village tavern, one of the hardest places I ever slept on. At five in the morning we were on our feet, and were permitted to go out and see the remains of the Austrian army filing past the controls on the highway. I stood it for fifteen minutes, but the sight was one of the saddest I have ever seen. Poor devils! What they had been through and how they had suffered! And now they not only got no thanks for it all, but had not even a home to go back to. No one had any idea what was going on 'back yonder,' and a good many were past caring. To face death, to give everything for a cause you had no interest in – that was the face of the majority of the Habsburg armies.

Before daylight (11th November) we were warned that the train would be moving and we got aboard. Slowly but surely we made our way forward, and just about one o'clock the top of the hill above Trieste was reached. There below us lay one of the grandest sights of Europe. I had not seen the sea since 1913, and I wanted to cry out with Xenophon's men, 'O thalassa, thalassa!' Taking the advice of the trainmen, we left the railway and took the trolley down the mountain-side. Very hungry and tired we reached a sort of hotel and got some food.

The whole town was *en fête*. That morning the king of Italy had been there, formally to take possession of the city, and one section of the population had given him a warm welcome. But the Slavs, with whom we were in touch before evening, had another view of it all. I found the same feeling toward the Italians as in Ljubljana, only more of it. We had astounding news when the afternoon paper appeared. The Germans had surrendered in France, and an armistice had been signed at eleven o'clock that morning! I was overcome, and there was noth-

Amateur at peace-making

ing for it but tears. But they were tears of relief and joy. Now the subject peoples of central Europe would be free, and a new era could begin! At last the 'wiosna ludów' had come. ('The spring of the nations' – the term used of the year 1848 when hopes of liberation ran high in Central Europe.)

But I had still other news. There were no official representatives of the Allies in Trieste, but at one of the big hotels I learned that an American Red Cross major was in town. He had come over the day before from Venice, accompanying an Italian lady of high rank, to meet the prisoners-of-war with whom we had travelled. As he was out, I left a note to say that I would call on him at breakfast-time the next morning.

Major Crockett of Boston was the finest type of New Englander. He heard my story, which I made as concise as possible, and said at once: 'You have a far bigger mission than you think. You may be the first man at all to get out from Central Europe. My suggestion is that you go at once to our Headquarters in Padua; but the place where you really should report is Col. House's Mission in Paris.'[3]

He agreed to take me with him on the Italian gunboat which was to leave for Venice at eleven, and to let my comrade Lieut Sarnek come with us. So again we set out, on a further stage of our journey. Never had I expected to make a visit to Venice under such conditions. On the boat we found a young French flight-lieutenant, who had been a prisoner-of-war in Prussian Silesia and had managed to escape into Bohemia a month before. He was now on his way home, and the two young officers, Pole and Frenchman, were soon fast friends.

We got to Venice about five, and Major Crockett directed me to the little hotel where the American consul was staying. I got some dinner, and saw for the first time the sign of the Red Triangle on the arms of three stalwart Americans, who were on service with the Italian army. The consul was very kind, and agreed either to pass me on to Padua or to hand me over the next day to the American admiral commanding in the Adriatic. I arranged to see him in the morning – but *dis aliter visum*. Lieut Sarnek had not been idle. From the Italian Town Command, to whom he had gone at once, he obtained two free passes right across Italy to Modane – for an *Agente Diplomatico Inglese* and for himself. 'We leave at eleven-thirty for Milan,' he said when I met him at nine o'clock.

What was I to do? So far I had followed the 'hunt' wherever it led; now Sarnek had become my leader. I thought it over and realised the soundness of his argument. From every point of view Paris was our objective. The rumour we had heard that Haller's Army was in Italy was false, so there was every reason for pushing on. By midnight we were on the way across the plains of Lombardy.

---

3 Colonel Edward House, adviser to President Woodrow Wilson, directed the American delegation at the Paris Peace Conference.

It was now the night of 12th November. I had been away exactly a week, with nothing as yet to show for it. Luckily we had enough money to go on with, and were heading in the right direction. My chief concern was: What is happening in Silesia? When shall I get back and how? As I learned afterwards, E had news of me, but of course I had none from Teschen, nor did I get any for long weeks. There was time enough for reflection on what had happened; and the nearer I got to people with whom I could speak, the more need there would be of reporting as fully as I could all I knew. Meanwhile, travel without sleep was tiring; and I was glad of a chance to rest a bit in Milan.

We stayed over a day and a night in the great city, and I had the good fortune to establish contact with the Red Triangle workers there, what was known in Italian as the *Fratellanza*, who gave me much information about what was going on by way of serving the Allied armies, as well as the address of headquarters in Paris. This offered at once the hope of finding acquaintances at the centre, who could then advise me as to my next step. But I had another and unforgettable experience. In the restaurant at lunch-time I observed near the window, sitting alone, a British officer, and after some reflection I decided to speak to him. He received me with great civility and listened with interest to what I told him. Then he startled me: 'You are in a difficult position. You may not know it, but no Briton has any right to be on the continent without an *Ordre de Mission*. You have none, of course, and I should report you at once; but if I do, you will be arrested, so I advise you to push on immediately with your journey, and good luck to you!' I thanked him for his courtesy, realising afresh that things were not quite so simple as they had seemed.

In the evening of 15th November we reached Modane – all three of us, Pole, Briton, and Frenchman, seeking admission to France. For the two military men the matter was not difficult, but for me, an unknown civilian, it was quite different. The flight lieutenant did his work well, however, and after an hour of argument he persuaded the control people to let me through. I have always felt that my being a Canadian helped me, and in any case the war was over. What could one mortal do to make mischief, even if he tried to? In a few minutes we were on the French side of the station, where I was told to look for the British RTO. I had no idea what that meant, but I found him and he proved to be true blue. Looking me over, he asked only one question: 'Have you enough money to buy a ticket for Paris?' to which I replied that I hoped so. He then said that a train was to leave in half-an-hour, and that I was free to go with it. As luck had it, I had barely enough, but I secured a second-class ticket – and had eight francs left. The next morning we were at the Gare de Lyon, in Paris. I had been travelling eleven days, but at last I had arrived.

Amateur at peace-making

By noon I had found the head office of the American YMCA and was received by the director, E.C. Carter. He saw at once that I had something of importance to report, and undertook to put me in touch with Col House's mission. The next morning I had a note from Hugh Gibson - later American minister in Warsaw - asking me to call that afternoon and see him. The result of our conference was that he gave me one of his secretaries for an hour, and I dictated straight to the typist a long report, based on some notes I had made. The poor secretary was kept later than he should have been, but the task was done. From a copy of this document, still in my possession, I take the following passages:

One of my Polish friends said to me long ago in Silesia that Austria is the finest example existing of an effort to make children love and honour a step-mother while their own mother is still alive. Now the step-mother is suddenly deceased. Complete local autonomy prevails. Almost every centre has its provincial government, for the most part composed of men who are honestly trying to maintain order. I shall show in a moment with what terrific difficulties they have to contend. First let me say in one word what I regard as the only certain way of deliverance.

The Entente, preferably America, should begin this very day to execute an occupation of those lands, not so much military as moral, for the space of at least six months. A mere show of force is sufficient. If the German armies were regarded as invincible until three months ago, one can imagine what must be the prestige in Central Europe of the troops which have beaten them in these three months to a pulp ... I speak of what I know when I say that even in the German cities of Austria, to say nothing of the non-German centres, the appearance of the Stars and Stripes or the Union Jack, on a mission of peace, would be welcomed with the wildest acclamation. Every existing local government would regard such a unit as the most welcome support, and would summon all law-abiding citizens to unite in making the strangers feel at home. These missions would have virtually nothing to do. Their mere presence would suffice. Unless matters have become much worse than they were ten days ago, there would not be the slightest fear of violence or assault from any side. In certain centres, for example Silesia, where the coal fields and the iron industry, situated right on the boundary of three nationalities, mass together most divergent elements of working men, a regiment of sober troops might be necessary; but elsewhere the 'occupation' would be more formal than physical. President Wilson has become the 'god' of these peoples, or at least their saviour. His name stands as no name has ever stood as the guarantee of a better future. I cannot say this more strongly, though I should write a whole page about it.

Following this I described at some length the danger from the side of the Green Guards, that is, the deserting soldiers who had set up quarters in forest and open country and were raiding the towns almost at will. I also spoke of the chaos existing in regard to getting the remnants of the Austrian armies sent home. But I gave most space to the fact that the central empires, though asking peace with the Soviets at Brest-Litovsk, had not allowed any of the Russian prisoners to return home, and that their presence might easily be the cause of grave complications as the winter advanced. Then I came to the situation in Silesia, which I knew best; and to the requests of the Poles, as I understood them from the council in Teschen and the legation in Vienna. I spoke of the settlement between the Czechs and the Poles as a sample of peace-making on the spot; and said something about the more difficult situation around Lwów, based mostly on what I had heard from the officers of the train that first night. Then I went on specifically as follows:

The following practical measures would serve greatly if carried out without delay. They would oil the wheels of alleviation until the 'occupation' suggested above could be made.

1 Intervention with the French military authorities to procure the release of General Haller and his Polish divisions, together with complete equipment, aeroplanes etc, and their despatching by the most practicable route to the Polish homeland.

2 Intervention with the governments of France and Italy to procure the release of all prisoners-of-war of Polish nationality, so that they may be organised into self-respecting military units, and brought home for service to Poland at the earliest possible moment.

3 Where not already procured, the stipulation with the governments in Ljubljana, Vienna, and Prague for the free and unhindered passage of such units of Poles fighting in the Austrian army as can be organised in these weeks around Ljubljana. Further, the assuring on the part of America, to the Slovenian people, that the necessary food supplies will be provided at an early date, via Trieste, for the use of such troops, as well as for the civilian population.

4 The immediate establishing of missions or consulates of the American government in the following towns, which I name because I consider them at the moment as presenting the gravest need: Ljubljana, Zagreb, Sarajevo, Teschen, Cracow, Lwów, Poznań, Warsaw, Danzig. I leave out the capitals Vienna and Budapest as requiring special treatment, and consider that Bohemia and Moravia are able to take care of themselves.

5 The opening of advisory or relief committees, preferably either through the YMCA or the Red Cross, in all the larger cities. These will co-operate with exist-

ing agencies for the relief and care of the poor and needy, the sick and the wounded, above all for the children.

I added two other suggestions, whose import was cultural rather than material or political. In the first place that a campaign of truth-telling should be set on foot throughout the Danube lands, to set right the perversions people had been hearing during four-and-a-half years – or even longer. Concretely I proposed that Professor F.W. Foerster might be sent to Vienna with a free hand, and with means to reach the *intelligentsia* by word of mouth and on the printed page. Secondly, I drew attention to the vacuum that was being created with the downfall of *Deutsche Kultur* as the gospel for all Eastern Europe; and to the need for action by the English-speaking world to help fill this gap. Then I closed with these words, borrowed from Kulisz:

Central Europe is today like to a great manor-house or chateau, which has suddenly changed hands. Those who were lords of the place for so long are expelled, and the common people who have done the work inside the house and in the fields, have come into possession. The whole structure is being rebuilt from top to bottom. Two things are to be introduced, of which there was little before: light and air! As Plato pointed long ago, both of these are hard to bear at first, when weak organisms, unused to them, are brought into sudden contact. The existing anarchy is nothing more than a disease which requires careful treatment and nursing; which must be kept free from infection, if possible, from without, and which will then heal itself in a few months.

My reference to 'infection' was, of course, to the threat of Bolshevism from the east, of which I had spoken at length in the early part of my report. That these fears were justified was seen a few months later when Bela Kun[4] took charge of things in Hungary.

Meanwhile, on the first afternoon, Carter had taken me to a session of an important conference of Red Triangle workers met to consider what was now to be done for the troops until they could be sent home. At that meeting one of the first people I found was Miss Elizabeth Clark, who at once announced my coming to the whole assembly, and I was even given ten minutes to speak. What I had to say, coming from behind the scenes, amounted to a mild sensation. Miss Rena Craswell (Mrs S.K. Datta) volunteered to look after me, and the next morning she took me to see the British authorities. I had an interesting half-hour with the vice-consul. Being a good Scot, he had a sense of humour. 'I ought to arrest you

---

4 Bela Kun, leader of the short-lived Hungarian Soviet Republic of 1919.

on the spot,' he said with a grin. 'That old passport of yours is only an interesting relic. You are breaking the laws both of France and England every hour you stay in Paris. By tomorrow at the latest you must clear out for London.'

He gave me some sort of document, which I have now lost. I was fortunate to get the extra day's grace, for on Saturday I was to have lunch with Mr Gibson, and talk over my report. That afternoon, however, I took the train for Boulogne, and arrived next morning safe in Southampton. Back on English soil, after nearly seven years! At every turn I was watched. Though they admitted that they knew all about me from Paris, they wanted to be 'sure.' A young officer in Southampton read the copy of my report; and was good enough to say that my comments on Bolshevism, as seen from Central Europe, were the best he had ever read. But a disappointment was in store for me. As a *repatrié* I could not go on to London for twenty-four hours! So I was hung up in what was then as dreary a place as England knows, and where I did not know a soul, till Monday morning.

Carter had lent me money, so there was no anxiety on that score. But the idleness was too great a contrast to the feverish movement of almost two weeks, and I took it ill. At noon on Monday, however, I was in the Foreign Office in Whitehall, asking for Mr J.W. Headlam-Morley.[5] He received me with old-time courtesy and let me explain why I had come. Then he interrupted to say that he would like me to come back at tea-time, and he would have one or two others to hear my story. Had I anything else to do? Yes, I had to report also to the War Office!

In the War Office I was received by Colonel Kisch. He asked me whether I could tell him anything about military matters, relative strength and weakness of forces, etc in Central Europe. Of course I could not do that, so he did not keep me. He returned some papers that had been taken from me at Boulogne, and said: 'You are a free man.' I was glad to hear it.

My meeting in the Foreign Office was longer and was very interesting. The first person Mr Headlam-Morley brought in was Alfred Zimmern, who had been fellow of New College when I was a student and whom I had got to know in the Palmerston Club. He at once identified me, so that was another milestone passed. After the two historians had listened to me for some time, a third gentleman joined us – a young man whom I had never seen before. His name was Namier.[6] When the conversation turned to the eastern front, in particular to what was going on around Lwów, Namier disagreed at once with my story. I soon realised that he was one of the 'experts' on Eastern Europe, owing to his having been

---

5 (Sir) James W. Headlam-Morley, professor and civil servant, in 1918 a Foreign Office expert on the German-Polish border question.

6 (Sir) Lewis Namier, born Bernstein-Namierowski in Galicia, in 1919 a Foreign Office expert on East European affairs. Namier wrote books and articles about Eastern Europe but is best known for his scholarly studies of eighteenth-century British politics.

Amateur at peace-making

born there and commanding three or four languages. He thus had access to the press that came through, of which I knew nothing. But the whole meeting was most cordial, and it ended with a request from Headlam-Morley that I would write for him also a memorandum, a sort of companion to the one I had done in Paris. This I did next day, and received in due course the following very nice acknowledgment:

Foreign Office
6th December 1918

Dear Mr Rose:

I am sorry for the delay in sending you the copy of your very interesting Memorandum – I thought you had received it last week ... Might I venture to suggest that perhaps the part dealing with Eastern Galicia, written as I understand not from immediate personal knowledge of that district, might be open to some criticism? All the part dealing with Austrian Silesia we found of the greatest interest and value. Mr Namier is very anxious to have an opportunity of seeing you again before you leave England, and I should be very glad if you would find time to come and see us here.

Believe me,

Yours very truly,

J.W. Headlam-Morley

Having discharged my duties with the ministries, I could indeed feel a free man. There was, however, one other chance given me at once of saying a word to an important person. Carter had sent me direct to Mr Lionel Curtis in London, who gave me a bed and even lent me a razor for a few days. The second morning at breakfast, I found myself beside Mr Phillip Kerr, of whom I had been told that he was personal secretary to Lloyd George. I took the chance he gave me when he put this question: 'What do you think should be done first in order to settle Europe down to peace and order again?' In effect I repeated briefly to him the points made to Mr Gibson, emphasising the value, in the large centres of the former Habsburg lands, of the peace work being done on the spot; and the need for moral support from the west in the form of 'missions' in khaki while the Peace Conference met. He saw the point at once and asked me for more details. These I gave as best I could, assuring him that I was a novice in such things and that only specialists could deal with the ways and means. The plan for sending missions to the important centres appealed to him, and what I had to say may have helped the cause.

And now a very practical question arose. I wanted to get a new passport and return to Silesia. This I was told was impossible. Curtis proved a wise friend. He said he would do what he could to help me get a passport, but on one condition: I was to go away to the country to rest and sleep for ten days at least. I certainly needed a rest, for I had been living on my nerves for over two weeks, to say nothing of the strain of the whole summer before that. So I had to capitulate, and went off to the west of England for a week. Thus ended the first stage of my 'Mission from Silesia.'

LONDON AND PARIS

While events took their course in Central Europe, representatives of the Western Allies (Entente powers) watched and waited in Paris. The military victors – Britain, France, and the United States – naturally played the greatest role but they were joined by other allies and the self-appointed representatives of hopeful Central European nationalities. The effort needed to deal with complicated political, military, economic, historical, and ethnic issues was enormous, so the Paris Peace Conference became a meeting place for technical experts as well as heads of state. Rose turned up in Paris as a private mouthpiece for the nationalities and gained entrance to their company.

The Polish question, Rose's principle interest, proved particularly thorny since two major rivals competed for western recognition. The Polish National Committee, headed by Roman Dmowski, had supported the Entente Powers from the outbreak of hostilities in 1914, since he saw Germany as the principle obstacle to Polish independence. Jan Paderewski, the world-famous pianist and nationalist, was loosely associated with him. Dmowski enjoyed good relations with western experts and their governments.

Józef Piłsudski, Dmowski's rival, had followed a contrary policy of co-operating with Austria-Hungary and Germany in order to defeat Russia, which occupied the major portion of Poland. He achieved the leading position in the puppet Regency Council organized after German victories on the Eastern Front in 1916 but, foreseeing the ultimate collapse of the German empires, refused to follow further instructions and was imprisoned until November 1918. Piłsudski returned to Warsaw to take full control of the government. His earlier career had earned him such prestige that he unified local councils. The Western Allies still viewed him with suspicion as a German sympathizer or, alternately, a dangerous radical (Piłsudski had once been a socialist). Several months of negotiations elapsed

Amateur at peace-making

before a national unity government was formed with Piłsudski as head of state, Paderewski as prime minister, and Dmowski as director of the Polish delegation in Paris. [DS]

Living in England during those first months after the war was difficult enough. I soon realised that everything was rationed with care - at least in London - and no one could get a meal without the necessary coupons. French friends were to tell me later in Paris that there had always been more food in France than in England, the latter denying herself all sorts of things so that the French would not go hungry. In any case, until well into the New Year more people on the Thames-side were going short on rations than the world believed.

I was back in town sooner than I should have been, since it was impossible to sit still when so many things needed to be done. As my letters to Canada show, I nurtured hopes all through December of getting a new passport, so that I could get 'home' to Ligotka for Christmas; but I was haunted by a sense of failure as an emissary. So far as I could see not a single thing I had suggested as necessary was being done; the inference was that I was a good diplomat. In time I was to discover that far more important people than I had also made urgent representations which those in authority did not heed. Actually, though I did not know it, some of the suggestions I made were even then being carried out.

As for the passport project, we made a blunder. My application had stated that I wanted to get back to Central Europe. There was the rub! The Foreign Office, it seemed, had no objections, but the War Office was adamant. We had Europe divided into two parts - the West and that behind the German frontier. Between them a cordon had been drawn, and no one was allowed to cross it. However, it soon became clear that, with the help of influential friends, I might have got papers to return to Paris. While we were finding this out I had other work to do.

As never before, for the time being London was the crossways of the world. Key people were arriving daily from the ends of the earth, and it seemed as if one might begin here with the rehabilitation of Europe. Paris, which was soon to succeed to this task, at least on the political side, had been too near the front, and was still too occupied with demobilisation. What I soon discovered was that there was almost complete ignorance, outside official circles, about Central Europe - in particular about Poland. For many reasons, this was not surprising, but it meant that the Poles were likely to have less than a fair chance of getting their claims listened to by the world; particularly in England, where there existed neither the traditional ties that bound Poland with France in the nineteenth century, nor the big and active 'emigration' that was to express itself effectively in the United States. The trouble was that I knew too little myself; at least, too little about contemporary affairs. When I reached Paris in November I still knew more about Jan Sobieski than about Józef Piłsudski; and more about Kościuszko than about Roman Dmowski and his work.[7] How that was altered I shall explain in a moment.

Fortunately, chances came to speak on what I could honestly talk about, and I took them. Curtis called me aside early in December and told me that he was unable to go to Oxford that evening to speak at a dinner in Balliol College, and wanted me to go for him. I went gladly - to find that the chief speaker of the evening was Sir George Parkin. The gathering was mainly one of men from the dominions; many of them had done war service, had been invalided out, and were now finishing the autumn term. Parkin spoke first, and gave me a fine opening by talking of the relations of the Anglo-Saxon peoples with one another. I followed up by enlarging on the opportunities, given to both Britain and the United States, to make a signal contribution to the new Europe by helping in every way the now emancipated Slav peoples - Poland (as the largest of them) *in primis*. I was complimented afterwards on the address by the master of Balliol himself, the famous historian A.L. Smith. This experience made it clear to me that people were eager to learn about the part of Europe which had been hidden so long by the curtain of Germany.

I was hardly back in London when a second chance came to say something - this time in the press. Thanks to someone in the Foreign Office I met Professor J.Y. Simpson, who had been making a special study of the Baltic regions, and he asked me to lunch with him the next day to meet 'Scotus Viator,' Dr R.W. Seton-Watson.[8] This was, of course, an unexpected pleasure, for I had got to know a couple of his books before the war came; and, on arriving in England, I soon heard of his work from others. He was very nice to me, as he always is with people who, like himself, are interested in helping the needy; but I soon discovered that we flatly disagreed over the Duchy of Teschen. For the sake of the railway, and for the economic strength the coal and iron would give, he was urging the incorporation of Teschen in the new Czechoslovakia. This surprised me greatly, for I had always thought of him as certain to put human claims, of a cultural sort, ahead of any material considerations. He at once asked me, nevertheless,

---

7 Jan Sobieski, king of Poland, and victorious over the Turks in the battle ending the siege of Vienna, 1683. Tadeusz Kościuszko, Polish noble, fought in the American Revolution, rejoined the Polish army, and eventually became commander-in-chief during the Insurrection of 1794.
8 R.W. Seton-Watson, historian and publicist on Central European affairs, published several books about the Habsburg empire before World War I; later Rose's colleague at the University of London.

whether I would not write something for his weekly, the *New Europe*. I did so, and it appeared under the title 'A New Idealism in Central Europe.'[9] My chief purpose was to emphasize the difference between the prewar artificial loyalties and institutions of the whole Danubian world and the forward-looking atmosphere of the new-forming nation states. There was not much in it about Poland, but I took occasion to point to the settlement at Ostrava on 5th November as a sample of the way things were straightening out. I quoted something an Austrian sergeant said to me in the train on the way to Vienna. He had been on long service in Congress Poland and was now getting home: 'I am certain now, and have felt it for a long time, that America has waged war on us to teach us the very things we needed to know.'

This article opened other doors. I was able to get something into *The New Statesman* under the title, 'Behind the Scenes in Silesia,'[10] which was certainly the first thing of its kind to be published in English by an eye-witness. Here my purpose was to show how many peoples of Central Europe suffered the horrors of war unwillingly, hating the things they had to fight and even die for, and all hoping and praying that the central empires would come down in ruin. Encouraged by this, I decided to try *The Times* itself. I knew that Wickham Steed was one of the editors, and I could fairly claim to have digested his notable book, published on the eve of the war, *The Habsburg Monarchy*. So I wrote him a note, and asked for an interview. He sent word that he would see me at six o'clock the next day. I think it was 17th December. I arrived in good time and sat down to wait.

Half-an-hour passed, and finally three-quarters, before I was called in. Steed apologized abjectly, and said he had been detained by a visitor from far away. But now he was free, and would be glad if I would tell him what I knew about Silesia. I at once picked his own pet ideas from his book, and gave him my views as to what should be done to meet the new situation. He was good enough to say that I was clearly a student of men and movements, and not just a tourist. Would I write something for *The Times*. He could not guarantee that it would be accepted, but he would do his best. Of course I agreed, and was getting up to go when he stopped me. 'Just a minute,' he said. 'I think you'd like to know who it was kept you waiting so long just now. You would never guess. It was Paderewski.' Of course I was taken aback, for I already knew enough of what was going on to realise that there was something afoot. After a moment I said: 'That is news. What is Mr Paderewski doing here? I understood that he was still in America.' I learned that the great Polish leader had been brought to Europe

---

9 *New Europe*, IX, 113, 12 Dec. 1918, 197-9
10 *New Statesman*, XII, 304, 1 Feb. 1919, 366-8

and, after a brief visit in Paris, was in London on his way to Danzig. A British gunboat was to take him, and he was going to explore the situation in Poland. That was something to think about. I went home wondering.

By this time, thanks chiefly to one man, the tireless secretary of the Polish Information Bureau in London, M. Sterczyński of Warsaw, I was getting to know the lay-of-the-land a little. I knew that 'Poland' for the Allies, particularly for the French, meant the National Committee in Paris, composed chiefly of National Democrats, and with the eminent Roman Dmowski as their chairman. Seton-Watson had told me things about Dmowski and the way he had acted in England that disturbed me. He had come over with a Russian passport and had pleaded for the Russian cause in a way that would put the Russians themselves to shame; only, when the revolution came, to desert it altogether, and to suggest to the Allies the creation of a fifty-million-strong Poland reaching to Kiev, to take the place of Russia as a check to German aspirations. All this meant little to me at the time; but I soon saw that, whether he was right or wrong in his claims, Dmowski had done much harm to the Polish cause while in England. This, however, was beside the point. What mattered now was that the Piłsudski regime in Warsaw, which was the *de facto* government of Poland, had no status in the West at all; and that, unless something was done, Poland might not be rightly represented at the coming peace conference.

Slowly but surely I came to realise what the trouble was. The Armistice of 11th November had left Poland under German occupation, ostensibly to keep the Bolsheviks from over-running it. (No one had any idea that the Poles would be competent to clear the land of enemies, and keep order!) Now Piłsudski, beginning his work on the very day of the Armistice, had arranged to send the Germans home, and set up a provisional government. It was a socialist administration, at least in appearance, and the National Committee people at once told the world that Piłsudski was making Poland Bolshevik! To make matters worse, the principle of the 'cordon' referred to above, drawn by the military people, made it almost impossible for anyone to get back and forth. So the truth was hard to get, and everyone was talking about 'those troublesome Poles' and the way they wanted to disturb the peace of Europe. The few who realised the facts of the matter were concerned about something far different. They saw the danger if Poland's forces were divided at the conference table, and hoped that something might happen to mend the breach.

Thanks to the Polish Information Bureau I was introduced to J.H. Harley, the author of *Poland Past and Present* and a great friend of the Polish people. He was acting as editor of the *Polish Review*, along with August Zaleski, and he asked me at once whether I would write the whole account of 'My Mission from Silesia,' as he called it, for the next number of the *Review*. 'If you can get it done

Amateur at peace-making

quickly,' he said, 'I promise you it will be put in the hands of all the important people who are to assemble for the Peace Conference.' That was a challenge I could not let pass, so I did some days of hard work on that paper. It was fuller than any of the memoranda I had written, and came out better because I had myself digested the materials better. I quote from it these passages:

A Czech officer, whom I met in Paris, said to me: 'No doubt Poland is at this time the prey of anarchy; but one must do the same with her as with Russia – leave her to herself, and she will come out of it.' I said at the time that the view was pure heathenism. My reason for doing so was that there are fundamental differences between the position in which Poland finds herself and that of Russia. Neither should be left to itself. That does not mean that the kind of intervention would be the same, for there is nothing more necessary than a wise diagnosis before any treatment is tried. Further, the Czechs, whose lands have known nothing of the horrors of war, whose internal organisation – the highest in Central Europe – has scarcely been touched by it, and whose industry has gone ahead by leaps and bounds, are not in a position to realise how deprived of almost every means of self-help the Poles have been, and in a great degree still are. Nevertheless, if I had known then what I know now, how well General Piłsudski is coping with the situation in Warsaw, I should not have dissented from the above mentioned view as strongly as I did.

Poland is not helpless, nor is her state a hopeless one; but she is being sorely tried and greatly needs help. Not to listen to her would be the same as if a liner, on getting the SOS call in mid-Atlantic, were to pass quietly on. Or, changing the metaphor, to know that in the next village an epidemic is raging, and coolly to decide that the one thing to do is to isolate the village. That is not worthy of a Christian civilisation.

Naturally, it is for the Poles to say whether they want help and what sort they want. He is foolish who goes anywhere uninvited. As all know, Piłsudski has wired his wish that no Entente troops should be sent to Poland without the consent of the Warsaw government. Surely there is only wisdom in that! But there seems to be tragedy in it too; first because General Haller, with the Legions, is still waiting in France, although Lieut. Sarnek delivered his letter to him a month ago; and secondly, because the Polish Mission, despatched from Warsaw two weeks ago to present the whole case to the Entente in Paris has been stranded, for some reason or other, in Switzerland. No one heard of their appearing in the West at all. Is it possible that, even when the Prime Minister deplores having no news from behind the Teutonic world, the men who have been sent to bring news cannot find their way to Whitehall? ... Somebody seems to be afraid of something.

The Entente will not do the right thing by Poland, if it does not lend a willing ear to what the existing government in Warsaw (even before the coming elections) has to say; or if it declines to receive the envoys of the said administration. It will also not do the right thing by Poland if it is content to sit idly by for weeks or months while other factors are at work (be they German or Russian, Gentile or Jewish), which have either a political or a religious axe to grind. Finally, it will not do the right thing by Poland, if, in settling the boundary questions of the future, the 50% basis is accepted as the *modus operandi*. Nothing could please Germany better than thus to reap, in spite of her defeat, a very rich harvest of her Germanisation. To assign to Prussia a wide stretch of territory because the census shows, in the year of grace 1914 let us say, 60% of the people were 'Germans,' is to put a premium on the most barbarous campaign of denationalisation that a modern civilised people has ever carried on ...

At the outset I had explained the main purpose of my mission on the same lines as set forth in my report to Col House. I spoke also of the chaos threatening in Central Europe as a whole, unless steps were taken to steady the agencies trying to tide over the interim. I concluded my paper thus: 'Those who see the difficulties to be faced, and are trying to look ahead, hope for one thing above all! That the Peace Conference will sternly avoid shutting any doors whatsoever. That was the mistake of 1815. The doors were shut, with the Holy Alliance set to watch them; and Metternich,[11] greatest scoundrel of his time, was left in charge of the Holy Alliance. The tragedy was that whole peoples found themselves on the wrong side of the doors. Let no one be served this way now.

An entirely different kind of service was made possible for me right through the weeks of December and early January by the English and Canadian Red Triangle organizations. My personal friendship, in some cases of long standing, with the leaders of these institutions, and their confidence in what I would have to say, made things even easier. Among them was R. Fletcher Argue of Manitoba. I soon discovered that very few of the men in uniform really knew much about the facts behind the war they had been fighting. Many of them were invalids, or convalescents. Many of them were waiting patiently – or impatiently – in their camps, until they could be demobilised. Time hung heavily on their hands, and they were ready to listen to anyone with a new set of experiences. The result was that both in a Christmas conference of camp-directors held in Oxford, and in a number of camps scattered up and down southern England, I had opportu-

---

11 'Forty years later I'm prepared to apologise to the shade of Metternich for this description of him. I was, of course, speaking from the point-of-view of all oppressed peoples.' [WJR]

Amateur at peace-making 81

nities given me to speak to thousands of men about why the war had come at all; and about what the results of it would be for the hitherto subject people of Eastern Europe. Most of them knew that Belgium had been overrun and that Britain had gone to war to keep her word with that little power; but Serbia, Poland, Finland, not to mention the Slovaks or the Slovenes, were little more than names to them. Everywhere I was welcomed, the more so as I had been behind the scenes and could tell them something of the mentality of 'the other side of the line' about which they were always curious. In London, too, in various centres set apart for the 'Tommies' to spend their leisure hours in, I was given a similar chance. How much good came of it one cannot say; but there was nothing else of that kind of thing done at all, since there was no one available to do it.

From time to time I had an opportunity to meet people of distinction. One would be anxious to question me, the next would be so full of something else that I was the listener. To the latter class belonged Sir Valentine Chirol, veteran journalist and authority on the Near East, who was so impressed by the 'Odyssey' of the Czech legionaries and their journey around the world to join the armies in France that he would talk of little else. In this connection, I should mention a short but pleasant talk with President Masaryk, who had just come back from America and was to leave shortly for Prague to take up his new duties there. It was clear he viewed the future with some concern, chiefly owing to the resurgence of nationalism among his own people. He foresaw the difficulties to be met with, if justice was to be had for the non-Czech elements in the new state, and by no means belittled them.

Christmas was at hand. My fine hopes of getting back 'home' to Ligotka faded away. The passport was promised more than once, but did not come. Neither did my 'story' appear in *The Times*, so that at last I went personally to see what was wrong. I learned that it had been set up, but the pressure of other things had crowded it aside. It never did appear, but I was paid for it and I used the money to buy some needed things for Silesian friends. Right at the end of my stay in London, early in the New Year, I found the press chief of the Canadian Peace Mission, J.W. Dafoe, of the *Manitoba Free Press*. He remembered me at once, and asked me to give him the manuscript. It appeared almost in full on the front page of his daily under the title, 'In Darkest Europe, and the Way Out.'[12]

The title was perhaps not quite fair, but I was in a rather pessimistic mood at the time. From letters to my family which have survived, I see that I felt the hopes of speedy and just settlement of Central European differences to be slip-

---

12 *Manitoba Free Press*, 1 Feb. 1919. Dafoe also published 'Turmoil and Confusion in Central Europe Graphically Portrayed,' ibid., 1 May 1919. Neither appears in Turek's bibliography. The *Manitoba Free Press* is now the *Winnipeg Free Press*.

ping away with every week of delay. Why did two full months pass after the end of the war before the peace-makers got together? Even today I do not know the answer to that question. But one thing is certain; not the people in London or Paris, but those at work in Prague, Warsaw, and other capitals of the new Europe were the real peace-makers at that time. And about all that we could know very little. Most of the news that came through was sensational, and often quite untrue. It was strongly coloured by a frantic fear of Bolshevism; and the charge that Poland had cast in her lot with the Communists made things look even worse.

'One needs endless patience in these days,' I wrote my brother on 5th January. 'The past weeks have brought news confirming almost every representation I made to the Powers on 18th November; and now when it is too late to save much trouble, they are making a beginning. If the Peace Conference bungles through, and gets a possible solution of even the gravest problems confronting Europe at this time, it will be a miracle. Every sort of mistake has been made; many are still being made. There is no guarantee for the future.'

The hours I spent with Sterczyński and a couple of brief talks with August Zaleski did not make me feel any more hopeful. They did help in my education, however; and when S took me one evening to the home of Dr George Świętochowski, who was practising as a physician in London, I had a fairly connected story to tell the group of Poles assembled there. Right here I should add that it was thanks to Madame Świętochowski that six months later my wife and I were able to meet Mrs Snowden and some other important people, among them the influential journalist E.D. Morel, famous for his defence of the coloured people in the Congo long before the war. He was now much disturbed about the 'unjust frontiers' Poland was claiming, notably about the 'corridor.' I was able to show him something he had never seen – the famous Spett map made by the Germans in 1912, clearly indicating to what an extent the 'corridor' had a Polish-speaking population. Having two copies of it, I gave him one – or rather lent it to him to show to others; I was never to recover it.

At last the day came when, thanks to the personal intervention of Lionel Curtis, I was told definitely that I should have my passport for *France* that evening. A week of January was gone, and I had been away from Silesia two full months. In the last hours a telegram came from Kulisz, which troubled me. It said: 'Stay in Paris to help our delegation.' That was the first plain news that came through to indicate that the settlement with the Czechs was not bearing the fruit we hoped for. My concern was deep, but it was somewhat allayed by other news of a better sort – this time for Warsaw. Paderewski had gone from Danzig and Poznań to Warsaw, had looked the whole situation over, and had given his hand to Piłsudski, agreeing to help him in the forming of a new coalition cabinet. The

Amateur at peace-making   83

National Committee in Paris were said to be greatly disturbed by it all. The English and the American press showed evident relief. At last there was hope of the Polish leaders burying their differences. Clearly Piłsudski had not gone 'Bolshevist' after all!

On 9 January I was back in Paris. Here I found plenty to do. Word had long since come from Dr Mott that I was to be used as seemed desirable in the American YMCA service; so I was at once provided with a uniform and trench-coat. An invitation came very soon to address a special meeting of all the American secretaries of the Paris region on the meaning of the war for the nations set free in Central Europe. This gave me a chance to tell them of the sufferings of Poland during the nineteenth century, and of the dreams of the great poets about a resurrection and the dawn of a better world. I made use of some of the ideas of Cieszkowski, and brought it all down to the actualities of 1919. They let me speak for an-hour-and-a-half, something no one else, they told me, ever dared to do! It was one of a series of meetings, and the first one in which the problems of the new states were brought up.

A second call came very soon, of another sort. In several parts of France the American Poles were being got together as 'Haller's Army,' with a view to their being ready when the chance came to move out for the homeland. A number of these camps were grouped fairly close together in Lorraine, and in every one there was a Red Triangle hut. Arrangements were made for me to go out and visit them, in order to talk with the men about the way Poland was getting on its feet – in general, to bring a word of good cheer. I have the *Ordre de Mission* before me as I write. It was made valid from 17 to 25 January, and the route was via Nancy and Bayon. As it turned out, we had the coldest weather of the whole winter, and I can still see in memory's eye the bleak open spaces of the Meurthe and Moselle country over which we travelled in open military cars to visit those desolate looking camps.

The men were everywhere glad to see someone from the outside who would tell them what was going on. It was not surprising to find that they were impatient. A hundred times I had put to me the question: Why are we held up here when Poland needs us? Are not the Bolsheviks threatening Europe? Why can't we go and help to keep them out? To all this I had no sufficient answer. I told them that there were complications and that everything possible was being done; but I made the mental resolution to tell some of the wise-acres in Paris what the simple soldier was saying, while they were disputing over politics. I found Poles from Western Canada, whom I had known as boys ten years before. They were there from all over the world, waiting to be given a chance to help set their homeland on its feet; but they were kept idle for months on the cold plains of Lorraine. In one camp I had the rare fortune to see a group of men who had just come in from Italy – prisoners-of-war taken from the Austrian armies in the Alps, still in the ragged uniforms and caps I knew so well, and half-starved. Among all there was one specific request: would I see to it that the Red Triangle people went with them to Poland? They did not want to go there unless Auntie YMCA (pronounced Imka) could go with them. Of course I promised to pass on the word.

Back in Paris, where the Peace Conference had assembled on 20 January, the opportunity came quicker than I expected. On making enquiry, I found that the prospects of General Haller getting away with a contingent were not good. It seemed that Wilson had the matter in hand and he was said to have fears that the army might be used in Poland, once it got there, not to fight the Bolsheviks but for party political purposes – to oppose the *de facto* government of Piłsudski. Those who told me this suggested that it might be well to sound out General Haller himself on the subject. I volunteered at once to do this, and had the good fortune to be received by the general the very next day.

He came to the very door of his room to meet me, took me by the hand, and welcomed me as he would an old friend. We talked for an hour about different things. I told him of my visit in Lorraine, and of what the men felt about the delay. I told him also of their wish to have the YMCA go with them to Poland. He smiled, and answered that nothing would please him better. 'Would I see that the head office of the YMCA knew his view?' I said I would. Then we spoke frankly of the main purpose of my visit. His comment on the whole matter was simple and to the point: 'Please tell all who wish to know that when I lead the Polish legions in France back to Poland, it will be to defend and stabilize our frontiers, and with nothing else in mind.' That was all, but it was enough. The sequel was to show that General Haller was a man of his word.

But now I must go back a bit to the first days after my return from London to Paris. As noted above, we knew already in London that the government in Warsaw had difficulty in getting its proper representation at the centre of Allied counsels – in Paris. Dr Dłuski and Professor Sujkowski had indeed been permitted to come, but I soon learned in Paris that the delegation proper, headed by Michał Sokolnicki, could not get a visa to enter France and were waiting in Switzerland. Clearly the National Committee under Dmowski's leading did not want them, preferring to keep a monopoly of their relations with the Entente. For a time it looked as though the Peace Conference would get under way, without any proper delegation from the largest of the new states about to be created by the coming peace treaty!

I put these facts as straight as I could, at the very first opportunity, both to the British and the Americans with whom I had contacts. Whether this helped or not I cannot say; but a few days later a message reached me that the Polish delegation had arrived, was at the Hotel Lutetia, and would like me to call on them. I did so, and found Sokolnicki, his secretary Michał Mościcki, and Lieut Hempel. We discussed the whole situation, and I undertook to try to get them in touch with the English delegates in Paris. Mr Headlam-Morley promised to see what he could so, insisting, however, that nothing was to be done which could in any way be regarded as 'official.' I thanked him, pointing out that it would be a pity if the people best qualified to explain the situation in Poland should be kept in the background and not allowed to meet with the very circles who most needed the information they could give. He agreed, and results came quickly.

I received word to bring Mr Sokolnicki to a certain place – I do not seem to have made a note of where it was – to meet Sir Esme Howard.[13] I think the hour set was six in the afternoon. We arrived and were received by Headlam-Morley in person. In a few minutes Sir Esme came in, and a conference began at once. I was permitted to remain, and listen. Speaking in French, Sokolnicki presented the whole situation in Poland in plain terms. He was nearly an hour in doing so, after which questions were asked. The atmosphere was most cordial, and one felt that, 'official' or not, the ice was now broken. Of this meeting Ambassador Sokolnicki has recently written some appreciative words in *Kultura* (Polish journal published in Paris).

My position in Paris was a favourable one. I had no axe to grind. I was in nobody's pay, for my salary from the World Student Christian Federation kept me. I was more in sympathy with the Warsaw government than with the National Council, but I had no desire to undo the fine work the latter had done for the Polish cause in a number of ways. Filipowicz had said to me in Vienna: 'We are grateful for all that the National Committee have done for Poland, but we cannot concede them the right to be the sole representatives of the nation at the Peace Conference.'

From time to time I was at the National Council headquarters. Here I met the anthropologist Jan Czekanowski of Lwów, the eminent biologist Michał Siedlecki of Cracow, and Bronisław Tetmayer (later Senator), who invited me to visit him in Bronowice – a thing I never was able to do. Either then or later I also got to know well the geographer Eugeniusz Romer, and there were many others whom I cannot recall today. One thing impressed me. By no means all of those who were helping in the council were satisfied with the tactics of their chief. I heard openly the criticism that he kept himself too much apart, and did not know what was going on around him. Again, when I applied, he refused to see me.

On my return from Nancy, which would have meant far more to me as a city had I realised what a part was played in its construction by the eighteenth-

---

13 Sir Esme Howard, British diplomat, delegate to the Paris Peace Conference.

century Polish king, Stanisław Leszczyński, the news was already abroad of the Czech 'invasion' on 23 January of Polish Silesia – an act that undid all the peace efforts of the previous November. Before the end of January delegates of the Teschen (Polish) Council had arrived in Paris, so that we could confer together. The general situation did not look good. As all know now, the powers were so disunited among themselves that nothing seemed possible in Paris except talk. Wilson's attention had been taken up with his idea to get the Soviets somehow drawn in – the Prinkipo plan;[14] and it seemed as if anyone could do almost whatever the might of his right arm permitted in Central Europe. The situation had worsened since November, and the Western Powers were largely to blame.

Copies of a useful document were put into my hands by the delegates from Teschen. It was a memorial of the Protestant pastors of the duchy, signed by twenty-five of them, with Franciszek Michejda at the head. It set forth simply the three reasons for the assigning of the area to Poland – geographical, historical, and ethnographical. In particular it emphasized the desire of Polish Protestants one day to unite in a single church, hoping that even the Polish-speaking Mazurians of East Prussia would also be able to belong. In a letter to my mother, dated 2 February, I wrote thus: 'Three days ago things looked very black here, but a kind Providence has cleared away the clouds. I'm hoping now to see things move. The one thing they won't do is get Poland opened up, as they should. General Botha's Commission is to go there on 8th February, I hear. I am to be with him tomorrow, to tell him what I know about the Silesian question ... Today I was able to give to Sir Robert Borden and to Mr Lansing's secretary copies of the Silesian pastors' memorial. I am also making it the basis of an article, to be sent by messenger to Dr Mott.

The reference to General Botha requires explanation. For some time the Allies had been realising that Poland did count, and that what was happening in Warsaw was of real importance for the peace of Europe. Plans were maturing for a big commission to go to Warsaw to see for themselves what was going on. Botha was to lead it, and several powers were to be represented. Lionel Curtis knew the general well in South Africa, and suggested that I see him for an hour to tell him what I knew. Unfortunately, the message where I was to go, and when, never reached me; or rather I got it too late. So that plan fell through. I have always regretted it for personal reasons, for he was one of the outstanding men in Paris at the time.

General Botha, however, fell ill, and the leading of the commission was handed to M. Noulens; Sir Esme Howard was to go as the head of the British sec-

---

14 President Wilson attempted to end the Russian Civil War by means of a conference of all Russian sides on Prinkipo Island off Constantinople. The Bolsheviks agreed to attend but their 'White' opponents rejected the scheme.

tion and Professor Lord as that of the American section.[15] I had met Lord in the Hotel Crillon, but he was too occupied to pay any attention to me. No doubt he was plagued by all sorts of people wishing to tell him what ought to be done. In any case he had no time to listen to what I had to say about Silesia. Then came a startling proposition from Mr Headlam-Morley. He was trying to get the people at the top to let me go in as a private emissary in Silesia, see exactly what was going on there, and make a report to Sir Esme Howard in Warsaw. Would I undertake it? Of course I agreed, though that meant disobeying the instructions given from Teschen. Anything, if only the 'cordon' could be broken down and contact established between those 'making' peace and those who were waiting for it 'to be made.'

The first days of February were full enough. I was in steady contact with various American agencies who were wanting to get a chance to do relief work in Eastern Europe; for instance, the Methodist church of the Southern States, who had three bishops in Paris, and were ready to go and help the hungry the moment an opportunity offered. I wrote for Bishop Lambeth a memorandum, of which I still have the original, telling them of the fine opportunity they could find in co-operation with the Polish Evangelicals to do both relief and spiritual work; but pointing out that Poland was mostly a Roman Catholic country, and that any efforts to begin missionary work among Catholics would be resented at once. 'No proselytising!' was in effect my counsel, and I put this as strongly as words would permit. Of course I gave the bishops the pastors' memorial, and told them details of the plans Kulisz had been making for educational work among the younger generation.

Meanwhile I had the privilege of a conference with Dr Eduard Beneš. He remembered me from Prague where I had been a visitor at his seminar, and we talked of the Easter days at Ligotka in 1914. I expressed my regrets at the action of the Czechs on 23 January, but he declared that there was no other course open. There were evidences that the Poles were planning a *coup*, and in any case the need for railway communication with Slovakia was such that it could not be denied. For him it was a foregone conclusion that the duchy would be assigned to Czechoslovakia, though he did not deny that the majority of the people were Poles in speech and sympathy. I left him, feeling the hopelessness of the whole matter and remembering that the pastors' memorial was dated 3 December. Clearly they must have had doubts even then as to the good faith of those who had made the settlement of 5 November.

Other visits and interviews were less depressing. I had tea one day with an American lady, said to be a 'princess,' who had hopes of becoming queen of Po-

---

15 Robert H. Lord, American expert on Polish affairs at Paris, Harvard historian, author of *The Second Partition of Poland* (1915).

land. I was privileged to attend a reception in honour of the Styka family, father and son, both of them painters of international reputation. I called from time to time at the home of Dr and Mrs Bronisław Motz, from whom I heard much about the course of the war both in France and in Poland. From them I received a personal letter to Lieut Świrski in Warsaw, personal adjutant of Józef Piłsudski, the chief of state. But one evening in particular will remain in my mind, when I had the good fortune to be invited by Curtis to dine with a small circle at the Hotel Majestic. It will be remembered that this was the 'home' of the British delegation to the Peace Conference, and no one could pass the doors unless he could show proof of legitimate and even important business.

Lionel Curtis and Lord Robert Cecil were the hosts, and there must have been about a dozen of us at table. Opposite to me was a small man, one of the heroes of the evening. His name was Bullitt, and they said he had just come back from a journey to Russia, where he had gone as a special agent of Wilson. I remember that he had much to tell, but I fear that I was not greatly interested. The reason was that on my right there was a still smaller man, younger than myself, with a high brow and fair hair. His name was Lawrence. There was an admiral of the American Fleet, and there must have been others: but I have no idea who they were.[16]

I had been warned by my host that there would be questions put to me about how things were going in Central Europe. Actually I escaped pretty well. With an emissary just out from Soviet Russia, and with the 'uncrowned king' of the Middle East at the table, it befitted me to keep silence. The evening was unforgettable. Of course the honours went to Lawrence; it could not be otherwise. Scholar, archaeologist, explorer, adventurer, architect of something nearer Arab unity than had been known for ages, and private cicerone in Paris of one of the most picturesque figures at the conference – who was able to dispute places with him? He was just a student generation younger than myself at Oxford, was in fact barely thirty; but what fame he had won! And how sick at heart and disillusioned he was on leaving Paris a few months later.

Two issues that came out in discussion will remain forever in my memory. One was the set of views Lawrence developed as to the contrast between the British and French attitudes toward the Arabs and their neighbours in North Africa and the Near East. In effect, he declared, the latter seek to make of the peoples of the southern and eastern seaboard of the Mediterranean 'good Frenchmen,' wearing Parisian clothes and speaking as nearly as may be with a faultless

---

16 William Bullitt, Wilson's personal envoy to Bolshevik Russia in 1919. His report was eventually rejected as too pro-Bolshevik. And, of course, T.E. Lawrence, 'Lawrence of Arabia.'

accent; while the British were anxious for something quite the opposite. They did not want the 'native-born' of any country to imitate them, copying their speech, dress, and manners, but rather that they should simply be themselves. He did not argue that this arose from any modesty on our part, rather perhaps the reverse.

Partly growing out of this discussion there followed a most exciting argument between our two hosts as to what should be done about Constantinople, or rather with St Sophia. It may be remembered that there were those who said that now was the time to restore it to its original place as the Mother Church of Eastern Christianity. Curtis took the view that to do this would provoke a reaction in the whole of the Muslim world, with dire consequences for our position in India. Lord Robert made light of these fears, holding that they were groundless, and that the right thing should be done regardless of critics. As all know, nothing came of the project, if such it was; and the Crescent still presides over the worship of God in that ancient sanctum.

I might add that I asked Lawrence whether he knew Dr Zwemer, whose books on Islam we had read in our study circles all over the New World, and who had spoken at Wernigerode in 1913. He replied in the affirmative, and to my further question as to how far that veteran missionary knew Islam, he gave this interesting answer: 'He knows a great deal about it, but he tends to create a picture of the Muslim world in his mind that does not always correspond with realities.' I have often thought of that remark since, for the same danger besets all of us. More than once I have come across the same phenomenon in the case of other 'experts,' and have wondered many a time whether I have not been guilty of the same mistake.

The fifth of the month has been in my life a fateful day. On the fifth I was married, on it I left Silesia in November 1918; I was resolved on the 5th of February, if possible, to start my journey back. And so it turned out. But at the last moment I had the greatest possible difficulty in getting a taxi to take me to the Gare de Lyon, and only the kind help of a French officer saved the situation. The next morning I was in Geneva.

THE SECOND PHASE

Rose's return to Central Europe involved him in fresh diplomatic complications. The Duchy of Teschen had become an object of controversy between Czechs and Poles, both of which nationalities inhabited the region. An early accord between the two groups broke down under pressure from Prague and Warsaw, resulting in the intervention of the Czech army over strenuous Polish protests. A decision was finally made in Paris to award most of the area to Czechoslovakia despite a Polish ethnic majority because of strategic and economic considerations. Poles carried bitter memories for years.

Rose later moved on from Silesia to central Poland, which became the focus of his activities for most of the next decade. [DS]

My return to Central Europe was a logical sequence to my journey out, but formally everything was reversed. As an emissary of the Polish Council seeking contacts with the Allies I had official standing, but based on a grand hoax. On my way back I had no official status and no documents to show what I was to do, but I was a *bona fide* Briton, with a *bona fide* passport, and with *bona fide* visas. The entry visa to Poland had been given by the Control Office already functioning in Paris, on the strength of a letter written by Professor Jan Czekanowski. To my regret I lost this letter, the only bit of evidence in black and white that I did any work at all for the Polish cause during those eventful weeks.

Friends in Paris, and others in Geneva and Berne, were disturbed on hearing of what was planned; still more disturbed to learn that I was going unarmed. At least I should take a Browning with me! At this I could only smile; neither in Austria nor in Czechoslovakia nor in Poland had I anything else but friends. I knew that a real welcome would await me - the first person to bring straight news of what was going on 'outside.' Never in my life had I carried a weapon, and I had no desire to begin now. As it turned out, the Red Triangle on my uniform, and indeed the khaki itself, were a sufficient protection anywhere.

In Geneva I had dinner with Phildius' father and mother, and got their son's address in Berne, to which I went on the same night. The next day I called on the Polish chargé d'affaires, my good friend from London, August Zaleski. He received me more cordially than I had expected. Never a man of many words, he was now able to see things in a more hopeful light than ten weeks earlier. Not that everything had cleared up - far from it. From notes in my diary I see that he still regarded the position of the joint Piłsudski-Paderewski regime in Warsaw as precarious. Dmowski still seemed to have the ear of the Allies in Paris 'largely because his opponents haven't got the measure of him.' 'To questions from Warsaw,' Zaleski went on, 'why nothing is being done to get Haller's army off to help out in Poland, he keeps replying that Wilson is unwilling to let it go, having become pro-Bolshevik.' That remark recalled the dinner at the Majestic at which Mr Bullitt was present, and the rumours going about as to plans for a meeting with the Russians on the island of Prinkipo. Zaleski welcomed the news that I was on my way to Poland, and advised me to go straight on to Warsaw, ask for an interview with Paderewski, and tell him the truth. If possible I should do the same with the chief of state. It was obvious that Dmowski himself was unwilling

Amateur at peace-making

to let the army go, since without it – his own creation – he would be left in a defenceless position.

'Dmowski seems to me to be after power,' said Zaleski. 'Even his own people admit that he has no programme.' Yet a programme for saving Poland, for keeping her out of the clutches of any outside control, seemed to be the crying need of the times. I reminded Zaleski that I had no authority to say anything for anyone. That, he said, didn't matter. The word of an independent person of goodwill was even more important. Of course, I was to investigate the situation in Teschen first, but the other should not be forgotten. Then he told me some startling news. The first American Red Cross train with medical supplies for Warsaw was to leave the next day from Zurich, and he was willing to ask the officer in charge to take me with him. He gave me a letter, and at three o'clock I found Capt Beard. He was willing to let me go, on my own responsibility, of course. So that was settled.

I was sorry to have so little time in Berne, where everything was fantasically beautiful under the snows of winter, even though my quarters were in a bathroom in the *Schweizerhof* – nothing else was to be had. It meant having but a short hour with Phildius and his wife, and we had a great deal to talk about. Nevertheless, to miss such a chance to get away would have been madness, and I thanked Zaleski warmly when I took leave. His last words were: 'If you should get to see the Commandant (the name used for Piłsudski by all of his colleagues of the Legions), tell him that I am always at his disposal.' I recalled those words seven years later when the man who said them became foreign minister of his country. Meanwhile I just found time to call on the kind banker who had acted as intermediary during the war, sending us money for our maintenance; and I found that he still had some in hand, which he at once gave me.

The journey to Zurich was made through a blinding snowstorm that recalled Manitoba days. Here too we had a long hunt before the three of us – the Swiss officer who has to take charge of the twenty men designated to convoy the train, a Russian Red Cross officer, and myself – found a place to sleep. The next morning I made a few purchases, including some chocolates, and at 11 o'clock we left for Buchs. Everyone knows how lovely that trip is along the lakes, and we saw it at its best. By sheer chance I stumbled on Pastor Melle, who had translated for Wilder in Vienna five years earlier. He told me that there was very little of the idealism and good-will left now, of which I had seen samples in November. The realities of a hard winter, lack of food, and a sense of the futility of the peace-making had done their work.

In Buchs it was still snowing. The day was Sunday, and we had to wait some hours before the train could be made up. It was evening before we got away. The conditions of travel, instead of being lonely and difficult, as I had expected, were ideal. A comfortable 'sleeper,' the most congenial of company, and regular meals. The captain was a Californian, my companion in the sleeper a corporal from Kentucky. The terms of our travel were that the railways regarded us as 'freight,' so we had to make way for passenger trains, and that meant going slowly. As things turned out, the intense cold and the snow held up all travel on the railways, and the journey to Vienna took sixty hours. More than once our Swiss convoys had to turn out and stand guard, while we stood helpless in the open country. Before we got to Innsbruck we found Italian soldiers guarding the line, and the impression we got was that they were none too friendly. But Captain Beard would stand no nonsense, and we got steadily on.

Arriving before daylight at Pensing, I suggested that we take the trolley into the centre of Vienna instead of waiting for the train to be moved slowly around the city to the North Station. My idea was that we should breakfast at the Bristol, in the Vienna way. It sounded good to the men, most of whom spoke no German and were willing to trust me. So off we went, but with sad results! I had reckoned without my host. There was nothing to eat, nor any hope of getting a breakfast anywhere. Two days later the municipal elections were to come, and the Town Council was holding up the food for that occasion! At least that was what we learned from conversation with the head waiter. So I had five hungry men on my hands. What was to be done? We soon found members of Professor Coolidge's mission – a branch of Hoover's American Relief Administration [ARA], but they had had coffee, and told us that there would be nothing for it but to wait until lunch time, and then go to the Italian commander's 'mess.' 'They are the only people who have food in Vienna!' was the comment.

I got the Polish visas for the party without delay. With the Czechs, for some reason, it took much longer; so we arrived at the Hotel Imperial an hour late. But they had heard of our coming, and gave us a royal dinner. I was tired out when we got back to our train, and glad to lie down. We got away from Vienna about five o'clock, and were in Oderberg (Bohumín) the next morning by four. Here I was to leave the party, so they got me up at once. As things turned out the train stood two hours waiting for a special express, they said, coming from Vienna. It pulled in after five, and I recognized that it was the Paris train carrying the Noulens Commission, which had been slated to start on 8 February. While waiting on the platform for my train to Teschen I heard from Polish porters of what the Czechs had been doing during these weeks. It was one-sided, as was to be expected, but I could see that nasty things had happened and much bad blood made. At six o'clock I got my train and arrived in Teschen to find the station in Czech hands. Without waiting I took the first local for Gnojnik, and was in Ligotka before ten.

The reception given me was overwhelming. I learned that E was in Teschen in order to be of service, if needed, with the 'Little Commission' as it was now to be called – the Allied mission which had arrived a few days before to 'keep the peace' between two neighbour peoples. I also heard that she had made the long and tiring journey to Prague some weeks earlier in order to put the case of the Poles in the duchy personally to President Masaryk.

The pastor was still an invalid. He had been home a week after being held by the Czechs under arrest in Ostrava for four days. E had been in the parsonage when he was arrested, and there was no reason given beyond that he was a leader in Polish national life. The experience had been a trying one, for no man was ever less political in outlook than he.

Before the day was over we had exchanged news. I had learned much about the local conditions; my hosts had learned what I could tell them of things in Paris. We then decided that I was to go to Teschen with the evening train, unless E came home with an earlier one. I reached Gnojnik after seven, but the station-master refused to sell me a ticket. I was told that I could not be allowed to go to Teschen that night. (I should add in parenthesis that the station-master and his family had been our cordial acquaintances right through the war, his daughter and her husband had been more than once at the villa. The latter was a corporal in the army, and was now very active, as I was to learn, in Czech interests.)

For a moment I was non-plussed, but at once I replied: 'I have business to-night in Teschen with the Allied Commission. Whether I have a ticket or not, I shall travel by the next train, and I suggest that you leave me in peace. This is an American uniform, and I'm on diplomatic business. He who interferes with my movements will suffer for it.' This I said quite openly, so that several people round about, some of whom knew me, could hear. It obviously made an impression, the more so as I walked past the sentinel onto the platform, to wait for the train. In a few minutes he came after me. The orders were from Teschen, from the Town Command. They were sorry, but they had to carry them out. I could not go! I replied that I would pay no attention to any order, unless they had it in written form. Of course they had none, as I suspected; so I said, 'I'm going; and advise you not to try to stop me.'

Again a pause, and then the station-master's son came out. I might go, but they would send a soldier with me, and I was to report to the station command when I arrived. The train came in; I went aboard without a ticket, and a soldier with his bayonet took up his station beside the door. Half-an-hour later we arrived, and I was guided at once to the command. Here I asked whether anyone spoke English, and finally got to the officer-in-charge, who spoke German. I told him that I could not see why I, a Briton, in the American YMCA uniform, was subjected to such annoyances in an Allied country, and asked to see the order for my detention. 'But there never was any such order!' was his reply. 'We had no word of your being here at all, and are very sorry for the annoyance that has been caused you.' He then asked me whether I could explain it. I said that the only possibility was some personal spite. (Later it became known that it was the son-in-law of the station-master at Gnojnik who had telephoned from Teschen to keep me from getting to the Allied Commission. He had done it on his own responsibility – part of a personal ambition to be a 'bigger' man than he was.) In any case I should have to report the matter to the commission, to whom I was now on the way. He begged me not to make an 'affair' of it, as such things were likely to happen in troubled times. I agreed, but said that there were signs of too much lawlessness in regard to personalities, and that I must report it. We parted on the best of terms, and I made my way to the Brown Stag Hotel, where I was told that I should find 'all the people.'

The commission was still at dinner, and could not be seen before nine-thirty. Later I was received in a formal manner that amused me greatly. The members stood in a row, seven of them, partly in uniform, partly in civilian dress, and I was asked to explain my business. I refused to take the matter officially but reported who I was and what had happened. I added that, having had some years' residence in the district and some knowledge of its history, I might be of some use to the commission, and was at their disposal; but I heard nothing more of them. Without being invidious, I can truly say that the personnel of the commission was not impressive. The English member was quite obviously given to his cups; the American was, as I learned afterwards, a mayor from a Middle West town, who looked harmless, and was certainly lost in the problems of Central Europe. One man did impress me, when I talked with him privately the next day, the secretary, Mr Dubois, who was afterwards director of the Ulen Company in Warsaw. Had these men arrived in Teschen in December, they might have been of some use. In the fact of a *fait accompli*, and of the downright methods of the Czechs, they could do nothing. Without agreeing with the Poles, who charged them with favouring the Czech cause, I should say that they were prepared rather to let things continue as they were than to lodge any stern protest against an aggressor, and so force any change.

The next day I reported to the chairman of the Polish National Council on what I had tried to do in Paris. He expressed satisfaction at the contacts I had made, and encouraged me with information on the events in Silesia. I decided to stay a few days before going on to Warsaw. It was a Friday, and I found my study in Ligotka exactly as I had left it three months before. Unfinished portions of my English translation of Cieszkowski's *Our Father* were lying about, not to mention other scraps of work. I tried to settle down to something, but found I was too tired. Again I went to Teschen, and discovered that a native of the duchy, the Austro-Hungarian consul, Karol Pindor, had returned home from the Far East, and was installed as competent interpreter for the Polish authorities. This made many things easier.

For the Polish cause the real trouble was the presence of a German minority in the Duchy of Teschen and of a half-assimilated group of 'Silesianers,' led by Dr Józef Kozdon. Intensely loyal to Austria until its collapse, all these people had sought to set up the claim for a sort of tiny Switzerland, lying between Czech Moravia and Polish Galicia. In this little domain, the moneyed classes would be the German mine, factory, and railway owners, and they would be complete masters of the situation. The Poles, and such Czechs as there were, would simply be their helots – just as heretofore. When the Czechs took possession of Teschen and of the duchy as far as Skoczów, these people decided that their hope was dwindling; so they were prepared to support the Czech claim, in the view that they would be better off as a part of the very large German minority in the new Czechoslovakia than as a part of the much smaller and very scattered German minority in Poland. Thus we had now the spectacle of Dr Kozdon, who had nothing but hatred for the Czechs before and during the war (calling them traitors and still worse), now standing in with them and making the task of the Poles with the Allied Commission as difficult as possible. Of course the hope did not die that, manœuvring one Slav state against the other, some way might be found to get a German 'Silesian Switzerland' after all. The lines on which I should report to Sir Esme Howard in Warsaw were thus clear.

On Friday, 21 February, just as I was ready to start on the journey to Warsaw, bad news reached me by wire from Switzerland. My brother had cabled from Winnipeg saying that mother was dangerously ill. Could I arrange to come home before Easter? So that was a new anxiety, which I had to carry as I went. The courier of the Polish council, a cavalry captain, undertook to get me through the lines; and a young American lieutenant named Bass went with us to take some documents to Professor Lord in Warsaw.

We got through without difficulty, and were welcomed at supper in Skoczów by the commander of the Polish forces, Col Latinik. I had the privilege of listening to his report on the situation, made to Colonel Tissi, Italian member of the commission in Teschen. Attacks by the Czechs were going on, four Poles had been killed. At supper the courier sat on my right, while opposite us, beside the two colonels, sat a Major Fordham in an English uniform. He spoke poor French, rather bad German, and no Polish – though he understood a good deal. The Polish commander was confident of his ability to hold on, but deplored the whole business. He begged me to put the case strongly in Warsaw. We had decent sleeping quarters in a private house, and I left the next morning for Bielsko. Late in the afternoon we were in Cracow.

For years I had looked forward to my first visit in Cracow, but had not expected it under such circumstances. We had been announced by telephone, and two officers of the Liquidation Commission were at the station to meet us. They gave us a warm welcome, and took us off at once to see the Castle on Wawel Hill. It was getting dark, but I recall my first view of the Florian Gate and its Barbican, as well as of the Grunwald Monument. At the office of *Głos Narodu* on the Rynek, I met for the first time a man whom I was to value highly as a fellow-worker in coming years, Tadeusz Żuk-Skarzewski. After dinner at the Saski Hotel we learned that the train from Lwów was late, so we had an hour or more at the Café Esplanade, which gave me an opportunity to tell something of my impressions of Paris and to learn much about things in Poland. On the platform I wanted to say 'Thank you!' but Captain Fanger interrupted me with words I shall never forget: 'Do not thank us. We have waited a hundred years for this moment when we can entertain visitors in our land, knowing that we and not strangers are masters here. The satisfaction is all ours. Come back soon!'

On arriving in Warsaw next morning we found our way to the Hotel Bristol. The Hoover mission people welcomed us, and we had a chance to clean up. I was hardly finished when in walked Dr Henryk Arctowski[17] whom I had met in Paris at the home of Dr Motz. He was with the Big Commission, as adjutant to Professor Lord. At once he said, 'You can share my room,' so I had now a roof over my head. As it turned out I had also the best possible guide to Warsaw, for Arctowski had been born there. We walked about for an hour or more. My diary says: 'Everywhere beggars, everywhere Jews, everywhere soldiers. In the windows fruit, gorgeous apples, butter, meat, even cheese. Also clothing of all sorts; but prices villainously dear.'

On arriving back at the Bristol I met Lieut Bass. He looked altogether crestfallen. All the journey he had shown himself rather superior to me as a civilian, and to his Polish hosts as well. He was convinced of the rightness of the Czech cause, and of the good deed of the Teschen Commission. Now he had got a severe wigging from the Big Commission people, and he begged me to go along and explain things. He was quite humbled. I said I would gladly come if they sent for me; but they never did, and it was better so.

The day was Sunday, so I could feel free. In the afternoon I got away to visit people of whom I had known for years – School Inspector Tosio (whose wife was an American) and his family. There I met the manager of the historic Home for the Aged Poor beside St Mary's church in the Old Town, a Mr Serafinowicz; and Dr Marjan Reiter, from whose school-books I had learned much Polish. The hours spent in the exchange of news and views remain in my memory today. Meeting Serafinowicz was a rare piece of good fortune, for he put himself at my disposal in succeeding days and showed me the splendid work Warsaw was doing, under the most trying conditions, to care for the children and the outcast.

17 'Distinguished explorer and meteorologist, later to lecture in Lwów University.' [WJR]

Amateur at peace-making

The next morning I made my way to the quarters on Królewska Street assigned to the British mission, and was soon in conference with Sir Esme Howard. It was quite informal; but I was able to tell him very simply just what had been going on in the Duchy of Teschen and make a suggestion or two as to dealing with the situation there. He asked me to write a memorandum for him, very short, and to hold myself in readiness to speak to the whole commission. He himself felt that the Czechs had made a serious mistake, and had hurt their own case by what they had done. Meantime, I was free to do what I liked, which was (of course) to get to know Warsaw. This was a most interesting experience. For a week I was able to wander at will, save for the time that I took to be shown samples of self-help in social relief; and I wrote the whole story after leaving, with a view to publishing it in London. Unfortunately, no one would risk the outlay, so it finally appeared in a Canadian weekly in Toronto in July 1919.[18] From it I quote:

I have felt very much at home in Warsaw ... only one thing made me uneasy. Not the sudden change in the weather from spring to such a blizzard as would be worthy of Manitoba's best, nor the fact that the prices of food and clothing are double what they are in Silesia; it was the uncanny though never impolite curiosity of the people.

I have been accosted, while waiting for the tram, in five different languages; each time with the offer to help, and with questions as to what news there was from the outside world. It was my good fortune to belong neither to a Mission nor to the Commission, which would have kept me indoors at a desk. I could roam the streets at will. I hadn't a car to ride in; and in the tram, if I conversed with a friend, all those around would stop talking, and prick up their ears to hear what the foreigner would say.

'That is the compliment paid by curious people to one of another blood, coming from far away,' said one of my friends when I told him. 'It is a great day in their history, and the sight of a stranger whom they can trust is a rare thing. We have had too many here of a far different sort.

The city was not attractive – how could it be after four years of war and occupation, on top of a century of foreign rule? It was amusing to hear Arctowski say: 'If I were a businessman I should start a paint factory!' Yes, that was it. Years of neglect, though little actual damage had been done by war. But the con-

18 'The New Warsaw,' *Canadian Churchman*, XLVI, 27, 3 July 1919, 425 and 433; and 'The Heart of Poland,' ibid., XLVI, 28, 10 July 1919, 442 and 450; XLVI, 29, 16 July 1919, 457 and 464; XLVI, 30, 24 July 1919, 474; XLVI, 31, 31 July 1919, 490 and 497

dition of the streets, the lack of bridges, the over-crowding of the tram-lines, the general misery of the poor in the face of zero weather – all this was terrible.

On Thursday morning I called again on Sir Esme Howard. There was now no need for me to appear before the Big Commission, for on the day before, Wednesday, 26 February, the Czechs had been obliged to withdraw, and Teschen was again free. It would be nice if I could feel that my efforts had contributed something to this result! *Post hoc propter hoc*! is too easy a doctrine, however, and I lay no claim. All I know is that both Howard in Warsaw and the people who sent me from Paris thanked me for the information I had given them. True, the agreement reached on 25 February was far from restoring the *status quo ante* on the basis of the settlement on 5 November 1918; but it did make the Czechs realise that they could not get their way by the use of force. It also gave both parties the assurance that their claims would be dealt with by the proper tribunals in Paris.

A few experiences of those busy days stand out in memory. I did not go near the Diet, which was already in session, under the leadership of the coalition cabinet set up shortly after New Year with M. Paderewski as prime minister and with Piłsudski as chief-of-state and commander-in-chief of the Polish army. This was a mistake on my part, as I can see now; but what concerned me more was the work going on, based on the measures of self-help organised by courageous men and women during the years of occupation, to meet the frightful physical and cultural needs of a city of nearly a million people. Among these were orphanages, homes for the aged, feeding stations, schools, and first-aid centres of all kinds.

What I saw convinced me once and for all of the nonsense we had often heard (and were still to hear) about the incapacity of the Poles as a people to deal with vital issues affecting common life. I had the good fortune to meet leaders in educational and religious life, engineers and social workers, business people and economists, and of course men of some standing in the world of letters and the fine arts. At the very end of my stay I had the honour of being received for a longer interview by the chief-of-state himself. Every day I found some time for sight-seeing, and apart from the Citadel[19] of grim memories, which I was only to visit years later, I saw most of the famous buildings of the city.

By contrast with Cracow, the capital of Poland is modern; although surprising remnants were to be found in the thirties of the older city wall, dating from the fourteenth century. Only one church, that of St Mary in the Old Town, is true Gothic. The rest are post-Renaissance, and the majority are in the baroque style,

---

19 The Citadel was a large fortress built on the north side of Warsaw to protect the Russian garrison in case of insurrection. It was also used as a prison to house Polish political offenders.

or, of course, nineteenth-century. Now, imposing as it is, at times even overwhelming, the baroque style has never attracted or inspired me as has the work of earlier ages. In its more chaste forms, as seen in Wren's London churches, it gives light and a sense of togetherness not to be found in the pillared abbeys and cathedrals of the Middle Ages; but it was easily spoiled by being overloaded with decoration and becoming almost theatrical. Nevertheless, the church of St Cross, in which Chopin's heart is enshrined, makes a great impression on the visitor, and when thronged with worshippers it is a place for prayer and for preaching which befits the busy thoroughfare of a great city.

One 'temple' towered above all others in Warsaw, one that was completely out of place and had no meaning (unless the wrong one) for the inhabitants: the *Sobor*, a vast Orthodox church built by the Russians, in the very centre of the city, on the square facing the Saxon Palace, where in due course was to stand the shrine of the 'unknown soldier.' Beside it was a towering campanile and, rich as it was in internal ornament, mostly in mosaic, this structure was as foreign to its surroundings as a mosque would be in Trafalgar Square. The decision taken later on to dismantle it was entirely justified, and this was carried out in the course of a few years, to the satisfaction of the whole nation. The needs of the small Orthodox population were adequately met by the smaller churches standing in other parts of the city.

Close under the charming St Mary's, in the heart of the Old Town, nestles the Home for Aged Poor. It was founded in 1388, a timber cottage, with 'room' for fifteen inmates. When its 500th anniversary was celebrated in 1889, there were 143 inmates of both sexes. Each of them had turned over his or her savings (not less than 100 roubles) and was guaranteed a room for life. When I saw the place the number was 242, and their maintenance was a major economic problem. For three years the institution had been beggared; the Russian authorities, when retiring in August 1915 before the Germans, had taken away the whole endowment fund of 500,000 roubles – no small loss. Only by a joint effort of city, church, and private agencies had the place been able to carry on.

But of more interest was the care of children. I visited nurseries, orphanages, and schools – Catholic, Protestant, and Jewish. In a Catholic day-nursery I found a happy circle of little girls, one of whom recited for me the famous rhyme which I turned thus into English:

Who are you, child?   A Polish mite.
What is your sign?   The Eagle White.
Where do you live?   Not far from here.
And in what land?   In Poland fair.
You love that land?   With all my nature.
Where is your hope?   In Poland's future!

Then my guide took me to see what everyone regarded as a model piece of work for abandoned children, the Jewish orphanage on Leszno Street, managed by a Mr Hosenpud. This remarkable man had been a teacher for years, and was president of the Jewish Teacher's Association. A believer, he took the view that Jewry is a religion and not a nation, and had many enemies among his own people, who were opposed to having orphan lads taught Polish, or brought up to play games, or introduced to the school curriculum that is regarded the world over as the road to intelligent citizenship. 'I am only standing at the gateway of this task,' he said; 'our work could be multiplied many times over, if we had the means.'

I stayed while the thirty or so little fellows had their noon-day meal. It was a really nourishing soup with bits of dumpling like home-made macaroni. I had a portion, and it was good. But I learned that they had no milk and got sugar only once a day, in their breakfast 'coffee.' They all looked fresh and well, and I made this note at the time. 'In the case of at least half, there were none of the traces of Jewish physiognomy. The removing of these children from their Ghetto surroundings effects a transformation not only in speech and manners, but also in countenance.' When I reported later on to a member of the Hoover (ARA) organization in London, I told him about these gallant workers for the children in Warsaw. Within a few weeks they began to receive help. Hoover's agents had been in Warsaw before I was!

In the very heart of Warsaw stands (or stood before the Germans destroyed it in September 1939) the Lutheran church. Nearby are two fine schools, founded and run by the Protestants, a high school, named after the sixteenth-century poet, Mikołaj Rej, and an elementary school. I visited both. The principal of the high school told me of his problems. The chief one was how to find room for half the boys whose parents wanted to place them there – not only Protestant, but Catholic and Jewish. I was interested to learn that Madame Paderewski had asked for admission for both her sons the moment she was settled in Warsaw. The number of Jewish boys who had to be turned away every year was enormous.

In the elementary school I got a pleasant surprise. This is how I described it at the time:

At my request to hear some singing, I was led to one of the nearest classrooms where a Roman Catholic priest was just beginning his lessons ... When they had finished singing, I asked for permission to say a word, and drew the attention of the class to the true meaning of liberty – a prayer for which they had just sung. I discovered that they sing both Catholic and Protestant hymns. The priest smiled at my look of surprise and said: 'We don't quarrel here over the matter of belief.

We have all one Gospel and one God.' I wrung his hand by way of thanks ... Few things pleased me more during my stay than just this episode; hearing such a declaration from a Catholic priest, who was teaching religion in a Protestant school (of course the class was one of Catholic children), in a land that had been until recently under Orthodox government.

Tuesday, 4 March, had been decided on as my last day in Warsaw. From my personal point of view it was to be the best. In the morning I called at the Hotel Bristol to pay my respects to Madame Paderewski, and to thank her for helping me to see so much of the relief work then going on. She had expressed herself, on a former visit, as doubtful whether the YMCA coming from a Protestant country could really be of service in a Catholic land like Poland, but this time she was very cordial. She begged me to urge all friends of Poland in the West to redouble their efforts on her behalf, and invited me to come to see her as soon as I should get back from Canada. I had an invitation to dinner at the house of friends, and we had just finished when Lieut Świrski arrived with the 'Commander's car.' (I should say 'the car of the chief-of-state.') He came in, drank a cup of coffee with my hosts, and then carried me off to the Belvedere.

The visit I now had the privilege of making with Józef Piłsudski, and the interview that lasted an hour-and-a-half, was to me the climax of my whole mission to Warsaw. My host was resting in bed, and he received me there. The whole occasion was completely informal and friendly. It was the only longer talk I had with this remarkable leader, and I wish now that I had made full notes of it immediately. I wish too that I had known far more about the man and his work than I did, for I could have used the time to better advantage. I was one of the first Anglo-Saxons to talk with him after the turnover, and certainly the first to talk with him in Polish. His first question was in English, 'Do you smoke?' and his last word was in English also, 'Goodbye,' but apart from that we chatted freely in Polish about all manner of things.

My first duty was to explain myself, which I did briefly. I told him why I had come to Warsaw, and what my chief concern was. I then told him about the Red Triangle work, and that the Americans would be with Haller's Army when it finally got permission to return to Poland. That was certainly the first news Piłsudski had of the organisation which was to help so efficiently during the next two years of crises, and whose services to the troops he was himself to observe. Then I gave him the message from M. Zaleski. That left us free to talk of other things. I can see the light in those sober grey eyes, as the chief-of-state responded to my questions as to the prospects and problems of the new Poland. He was suffering from a slight cold, and coughed from time to time. But he told me that he had no patience with doctors. His view was that where work had to be done one must do it, and not spare oneself. That had always been his life principle, and perhaps on that account he had been made into a sort of hero. 'My adorers have put me in a false light,' he said. 'At bottom I'm sort of a barbarian.'

I soon saw that he meant this seriously. Unwilling to 'conform to the existing order in Russia, he had elected to be an outcast, and had lived more or less a savage life. He repeated the words later on: 'I am a lover of fighting, a bit of a barbarian. You in the West have your sport of all kinds, we have this constant warring instead. Those who talk of eternal peace on earth are mistaken. There will always be striving, and with it rivalries. This kind of thing builds up character. There is no other way.' Piłsudski was little interested in what was going on in Paris, but eager to talk of what was happening in Poland. It was clear that he had no doubts about winning: 'The end is assured. You could call me an optimist by nature, but in analyzing situations I incline to be a pessimist. About the ends in view we can have faith, but about the means of achieving them, it is harder. The evil lies in human nature, and we must deal with that. For Poland, military training is essential. Our nation has been in subjection, and has not learned to discipline itself, to be master of itself. To learn this is the first thing. Time will tell whether we can be masters of others.'

From time to time my glance left the face of the chief and rested on the only ornament in the room. It was a small Madonna by Raphael, hanging on the wall over the bed. I did not then know how much Piłsudski owed to his mother, but I understand now why that Madonna was there. In the man before me was a rare combination of head and heart. A romanticist, yes; but sternly practical and calculating all the while; reckoning cooly with the difficulties, but stubbornly refusing to yield. And one special note: 'What we Poles have to do is to find our way, by a single mighty effort, out of the eighteenth century into the twentieth. I am proud that I have the privilege of leading in this great work.'

I mentioned my modest beginnings by way of knowing the past of Poland, her thinkers, her mistakes, and her problems. Piłsudski drew attention at once to Poland's place on the map. Between the east and the west, with something of both in her make-up, the still strong semi-feudal social structure on the one hand, but a mighty urge to individual liberty and equality on the other. He spoke of the presence of magnates and nobility, by contrast with the Czechs and the Serbs. 'We are more like the Croats,' he said. 'This we must keep in mind in all we try to do. Just as we must also keep in mind the power and influence of the Church. We cannot think in Poland, as yet, of a separation of the State and Church – as in France.'

I drew his attention to the new socialist Russia. He responded at once. What the Bolsheviks were doing was hateful to him. He had fought Tsarist Russia; he would do the same with the new Soviet regime. For Poland such a system was unthinkable. 'We must win the future,' he said in a striking phrase, 'but without destroying the past. That would be a glorious thing to achieve.' The chief task was that of unification; to possess a single school system, a single army, a single Polish administration of justice. It would take time, but nothing else would suffice.

The night train took me back to Cracow, and the next evening I was again in Teschen. Ligotka was still behind the Czech lines, so I made my report to those interested before going home. Here I found that E had everything ready for our long journey 'out.' We did it by stages; first to Prague, where Mr Fitzgibbon Young, as secretary of the new legation, gave E a provisional *carte d'identité* and where we renewed old acquaintance from prewar days. When we told our friends of what was going on in Silesia, more than one expressed regrets. 'Friendship with the Poles is of more value to us than a strip of territory' was their way of putting it. Of course few of them knew of the strategic and economic significance of that particular strip.

The journey to Berne proved rather tiresome; but we arrived safely, to find there Frank Savery as vice consul who at once provided E with a proper passport.[20] As *repatriés* we had to take the roundabout route via Evian-les-Bains into France, and so were a day longer in getting to Paris than I had expected. We were given a warm welcome by many friends, some of whom seemed never to have expected to see me again.

It would be of small value to comment here on the almost tragic atmosphere of indecision, the sense of frustration, that were to be felt in Paris at this time. What disturbed us most was that Haller's Army had not yet got under way, nor did anyone know when it would. The only real step forward, so far as the Polish cause was concerned, was the consolidating of the representation at the Peace Conference. Party rivalries were no longer in evidence, and the interests of the new state were supreme. I got in touch at once with Mr Headlam-Morley, who thanked me for the help I had given in the Teschen matter.

A few days later he asked E and myself to lunch; but he warned me that the boundary decision appeared to be going in favour of the Czechs. 'We shall have at lunch with us a new member of the British Mission here, who is acting as rapporteur for the Czech cause. His name is Harold Nicolson. Don't say anything that will embarrass him, as he can't help what is happening.' I promised to 'be good,' and looked forward to the occasion with interest. The talk during lunch was of everything, including the notable book, *The Four Horsemen of the Apo-*

20 'Savery was British consul, then consul general, in Warsaw during the whole inter-war period, and made himself one of the first living authorities on all things Polish – language, history, and institutions.' [WJR]

calypse, but we did discuss the situation in Central Europe as well, partly because of what had happened in Budapest, where Bela Kun had just got his innings. The guests knew that we had just come out from Silesia, so I remarked to Nicolson that I had heard of the decision that Teschen was to go to the Czechs after all. 'I'm afraid it will,' was his reply. 'You realize what that means,' I went on. 'A very considerable Polish majority on the wrong side of the frontier, when it was all unnecessary. Won't this make the prospects of trouble in the years to come much greater?' He agreed that this was true, and added a word that I have never forgotten: 'We shall have to look sharp.'

By 'we' he meant, of course, the League of Nations; and he clearly lived in the hope that it might be able, either to show its spirit over all Europe or, for lack of that spirit, to play the part of an effective police. Perhaps I was in a doubting mood but that remark has always seemed to me to deserve the comment made by Jan Hus when a woman threw an extra faggot on the flames at Constance: *Sancta simplicitas*! Nicolson remarked that he had great faith in Masaryk and Beneš, in their efforts to smooth out difficulties. Time has shown that 'we' could do neither the one nor the other of these two things; and that even a liberal constitution like the Czech was no adequate guarantee of justice for minorities.[21]

The next day I had a long hour with Wickham Steed, in which I told him many of my latest impressions from the trip to Warsaw. He said to me: 'You must go and see Dr Beneš.' I consented, and went along to the Czech headquarters the same day. The secretary took my name, and came back to say that Dr Beneš was very busy, but if I would wait he would try to see me. So I sat down and waited. After three-quarters-of-an-hour I reminded the young man, who went in again. The answer was that unfortunately no interview was possible, but would I give my message to the secretary. This was difficult for my French was very bad, and he spoke neither English nor German. So nothing came of that. I doubt whether what I had to say would have helped in the least.

We were busy enough during those days, though there was nothing that one could do. I was waiting for the arrival of Dr Mott from New York, so that my 'furlough' could be arranged, and we were entertained by various friends. One evening thanks to the courtesy of Professor Romer, the eminent geographer from Lwów, we had the privilege of being at one of the reception dinners given by the Polish delegation. It was here that I met Stanisław Patek (the able lawyer who had defended so many of his countrymen against injustice under Tsardom), soon

21 'It should be noted that the minority groups in the Czechoslovak Republic were in many ways better off than in any other of the restored countries of Europe; but they were far from enjoying the status they would have enjoyed on the right side of the frontier.' [WJR]

Amateur at peace-making

to be ambassador in Tokyo. He took E in to dinner. On such an occasion one forgot, so far as possible, one's disappointment at the predatory spirit of mankind, and enjoyed the society of kindred souls, as well as the hope of a better future. Poland had survived her initial difficulties, the winter was over, summer was coming. All this gave grounds for optimism.

My hope of seeing General Haller again was disappointed, for he was out off in the provinces with his troops. It was now decided that the Red Triangle people would accompany their military units when the exodus for Poland began, but no one knew when that would be. A note from Mr Headlam-Morley, which I still have, asked me to dinner to meet Colonel Cornwall, who was to go out to take over the Teschen mission; but I think this was changed and another man went in his place. Just before leaving Paris I called at noon at the Majestic Hotel to say 'au revoir' to my esteemed 'employer.' I found him just ready to leave, in fact a taxi was waiting at the door. He asked me to get in with him, saying that he was on his way to the Hôtel Crillon, and had only enough time to get to a meeting then. With a smile he held up the bundle of papers he was carrying. 'You would never guess what I have here,' he remarked. Of course I could make no conjecture at all. Then he went on: 'It is the first draft of the Constitution of the Free City of Danzig.' Then I knew that another decision had been taken, and that again many people would be dissatisfied.[22]

Dr Mott arrived, but he had caught a heavy cold, and for a couple of days could receive no one. When I got to see him, he was kindness itself. Nearly six years had passed since we had met, and he looked older. At once he said: 'Of course you must go home, you have been away nearly seven years, and that's long enough.' So that was settled. Then I learned something else. The Red Triangle people were already at work in Czechoslovakia, and complaints were coming from Prague to the headquarters in Paris about my 'political' activities. Dr Mott told me about this and asked me what I thought. Of course I could see the Czech point of view, but I pointed out the essential thing: that I had begun the work at a moment when there was agreement between the neighbour Slav peoples and when the end in view was to realise on the spot the liberties of both, consequent on the collapse of the Habsburg empire. Dr Mott understood, and in fact did not need the explanation, for I had written him fully in America. But he counselled, nonetheless, that from now on I drop the whole thing, and return to my work among and for students. I agreed, and it was thus that 'My Mission from Silesia' ended.

22 The City of Danzig (in Polish, Gdańsk) was an important port on the Baltic and was claimed by both Germany and Poland. The Paris Peace Conference made it a Free City under League of Nations supervision. World War II broke out over Hitler's desire to annex the city.

It will not be out of place to add that, although I felt an injustice was done to the Polish people of the duchy by the settlement of 1920, which made the Olsa River the frontier, thus cutting the town of Teschen into two parts, I maintained complete silence on the subject for twenty years. There was plenty that one might have told about; but all discussion of grievances could only make the prospects of neighbourly relations between Slav peoples living alongside the German Reich more difficult. That many of those Poles who had been shut out of their own country thought the same thing was clear from their reluctance to let me have any details as to what was being done to deprive them of cultural and economic equality with their Czech fellow-citizens, even though I asked for information again and again.

Only when, in 1938, alongside the Nazi demands on Czechoslovakia, the Polish government asked for a revision of the frontier that would mean a return to the agreement of 5 November 1918, did I break silence in the teeth of general indignation in Britain to explain in the *Contemporary Review* (thanks to the kindness of Dr G.P. Gooch) the reasons for what Warsaw had done.[23] The main ground for justification of the action was to keep the territory, in particular the railway junction of Oderberg-Bohumín, from falling into Nazi hands. Maturer reflection and the frightful happenings of the forties have made me change my view on the whole issue. Judged by itself, what the Poles demanded was fair enough; in the light of larger issues their action was unfortunate. I can now see, though one must regret it, that local groups must sacrifice their rights when vaster matters are at stake. Nevertheless, I could still wish that the trunk railway and the Jablunkov Pass and tunnel lay twenty miles farther west. In that case there need have been no conflict at all.

---

23 'Czech-Polish Understanding: The Teschen Question,' *Contemporary Review*, CLIV, Nov. 1938, 570-5

4
Liberated Poland 1

We had roughly three months at home; but only if the word is understood in the general sense of 'the New World.' My mother survived the ordeal of her operation and was soon on the way back to health. We restored contacts with kith and kin after seven years' absence; and took advantage of many invitations, both in the west and the east, to speak on the prospects of salvaging war-torn Europe. One of these, an important one, did not see fulfilment. I was invited to address the Canadian Club in Winnipeg, but the luncheon had to be cancelled because of the now famous general strike.[1] For some days the atmosphere was tense in the city, and two of my old friends came in for much criticism: William Ivens, a Warwickshire-born lad, who had graduated from college just after me; and J.S. Woodsworth, regarded by many as the villain of the piece, and soon to become the founder of the third party in Canadian politics, known as the CCF [Co-operative Commonwealth Federation].

For most of the people of Canada and the United States the war period had meant unusual prosperity – artificial, as always under such circumstances. Being primary producers, they found markets for their output such as no one had dreamed of ten years earlier. The slump, bound to come, had not yet set in; and many people refused to believe in such a possibility. Nevertheless, certain wartime occupations – those of the great sea-ports, for example – had already been

---

1 Rose appeared before an audience at the Polish Sokół on 27 April 1919. His speech, which he delivered in Polish, claimed that the Polish government represented all political orientations and that Piłsudski, the head of state, was a 'genius.' *Gazeta Katolicka* (Winnipeg), 29 kwietnia 1919. Headline: 'W Polsce Zgoda i Harmonia' (In Poland Concord and Harmony).

almost dissolved, and thousands of (mostly unskilled) workers were idle. Ex-army men increased the numbers of unemployed, and the view prevailed that nothing was being done by the authorities to meet the emergency. The loose organization called Independent Workers of the World (to outsiders IWW, came to mean 'I won't work'), and still more the One Big Union movement, became a potential threat to internal law and order; and the red herring of Bolshevist propaganda was drawn across an already anxious trail. For this the Moscow reformers were chiefly to blame. Had they been wiser, they would have stuck to the slogan adopted later, 'Socialism in One Country,' instead of trying to stir up people everywhere to revolution. What really matters for our story is the fact that, in the words of P.W. Slosson, 'Soviet Russia quickly replaced Germany as the villain of international politics.' The same writer goes on to quote A.G. Gardiner: 'The public mind [of America] was hag-ridden by the spectre of Bolshevism.'[2] People 'saw red' everywhere; strikes broke out even where conditions did not justify them. The result in the US was the unfortunate Attorney-General Palmer regime of reprisals, during which emotions got the upper hand and even race riots with bloodshed followed.

The middle of July found us back in London. One of my first tasks was to read the proofs of the Cieszkowski volume, *Our Father*, which was published later in the year by the SCM Press. Had it come a year earlier the sale might have been good; as it was, the interest called forth, though real, was slender in dimensions. The Preface was dated 'Peace Week.' We were in the vast throng in Trafalgar Square which welcomed Woodrow Wilson to London, but did not get sight of him.

Then came Paris, where during two weeks I had my first experience of the Red Triangle Service of Supplies. A carload of badly needed articles – foodstuffs, clothing and materials for sports and games – was ready in the warehouse to go to Poland (whither in April the first group of YMCA had accompanied Haller's Army), provided someone would load it for shipment to Antwerp. I undertook the job, and in a short time everything was ready. Along with it I sent two boxes of personal effects, one of which, being too slightly cased, was rifled in Danzig *en route*. This was the only loss of any kind we sustained during all those troubled years. A better-made box, containing books and a few wedding presents, had reached Antwerp from Canada just before the outbreak of war and was finally delivered to us early in 1920.

We were now ready for the last lap of our journey, and I chose at once the direct route across former enemy territory, via Cologne and Berlin. Strictly speaking, this was still forbidden soil, but tickets were not refused us and we set out

---

2 Preston William Slosson, *The Great Crusade and After, 1914-1928* (New York 1931), 79

with confidence. Not only were we shown no kind of discourtesy, though I was in 'uniform' and had an American colleague with me, but at all stations we found both porters and officials as helpful and reliable as of old. In conversation they were matter-of-fact, but nowhere resentful. On the contrary they seemed to be glad to talk with someone from the outside world. The British control officer at the new Polish frontier was rather taken aback at the sight of us, but he made no difficulties. In a few hours we arrived, for the first time, in the interesting city of Poznań.

Here we found Professor Adam Żółtowski, whose work on *Our Father* had been of great help to me, and his lady; and, thanks to their kindness, we got out to the country home of the philosopher himself, where the son gave us a warm welcome. He listened with interest when I told him of the coming appearance of his father's book in English, and asked me to keep in touch with him during our time in Poland.

But my first visit to Poznań was memorable for another reason. A friendship began then with one of the noblest men I have ever known, lasting until his death during the Second World War - Bernard Chrzanowski, citizen, lawyer, and public servant. Before 1914 he had been a member of the Reichstag in Berlin; and though slight of stature and mild of manner he had dared more than once to arraign Prince Bülow[3] and his colleagues before the whole world for their policy toward his fellow countrymen. Incidents that could not be put into the newspapers thus found at least some publicity in the German Hansard - things no one could deny. Now, with the power of the Reich swept away, he was busy with the task of ordering the school system in a free Poznania.

A sample of his fearlessness, even toward his own people, deserves recording. Not far from his office was the site on which had stood a statue of Bismarck. This had, not unnaturally, been thrown down when the German forces were turned out in December 1918, but the pedestal was still there. Chrzanowski took me to see the spot, and remarked: 'I tell my fellow Poles that they should have left Bismarck standing, and even laid a wreath at his feet. It was his whip that made men of us.'

On our arrival in Warsaw a problem arose. The Connecticut lawyer who had been in charge of the Red Triangle group that accompanied Haller's Army had been called home, and his place had been taken provisionally by a businessman who had little or no experience of social work. He at once asked me, and quite rightly, whether I had come to Warsaw to report to him, as had our travelling companion. I answered him in the negative, and he was nonplussed. (Actually,

---

3 Bernhard von Bülow, German chancellor 1900-9, favoured German nationalist measures against the Poles in the German zone.

until Dr Mott's visit to the liberated lands of Europe in the following May, I was still on the payroll of the federation; and in any case my concern was with the student community.) He probably wondered what all this meant, and even thought that I was some sort of 'freelance,' with a mission to report on what was going on. Fortunately, the matter was soon cleared. Edmund Chambers, one of the two Canadians who had learned Polish in Silesia before the war, had been a chaplain with the army in France and was now a volunteer worker with the YMCA. He had learned Latin under me in college, and could explain the whole situation. An understanding was soon reached, and neither then nor later did I ever have any conflict with my Red Triangle colleagues.

The time was high summer, and the universities were empty. I therefore decided to go to Silesia for a fortnight's rest, and take stock of the general position. We were given a warm welcome there, though people were depressed by the interim boundary settlement, which had awarded half of the duchy to the Czechs. This included the Protestant parishes we knew best. It also meant that all our belongings were on the other side of the new line; and I owe it to the courtesy of the American Red Triangle workers on the Czech side that a lorry was put at our disposal for their transfer. True, I had to listen to a curtain-lecture from one of them, who had heard from Czech sources of my mission to Paris, and said that if anything of the kind happened again 'he would have me sent home.' As it turned out, he himself was moved shortly, while we began to settle down for what proved to be eight years of hard, though useful work.

Pastor Kulisz was now installed in the big Church of Jesus in Teschen, and a large room in the manse was put at our disposal for the time being. It seemed best that E should stay for the present in Silesia, while I began what was to be a roving commission, with Warsaw as 'Home Base.' As it turned out, this arrangement had to continue until the following July; then I was posted to Cracow and we had rare fortune in getting a comfortable flat. Here we lived until 1925.

In such a time of reconstruction, indeed of war, since Poland was not really at peace until September 1920, a variety of things pressed for attention, and none of them could be done properly. One had first to do a great deal of patching-up the old, before the new could be put in its place. Relief work of all kinds was imperative, but this in itself amounted only to clearing the ground for future building. On this account what follows has not been arranged in chronological order but rather according to the task and the duties involved. In actual fact I was engaged on several things simultaneously, and they were not always well done in consequence. Nothing like a complete record has been attempted, but enough has been said to give some honest picture of those times.

The fields of interest and activity will be dealt with in the following, more or less logical, order:

Liberated Poland 1

1 European Student Relief (ESR)
2 The Student Christian Movement (SCM)
3 The Red Triangle
4 Training workers – Osada
5 Cracow city
6 The Polish Association
7 Poland's 'Manchester'
8 Further study
9 Places and people

But, to start with, a few pages of general introduction to the whole story.

It was a condition of Polish independence that all three empires sharing the guilt of the partitions should be broken in pieces. Only this could permit the liberation and unification of a nation numbering at the time nearly twenty million souls. Not all of these were set free, but at least 90 per cent of them achieved this ideal; and when, two years later, peace had been made after the repulsion of the Bolshevist threat, the new commonwealth numbered twenty-seven million citizens. This meant a population, and an area, nearly two-thirds that of France.

These people had been subject for more than a century to alien powers – one of them Lutheran, another Orthodox, the third Roman Catholic. In an age of mighty changes they had been separated by tightly sealed frontiers, and allowed to do little or nothing in common. They were now faced with the difficult task of learning to live together and to work out a common destiny. Many of the non-Poles living in the republic were not well disposed to the new order of things, but it is safe to say that only the Germans, numbering less than a million souls, would have preferred to belong to any neighbouring country.

The vast majority of the population lived on and from the land, and a good half were only two generations removed from serfdom. Many of the older men and women had been born in that condition, and could recall what they had heard from their fathers about it. Now they experienced a second liberation, and it seemed indeed a miracle. But the level of cultural and economic life in the new state was very unequal. Students of such matters were soon to distinguish three regions – Poland A, Poland B, and Poland C; of which the first comprised the lands adjacent to the western frontiers, whose standard of living approximated that of Eastern Germany, Bohemia, and Moravia; the second lay for the most part east of the Vistula and lived on a level nearer that of Russia; the third denoted the south central provinces – densely populated, possessed of rather poor soil, and in consequence unable to produce enough food even to nourish its own inhabitants. This fact alone presented the new regime with a whole galaxy of by no means simple problems.

Four-and-a-half years of war and military occupation had left the country stripped of almost everything needed for daily living, to say nothing of the huge task of rehabilitation and improvement. In respect of foodstuffs, even in the hard winter following the war, the Poles were better off than their neighbours, but means of communication had been so crippled that distribution was haphazard and the plight of the cities pitiful. Someone had therefore to undertake a huge work of relief, and this was realized at once by the emissaries of Hoover's goodwill agency, soon to be known as the American Relief Administration – ARA for short. The needs were most acute in regard to housing, clothes, and medicinal supplies; the worst sufferers were the children.

It was well that the majority did not realise how critical the situation was, how vast the needs, and how slender the resources for meeting them. Many of the common people had never known real comforts, and so were the more ready to put up with continued privations. The range of things the West would regard as necessities, but which were quite unobtainable (unless from abroad), was colossal. Some, it is true, could with luck be had on the 'black market,' but this was truer of luxury articles than of utilities. Paint and putty would be sought for in vain, and even glass and nails were scarce. In the hospitals, patients were lying two-in-a-bed, if that name is not too sumptuous for the broken-down cots that had survived the war. Only leftovers of bedding of any kind were to be found; and every scrap of sheeting had been torn up for bandages. Surgeons were doing their work without rubber gloves, and often with the most primitive instruments. Repairs for machinery or even the simplest tools for work in wood or iron were not to be bought. If something broke down, it was unusable until the missing part could be imported. Perhaps the chief reason for this was that under the imperial system manufacturing of all kinds was concentrated in neighbouring lands, with the Polish world reserved as a colonial possession. At the same time five years of war and occupation were bound to exhaust resources of all kinds.

Meanwhile Poland was still at war. The peacemakers in Paris had settled fairly quickly her frontiers on the north, the west (save for Silesia), and the south; but nothing had been done about the long frontier toward Russia. Moreover, the whole of Europe was disturbed (more than was necessary) by the threat of social upheaval coming from Bolshevism; and the neighbour peoples, owing to their place on the map, were the most exposed to whatever might come. The Western Powers were still supporting attempts on the part of 'White' Russians to overthrow the new regime of Lenin and Trotsky; and the Poles could hardly help being drawn into the struggle. The quite unnecessary war of 1919-20 was the consequence. As if by a miracle, Central Europe was saved from being overrun by the Red Army, and peace was concluded in March 1921.[4] However, the issue trembled in the balance for more than a year; and perhaps the only good thing about it for the Poles was that, in the face of a grim threat, they had to learn quickly to stand together and forget many differences created during a century of partition.

Inside this national issue, and pressing for attention, was a smaller but vital human problem: Who was to care for the great numbers of refugees finding their way home from nearly every point on the compass – in particular prisoners-of-war and the uprooted civilians who were scattered all over Russia and the Danube lands, and who wanted nothing so much as to get back to the place where they had grown up. All were destitute, many were ill, and the threat of epidemics (cholera and typhus) was imminent. To meet this, a splendid mission led by Colonel Gilchrist and others got to work, and a *cordon sanitaire* was established on the existing eastern borders, with all available resources to enforce it. In this exacting, even dangerous work, volunteers from many relief agencies took part, and some laid down their lives. What concerned the rest of us was that everything possible be done to care for those who passed the cordon, to help them back to normal living, and to restore them to a place in a settled society.

Let no one think that this huge enterprise was left to relief agencies. The Poles had been engaged in it even before peace came, for they knew well the value of human material; now they were at it more than ever. During my visit to Warsaw in February I had sat in on a meeting of economists and engineers at which a full discussion took place on the available resources of the country – food, raw materials, and credits of all kinds, as part of an over-all planning of rehabilitation. Those people were going to work in a business-like way, surveying the field of need, taking stock of supplies, and laying down an order of priority for the whole task of reconstruction. For the first time they could go to work in the assurance that what they were doing would serve their own nation and not the well-being of aliens.

Since early in the year, parliament (the Seym) had been meeting regularly and a coalition government was in charge. Things of national concern and importance were in its hands, but so far as possible each district was made responsible for local needs. This wise policy paid high dividends in the western provinces of the country, where the ravages of war had not been known, and which were more advanced in culture and well-being than the areas east of the Vistula. In

---

4 A surprise Polish flanking movement halted an apparently irresistable Soviet offensive only twenty miles from Warsaw in August 1919 and forced the Red Army to retreat. The battle became known as the 'miracle on the Vistula.'

any case the whole task was to prove easier in the central provinces than it did on or near frontiers, where military operations were still in progress.

It is to the credit of the nations who had won the war that they realised how much there was still to be done if they were not to lose the peace. The generous help given to the peoples set free when the empires of Habsburg, Romanov, and Hohenzollern tumbled was not only a work of charity; it was dictated by common sense, for to have allowed the four-score million people of Central Europe to remain in semi-starvation while wrestling with the work of reordering their lives would have been folly. In retrospect I can see what few of us realised at the time: every relief worker could regard himself as a soldier in a battle with forces of disruption, or a builder sharing in the creation of a new fabric of humanity.

Fortunately, Poland had sufficient foodstuffs within her borders to remove the threat of famine, but with one important reservation − the getting of the bottle to the baby. Never properly equipped with either roads or railways, innocent of canals, and far behind the west in experience, the country could have people starving in one province although a hundred miles away there was food aplenty. The crux of the problem therefore was organization and transport. What sadly lagged was the last-named, for sheer lack of roads and vehicles. Somehow this hurdle had to be taken, and the immediate need met, before the attention of the public could be directed to long-range rehabilitation.

It is a fact that an agricultural land can recover from calamities much faster than one that is highly urbanised. Given one good crop, people would be free of anxiety; for this reason every effort had been made in the spring of 1919 to get as much soil under seed as possible, and to husband the surviving resources of livestock − cattle, pigs, sheep, and poultry. These were better in the western provinces than in the east; and they were drawn on to help provide food for the two or three larger urban centres − the capital, the textile region around Łódź, and the big industries area of the south-west, where a struggle was still going on with the Germans for the possession of part of Silesia. How our relief agencies helped to raise the nation out of something near to despair, and to get back their self-confidence, will appear in these pages.

1 STUDENT RELIEF

The story of European Student Relief has been told in straight-forward fashion by the late Dr Margaret Wrong.[5] In a single, but important sector of the whole front, I was to play some part during the years 1919-21. Better said, I was to

---

5 Margaret Wrong, *Ideas and Realities in Europe* (London, Student Christian Movement Press, 1925)

Liberated Poland 1

initiate the work, hand it over to a full-time director, and then help wind it up after the major task was done. E shared in the general task of relief for needy families in Cracow, where we settled down in the early summer of 1920, and she did a special job with a destitute group of 'exile' students from the Ukraine.

Conditions in the universities were pathetic, and what we did to alleviate the suffering illustrates most of the problems raised by the general task. One had to start by getting the facts, no easy matter. Some of the neediest were most backward about letting us know of their condition; while some of those most forward in appealing for help were least deserving. At times one had to get outside the student group to find out the truth. It fell to me to visit again and again most of the six universities in the new Poland, of which three - Wilno, Poznań, and Lublin - were in process of formation. Even in the two that had functioned before the war, Cracow and Lwów, the situation in regard to housing, food, and equipment was bad. Warsaw, which had been able to reopen under the German occupation (after being closed for most of the nineteenth century), was little better; actually the need there was greatest of all since, now the capital of a free country, it tended to draw more students than could possibly be accommodated.

Relief work, under such conditions, is at best a scramble. It ministers to elemental wants; but after meeting them for a week, one finds that they are as clamant as ever. To provide temporary supplies of food and clothing is useful; but to take the longer view and do something about housing is better. Nothing is more fatal for the worker than to succumb to feelings of pity or sentimentality. He must use his head, and even then there will be some waste. Two factors govern the amount of help that can be given in any area - supplies to be drawn on and means of transportation. Only in time did I come to realise the importance of the latter.

Our major anxiety in regard to supplies was taken care of by the presence of the American Red Cross, which shared everything possible with the civilian population, and the Hoover's ARA. The former's main business was, of course, to serve needy people in uniform, including prisoners-of-war; but the Hoover mission had a free hand to assist all *bona fide* relief agencies, whether Polish or foreign. Among these last were the Friends' Service Mission, the Joint Distribution Committee (Jewish-American), and our own ESR. The Red Triangle people showed their good sense in not refusing help where a case could be made out, and they were fortunate in being able to draw on large stores that had accumulated in France but, with the quicker ending of the war, had not been needed there. A special group, known as the Grey Samaritans, was composed of young American women of Polish extraction, who made the villages their peculiar care. Trained by the YWCA, they were brought to Poland by the White Cross, organised by Madame Paderewski, and everyone had to admire the courage and devotion they showed in a difficult field.

As for the student field proper, it numbered close on 20,000 men and women even though the armed forces were still mobilised. The majority were away from home, many had no home of any kind, some were completely orphaned. The desperate overcrowding in the cities made it difficult even for those who could pay to secure living quarters; perhaps half were without any funds, and as near naked as the law allowed. Those who could find any kind of employment, and in some places this was possible, combined work with their studies, a useful thing if their health was sufficient to stand the strain. But for this they needed regular meals, and regular sleep. Hundreds were in one or another kind of uniform – or leavings of the same; and scores were to be found sleeping at the railway stations (though this was forbidden) or even under bridges. Around me in the classroom in the fall of 1919 I saw odds and ends of American, British, ex-Austrian, and ex-Russian military clothing, apart from the improvised Polish uniforms on those who had got a few months leave-of-absence for study from their units. It was a motley sight.

Many had been prisoners-of-war in Italy or in Russia, and had found their way home with great difficulty. Their courage and sense of deliverance carried them through every obstacle, in some cases foot journeys of hundreds of miles. Yet it might have seemed to them that their newly-liberated homeland did not want them. I found not a few who, having no other place to go, were taken in and cared for by 'women of the town.' The authorities did all they could, but it was hard to get a gallon into a pint pot! Hence the need for urgent, if only emergency, action by outside agencies.

At the middle of the century we have become accustomed to relief work of all kinds in many parts of the world, but thirty years ago the thing was relatively new; so we had to learn as we went along. Starting with the food problem, we set about providing supplies for existing student *mensae* (the Latin word for 'table') had long been used to designate a student-run eating establishment. The next step was to find and equip more such 'restaurants,' so that a wholesome dinner could be had for about sixpence, with a light breakfast or supper for half that sum. Neither quarters nor equipment could easily be found, but some way the thing was done. In Warsaw huge barracks near the Poniatowski Bridge were secured from the army; and in this wilderness of former army quarters, feeding, sleeping, and amusement facilities were set up which cared for hundreds of men. Even the central offices of ESR were placed here.

In the severe Polish winter, to be without underwear or an overcoat, even if one had some sort of suit of clothes, meant the risk of chills or even illness. The same was true in the matter of footwear. But no less essential if men and women were to get on with their classwork were books, note-books, pens and pencils, and, in the case of science people, slide-rules for the engineers and scalpels for those in medicine. These last were simply not to be found in the country, and we had a lot of fun bringing them in from elsewhere - not always legally. The book shortage was due both to the fact that for years nothing had been published and to the special reason that before 1914 there were only two universities where teaching went on in Polish, whereas now there were six. Medical, technical, historical, and economic textbooks of almost any date, and in any European language, were at a premium. A class would send one of their number to us to beg for some needed work 'at least one copy'; they would then have it read to the group, who would make notes; or, in some cases, would manage to have the whole thing written out by hand and passed around. Scripts of this kind were much sought after, and some students earned their living by copying them when they should have been sleeping.

Such was the general picture, when peace came, in every one of the liberated countries, but the attention of the outside world was not rightly drawn to it for more than a year. Only in January 1920 did Miss Ruth Rouse, representing the federation, discover the urgency of things on a visit to Vienna. Telegrams went off at once to the British SCM and in a few weeks supplies began to be assembled in many countries. What the Red Triangle had been doing for at least six months as a side-line in Warsaw was now organised as a separate and growing activity, and workers, American and Polish, were set aside for that task. In due course volunteer workers, for shorter or longer periods, came from various English-speaking countries - Scandinavia, Holland, and France. With the demobilisation of the armies after the 'miracle of the Vistula' in the late summer of 1920, the real job began.

During the previous year I had been visiting the universities as a Red Triangle worker and had got to know a good many of those responsible for their development - such as was possible under war conditions. For a while in the early spring a special mission had taken me to the United States,[6] but I got back just before Dr Mott was expected in Poland, coming on from Prague. As will appear in a later chapter, his visit cleared up many things, one of them being my own status; but the real change for me came when I was asked to settle in Cracow and help with the quartering of the Red Triangle HQ there. The Russian armies were advancing toward the Vistula, and over half of the Warsaw staff were moved from the capital during the critical weeks. When the crisis was over they returned to Warsaw, and I set up the Student Relief Office in the Protestant school on Castle Street.

6 Rose accompanied Father Oraczewski on a tour of the United States and published a booklet entitled *A Visitor from Poland* (New York, March 1920) describing Father Oraczewski's philosophy of social action. The item is not listed in Turek's bibliography but a copy can be found in the archives of the *Winnipeg Free Press*.

Of course the headquarters of ESR, with a Harvard man on furlough from India, J.C. Manry, in charge, was rightly placed in the capital; and a very able secretary found in the person of Jean Chisholm, a Scottish lady from Edinburgh – now Mrs J.O. Wilson of Quebec. I had charge in Cracow, and kept an eye on Lwów, where the need was even greater. Every week or so I went to Warsaw for conferences on policy, since I knew the general situation in the country better than others. In all our work we had the help of devoted Polish colleagues, both men and women, and it was they who carried most of the burden of actual relief.

Into our Cracow office there soon began to come a stream of needy people, many of whom I got to know personally. A sample of these I recall even today, a student who was to graduate in medicine five years later and become a useful practitioner. When I first saw him he was in rags, having just found his way back (actually by begging) from somewhere in the Ural mountains. For a month he had not dared to take off his boots for fear that he would not be able to get them on again! His feet were wrapped in rags, and it is a wonder that he escaped blood-poisoning. With care we got his wounds cleaned and healed up, found him some clothes and a place to live, and put him back on the road to recovery. One day, while we were handling cases of this sort, a stranger walked in to see what we were doing. He gave me his name, that of an already known novelist, Jan Wiktor, and said that he had heard of our work and wanted to see it. Later he sent me a copy of one of his stories with a dedication which I greatly prize.

But for the most part I was busy with advisory duties, and with liaison work of various kinds, thanks to the fact that, apart from Chambers, I was the only 'foreigner' who spoke Polish. On this account I was invited to be in Lwów when the 'medicals' there were opening their new 'mensa.' I had already watched the engineers of that university build their own residence, and we had given them some assistance. Now, I was present at the opening of this new amenity and here I met the rector, one of Poland's greatest men, the poet Jan Kasprowicz. The son of a small farmer in Poznania, he had literally 'made himself' into a professor of comparative literature, not least by his celebrated translations of the English poets. Though possessed of no academic degrees, he had won his way to fame, and was now head of the institution that had harboured him. It was a rare privilege to meet him, and to hear him speak. When asked to say a few words, I paid both him and his colleagues a tribute for the work they were doing. Among the latter were the well-known geographer, Eugeniusz Romer, whom I had met in Paris, and Henryk Arctowski, the meteorologist, who had taken care of me on my first visit to Warsaw. The rector asked me to come and stay with him in his country cottage near Zakopane, something which (to my subsequent regret) I was never able to do. But I lent him a book or two he badly needed, and mourned with many others his untimely death a few years later.

In Cracow, with the help of the Red Triangle, we got hold of the barracks that stood just off the street of the Carmelites (much smaller than the great Bloch barracks in Warsaw), and here we created a hostel for a hundred students of the new Academy of Mining that was taking shape – the first of its kind in this part of Europe. The management was in the hands of our women workers, and it relieved the housing situation during two critical years. But in one of our plans, or hopes, we were completely baffled. My Red Triangle colleague, the New England-born Oberholzer, who had pioneered the work in Cracow, suggested to me that we try to get the existing student 'mensa' to introduce the cafeteria system, offering to pay for the installations. Students would serve themselves and many more meals could be handled in shorter time. But the novelty of it all was too great, and after a try-out on a small scale the project was abandoned.

The other universities were not being neglected, but their problems were less acute. Poznań had escaped war damage, and some sort of housing could be found for needed institutions. The food issue was also easier of solution here. In Wilno, and in the new Catholic University of Lublin, the numbers of students were much smaller and such help as we could give was mostly in the matter of supplies. In the former I found as rector the distinguished biologist from Cracow, Michał Siedlecki, whom I had also met in Paris. More will be said later of my visits to this charming old-world city, set far away in the north and completely snowed-up in winter. In Lublin, on my first visit, I found a man in charge of the Red Triangle work who was to do me a signal service later, Eric P. Kelly, a graduate of Dartmouth College in New Hampshire. One of the most unselfish men I ever knew, he and a colleague were handling a very difficult situation, and in masterly fashion.

In Cracow, and by a lucky chance, we stumbled on a special need which we were fortunately able to meet. I knew that ESR was backed not only by the student world outside but also by the teaching staffs; and this meant that needy professors and their families had as much right to help as the younger generation. In conversation with the rector of the university, Dr Stanisław Estreicher, I raised this matter, and was met by a look which I shall never forget. 'I have three or four older men on the staff,' he said, 'who have almost nothing to live on. They are retired, and we have no proper pension fund as yet. If you could find some food for them, it would be a heavenly act; but I warn you that they are so sensitive that they will never admit their need.'

We took counsel, and I went off to the ARA people to see what could be done. With their usual generosity they put at our disposal a dozen of their precious 'sacks' of the most concentrated foods, repeating the gift every two months during the winter. Each of them contained bacon, sugar, flour, and dried fruits, and all I had to do was leave one on the doorstep of each of the destitute families. As it happened, I was later to get to know two of these men and their wives rather intimately, and only then did I learn how much this benefaction had meant to them. Both were scholars of European reputation, and one was to be a member of the board that examined me in 1926 for my doctorate.

A word is in order about the spirit in which this help from outside sources was received. There were those who did not like 'charity' in any form. Never had they, or their fathers before them, seen strangers in their country anxious to help but with no axe to grind, and they were suspicious; and there were some whose pride was hurt in the taking. At one Conference of Relief Workers from many lands (held outside Poland) I sat and listened to student delegates from the universities I knew belittling the service rendered by ESR and declaring that no more was needed. On my return to Warsaw I mentioned this fact to a high university official, and he was very angry. 'Young fools! What do they know about the need!' was his comment. He made no bones of saying that it was only thanks to a grant in cash from our funds that the Residence for Women Students in the capital was getting a roof before the rains and frost of winter would set in.

Fortunately this kind of resentment was a scarce article, partly because of the wise and understanding way relief agencies went to work. Our main wish was to put people in the way of helping themselves as soon as possible; and a fine example in this regard was set by the Friends' Mission under Dr Haig and Miss McBride. Every one of us felt the challenging character of the whole situation. In the universities in those years there were men and women of all ages, not a few of them mature teachers or professional men and women, who under the prewar conditions had never been admitted to higher studies. Their daily bread was earned by four o'clock in the afternoon, and then they would attend lectures in the subjects of their choice.

One case in particular stands out in memory, and it could be matched by many others. J was a school inspector in the capital, and had been occupied day and night since 1915, when the Germans gave the Poles permission to reorganise (indeed to create) their own secondary schools. He had two grown-up sons, who were anxious to study but had to earn their way since the father's salary was far from able to support them. When they complained that this double duty was too much for them he said: 'All right, boys, I shall register at the university myself, and show you whether it can be done!' He did so, and undertook afresh what he had begun twenty-five years before – his own field of geology. The sons liked the idea of a race and raised no more objections. When I got to know the inspector he was on the way to his degree, which he secured when well over sixty. I saw one day in his home the pile of books, in four languages, from which he had drawn the materials for his thesis.

Nevertheless there was a shadow side to all this. As noted already, not a few of those most eager to study were physically unable to stand the strain. This was in part due to the privations of war years; but it was also due to the too widespread presence of that scourge of humanity, tuberculosis, which flourishes in years of short rations. The universities of Central Europe had maintained their own sanatoria even before 1914, but some of them had been rendered unusable by war abuses, and in any case they were quite inadequate to meet the needs. Rest-hostels were to be found in the valleys of the Carpathians, but they were short of equipment or in need of basic repairs. Those owned privately had to charge prices beyond the purse of students, and there seemed no way out of the impasse. ESR did something to help in this field, chiefly again with food supplies, but one particular situation arose in which I was asked to make a visit and a report. It is worth recalling, in part for the adventure involved.

A rest-home (not meant to be a proper sanatorium) in the picturesque town of Szczawnica in the Polish highlands was being refitted, but the roof showed signs of collapse and there was no money for the job. I was asked by our HQ in Warsaw to make the trip, see the place, consult about costs, and make a report. To get there meant a fair journey by road after leaving the railway at Nowy Targ, and I knew that it would be a long day's effort. As it turned out the road was fairly good, and a Jewish firm had recently got hold of a couple of aged autobuses and was maintaining some sort of service. I arrived safely before noon, and had soon made my investigations. The bus was ready to start back, and I had hopes of catching the late afternoon train home. But first we had engine trouble, and finally, about four miles from the station, the bus slowed down on a rather steep hill and refused to move. I soon saw that there was no hope of recovery, so I set out on foot, hoping that the train might be late and I could still catch it. A peasant cart came out of a sideroad a little later, and I got a ride for a change. From the top of a rise, half-a-mile from Nowy Targ, I saw the scene – the station lay between me and the town, and the train was in sight coming in from the south. By hurrying across the fields (the road made a circle around them) there was just a hope that I could catch the train – for once it was on time! I gave the farmer some silver, and started to run. The train left the station before I got there, but very slowly, on an uphill grade. I caught the last coach, and swung on. But I never tried to do it again.

2 THE STUDENT CHRISTIAN MOVEMENT[7]

It was the prospect of working among students that prompted my decision to remain in Europe in 1913; seven years later the same purpose animated my work, but in wholly different circumstances. From the subject peoples of a dozen coun-

---

7 See Ruth Rouse, *Rebuilding Europe: The Student Chapter in Post-War Reconstruction* (London, Student Christian Movement Press, 1925).

tries fetters, felt most of all by youth, had been removed, and the atmosphere was wholly different. Now, when a call came, minds and spirits were responsive as never before; both men and women were eager to fit themselves for the highest service.

What at the time had seemed to be a hardship – to be confined in a little corner of the continent during years of feverish conflict, could now be seen in a different perspective. In Prague I had begun work with little fitness and even less preparation; now almost everything was reversed. I could communicate freely with those around me. I had been through a time of testing along with my fellows, and had made some headway toward an understanding of their past and of their aspirations for the future. In short, we had plenty of things in common. Even my work on Cieszkowski was a help, since it gave me a modest standing in academic circles; and all I had to do was continue on the lines begun, so as to meet whatever chances might arise. By learning with those about me, I could enjoy the fellowship of common action.

The emergency work described above, and my service with the Red Triangle to which we shall come, were episodes only – though important ones. Relief work was one thing, but the real purpose in my mind was quite another. It was thus a blessing that the organisation of SCM groups was well under way before student relief as such began to function; had it been otherwise we could hardly have escaped the suspicion of 'buying souls.' As it turned out, this charge was never laid by any honest observer. Conversely, there were cases of real need among those belonging to the SCM for whom nothing was done so that no one could say that they were influenced by thoughts of 'loaves and fishes.'

We found a few people who recalled the visits made in Cracow by Miss Rouse and Wilder before 1914, but they were long since out in the world. During the first postwar year I got to know a good many students, in particular those who, being on furlough from the armed forces, enjoyed the privileges of the Red Triangle canteens and club-rooms. From time to time discussion groups arose, in which a wide range of subjects were dealt with – politics alone being excluded. In Warsaw I attended lectures when possible, and so made some contacts; but nothing more than casual relations could be established in these circumstances.

Then came the visit of Dr Mott, as head of the war work of the American YMCA, early in June 1920. Though occupied chiefly with this big task, he never forgot the student field; and it was auspicious that he was invited to speak in the Convocation Hall of the University in Cracow, with the rector in charge. In the audience were professors and students, but also many townspeople; and the address of welcome was given in English by Professor Leon Marchlewski, who was three years later to become chairman of the board of the Polish YMCA. At the end of the meeting I was permitted to say a few words in Polish, and from that time my good relations with the people of Cracow were established. A few weeks later, E moved from Teschen and we settled down for five years' residence.

Dr Mott asked whether three students could be selected who could come to Warsaw for a conference, and this was done. A score of young men and women met for a full day, coming from three universities. It was decided that one of them, Tadeusz Mitana, should be sent as a delegate to the summer conference of the French SCM; and that two students, one man and one woman, should be chosen to attend as observers the coming general meeting of the federation - to be held in Beatenberg (Switzerland) late in July. To this latter I was also invited, where I should have my first chance of seeing the federation in action and of realising how it had maintained its fellowship throughout the terrors of the greatest war in human history.

Man shoots, but God carries the bullet! So runs the Polish proverb, and now we were to see its meaning. The war with Bolshevist Russia took a fateful turn, and the two people designated for Beatenberg decided that they could not leave their country in such a crisis. On 21 July I had a letter, signed by both, asking me to act as their deputy. This request put me on the spot - if they had such confidence in me, I was bound to consider myself one of their number, and make the same decision. I remained in Poland, and thus missed my one chance to be present at a federation conference.

Deliverance from invasion came in August, and the end of hostilities a few weeks later. The universities were formally reopened at the new year, and classes were crowded. In November I had been given a chance to deliver three formal lectures in the Copernicus Hall of the University in Cracow on 'The Spirit and Work of the YMCA in America' and this opened new contacts.[8] About the issues raised by these lectures more will be said in subsequent pages. They gave me a certain 'notoriety,' undesirable in one way but not unhelpful in others. February 1921 proved to be a month of significant happenings. Theodore Abel, a law student in Warsaw (and later in Poznań), had gone with the head of the Red Triangle Mission to the Quadrennial Students' Conference in Glasgow, and he returned with a sense of high responsibility. Mitana had learned much during a month's stay in France. In the course of ten days committees were set up in three universities, and study groups were formed to concern themselves with social and spiritual issues. The numbers were not large, but the temper of those who came together was the best. What is more, as I was able to visit them and sit in at their sessions, I rejoiced to see how much they had in common - no

---

8 *Duch i Praca Y.M.C.A., Chrześciajańskiego Związku Młodych Ludzi w Ameryce* (Warsaw 1920)

small triumph after a century of partition and ignorance of each other's minds. Thirty years later friendships formed in those groups are still alive and firm, in spite of the horrors of a Second World War.

Few experiences have ever given me more satisfaction. The men and women concerned were doing things themselves, in response to a sense of need, and no one played the part of passenger in the boat. Only on one occasion did a jarring note creep in when an over-eager patriot raised a warning about outsiders of any kind being associated with a Polish association. He was promptly overwhelmed by his neighbours and accepted with grace the verdict of the majority.

During the following months groups met regularly in three universities, that in Lwów being somewhat smaller than the others. Steering committees handled all business, and dues were exacted to cover incidental expenses. Someone gave the initiative in planning a summer conference, and this was arranged, in two parts, in the middle of July. We secured the use of a school in Goleszów, a village east of Teschen at the foot of the Carpathians, and I got the Red Triangle people to lend some cots and blankets for the week. My own contribution was six sacks of wheat from Eastern Poland, which we got ground locally and made into the best whole wheat bread I ever ate.

During three days nearly thirty 'leaders' met for discussions and periods of meditation, and then came over fifty others for the general meeting. For the most part these people were completely strange to one another; but none of the differences arising, whether of creed or tradition, caused serious difficulty. Several seniors were present, the most eminent being the veteran philosopher from Cracow, Professor Rubczyński, who wrote a sympathetic account of the meeting in a Cracow journal. Pastor Kulisz came to a number of sessions, and helped us much. The students conducted morning periods of a devotional nature, one of them centring around the theme of Martha and Mary – their diverse outlooks on life.

The main business of the Leaders' Conference was to decide on a sort of basis or constitution, as well as a name for the association. The last was agreed on as *Christian Union of Polish Students*, and the main clauses of the basis were these:

1 Wishing to consecrate our powers to the service of our country and humanity, we feel that we must begin with a change of heart in keeping with the teachings of Jesus Christ. We believe that all social development is the fruit of the men and women who make up society. Further we hold the Christian Ethic to be the most vital means of progress both of individuals and of nations.

2 In keeping with our faith and conviction, we declare:

a) That our first purpose is to develop our lives in keeping with the teaching of Christ, in order that its principles may be realised in practice;

b) That we desire to extend a hand to all who, without regard to their religious convictions or church relations, wish sincerely as we do the moral regeneration of our age;

c) That we exclude all Party politics from the discussions of our Union, leaving each member to decide whether he or she can belong to a particular organisation without compromising the principles of our Union.

3 We hope to achieve these ends:

a) By entering into the life and teaching of Christ through a careful study of the Gospels;

b) By getting to know the works of the poets and thinkers of our own and other nations;

c) By discussion of social questions and taking part in social service, always keeping to the view that such questions must be solved in a Christian way;

d) By drawing closer to the students of other nations with a view to co-operation in the spreading of Christian truth;

e) By creating warm relations of friendship in life and spirit among those who accept the aims of the Union, so that each may help the other to get nearer to the ideal set by Christ, whether for individuals or for the community.

These rather demanding terms were accepted after a good deal of discussion by the general conference, and from that time they took the place of the somewhat varying 'constitutions' in use in the local unions. When one realises that two-thirds of those involved had grown up in the Roman Catholic faith, while the rest were either Protestants or Orthodox (with a few who claimed to be attached to no church), it must be admitted that the results achieved were encouraging. Neither then nor later was the suggestion made that the Polish SCM should apply for formal admission to the federation, it being felt that this could only become a matter of contention. But one practical 'lead' was given, which brought the issue of life vocation home to all. Among the pressing needs of the new Poland was that of teachers for rural communities, many of which were without schools of any kind. The attention of members was called to this fact, and high priority was given to this kind of work in fulfilment of the ideals set out in the basis. I was able to confirm later with my own eyes the gains for the nation thus won.

Two weeks after Goleszów I got away to attend the second Southeast European Conference of Students (counting that of Ligotka 1914 as the first), which was held at Sonntagsberg, not far from Vienna. E went with me, and we had a chance to renew friendships with Wilder and other friends of former years. I was the bearer of a message from the Polish SCM, from which I quote these sentences:

Those who do not know our movement at first hand tell of us that we are the victims of influences coming from abroad, notably from America ... There are some who point even to certain sects, of which we are said to be mouthpieces. We therefore declare that we are not in any way dependent on anyone whatsoever. We do desire to profit by the experience of others, and we should like to make our own the ability and skill that others have developed, but this is far from meaning any kind of organic or inner dependence. The sources of our spiritual convictions are not to be found beyond our own frontiers; they were growing in the hearts of many people long before our organisation came into being. Often these people did not know one another until they met in the SCM ...

We do not at all seek to find in our view of life a refuge from the evils of the world; nor do we belong to the type of disillusioned social apostles who long for quiet in which to get their breath, and find relief when ideals have gone bankrupt. We know that Poland has too much apathy and helplessness ... We gather power and enthusiasm from the feeling that our union has grown out of the needs of today. There is no greater social necessity than work that will help every man, in whatever trade, profession or party, to be true to the Christian principles of righteousness and love.

The year 1921 was a time of transition and testing in the new Poland. With this went a good deal of stock-taking of many kinds. Voices were raised to proclaim that the 'American invasion' was dangerous, and that an end should be put to it soon. To this there was prompt reaction, and the debate itself was useful. The SCM was the scene of much discussion, and many opinions were expressed in the course of local meetings during the winter. The decision to hold an Easter Leaders' Conference in Cracow was welcomed, and close to thirty men and women were present. As guest we had one of the best known of the younger clergy, Father Władysław Korniłłowicz - one of four brothers who did yeoman service to their nation, though each in a different way from the others.

It soon became clear that while Father K was with us in spirit he was far from happy about our basis of union. True to the teachings of his church, he wanted the movement to be Roman Catholic, both in spirit and membership. The term 'Christian' did not satisfy him, and the presence of non-Catholics was an offence. At the same time, he realised that any effort to drive our people was bound to fail, so he did no more than talk earnestly to the whole group (or to individuals) about what was the best thing, compared with which what we had was a second best. All this was not only fair but was highly edifying, since it made our people think more seriously than before about what the West had been facing for centuries. No resolutions were taken, save one – to refer the whole matter to the local unions, and make it the chief issue at the summer conference which was arranged for the last days of June, in the historic city of Sandomierz on the middle Vistula.

Here we were fortunate in having the help of one of the finest teachers and writers on Polish thought, Professor Józef Ujejski of Warsaw. Friendly in his attitude to what we were doing, he was well aware of the difficulties faced both by our individual members and by the organisation as a whole. With some justice we could look to him for guidance, just as we depended in Cracow on the constant good-will of his older colleague, Professor Chrzanowski.

In a report letter to Dr Mott, I had told him about the two extreme currents to be found inside our ranks; the one desiring that we become a strictly 'religious,' that is, theologically Catholic, society; the other advocating complete emancipation from creeds and dependence on what the Quakers call 'the inner light.' Between these were to be found the 'middle of the road' people who stood by the idea and ideal set out in the Goleszów basis. Our Sandomierz meeting had then one major purpose – to arrive by discussion and a vote at some solution of this issue, since if left open it could lead to much waste of time in the groups, or even to a break-up.

The prospects of a happy ending to the controversy were much improved by the return, early in June, of Mitana from the federation conference in Peking. The generosity of an American friend had made it possible for a few delegates from European countries to go to this important meeting, who could not have been sent by the movements they represented. Mitana had joined the French delegation at Marseilles in April, and seen much of the world in their company. It was my good fortune to have a long talk with him in Cracow shortly after he got home, and I saw that he was in no doubts as to what action should be taken at Sandomierz. All the same I went to the conference with some anxieties, hoping in my heart that what had been so well begun in the previous year would not be undone now.

At a special session provided for in the programme, Father K put his case well; and he got some support from members to whom their church affiliation was the most important thing in their lives. The extreme party of the other wing said their say also, while not a few expressed the hope that we should not meddle with the basis adopted a year before. Professor Ujejski had consented to act as chairman, and to say a word at the appropriate time; but he felt the gulf existing between the two opposites so acutely that he asked to be relieved of his office. It was clear that he did not agree with Father K; nevertheless he was not ready to express his differences in open forum. Theodore Abel, later to become professor of sociology in Columbia University, New York, was asked to take the chair, and he at once made a strong plea for continuation on Goleszów lines, arguing against the swapping of horses in mid-stream. Mitana then added his views, and after some more discussion a vote was called for. The majority was large in favour of the Christian, as opposed to the Catholic, position – a distinction many regretted because for them it did not exist. The upshot was a secession on the part of some Warsaw students, who formed a new circle in the capital; but what pleased me was that the separation was effected with goodwill on both sides. The personal friendships of earlier days carried over into the new order.

This battle cost us nearly two days of time, but it was worth the trouble. Our people matured in consequence, and I was able to report to Dr Mott: 'By the grace of God we shall keep an atmosphere of broad sympathy for all, while at the same time holding to the Christian basis as the one sure way of satisfying the needs of the present day.' (It is worth noting that our groups in the universities, even before this, had in student jargon been dubbed 'the Christians,' and this name stuck in the years to come.)

The issue faced during those months was, as I felt then and still think, one of vital significance not only for Poland but for Western Christendom. A study of the history of the subject peoples of Europe during the nineteenth century will show how important church affiliations had become. In the case of the Poles their position between Lutheran Prussia and Orthodox Russia called for a reinforcing of patriotism through theology, the wisdom of which may be questioned by outsiders but was never doubted by those involved. To perpetuate this kind of thing into a new age when independence had been won would raise many difficulties, and might even imperil the faith. Apart from the fact of strong non-Catholic elements in the country – Evangelical, Orthodox, and Jewish, the identification of national loyalties with Catholicism would mean a prolonging of the gaps that had separated the Poles from the Anglo-Saxon world. In older days Protestantism meant for them Lutheranism as they knew it in Prussia, and nothing else. This, as they knew full well, was both a mistake and a pity.

As will appear from later pages there existed a fear on the part of zealous Roman Catholics in regard to the presence of 'foreign' Christians in the country – a fear that was quite ungrounded. We newcomers were charged with propagating 'indifferentism' – a word taken from the French and meaning that we thought one way to heaven was as good as another. Some of the clergy even charged us with proselytising, or 'stealing souls.' Neither of these fears had any justification. In all our work, and I was in touch with most of what went on, I know of no case where a loyal Catholic was enticed away from his church. Conversely, I know of many who, as a consequence of belonging to our groups, were brought back from spiritual indifference to the status of 'practising' believers.

We had a concrete example in Cracow. One of our woman students, run down in health by a combination of earning and learning, was in hospital, and E went to see her there. While the visit was on, a Catholic Father came along, one of the men who gave much time to pastoral work under difficult conditions. Conversation was general, but the Father asked the patient whether she went to confession. The reply, 'I do now!' provoked the further question as to what was meant by 'now.' To this the answer was, 'Well, you see, Father, for a long time I had almost lost my faith; but since I came in touch with the SCM I have found it again. Now I go regularly to confession.'

At Sandomierz I asked to be allowed to resign from the council of the movement, though as a registered student in Cracow I had every right to be on it. My reason was that my duties with the YMCA were getting heavier; but I also felt that withdrawal might help to quiet the fears of certain people. My request was accepted, but I was then asked to become chairman of a Committee on Methods of Work, and to continue when possible to visit the university groups during the academic year. As things turned out, an extremely busy year was ahead, and I delegated others to make fraternal visits whenever possible. Some of our students were not only mature, but also well fitted for such work, and the more experience they got the better.

The third summer conference of the SCM was held in July 1923 in the People's University at Dalki, near Poznań. This institution had been founded by Father Ludwiczak on the model of the Danish Folk High Schools created by Grundtvig after the defeats of the sixties – a piece of work from which all the world can learn. To my great regret I could not be present. As recounted elsewhere E and I were away on furlough during which I saw a good deal of the SCM in Canada. From this absence we returned in January 1924, and my first report included these comments:

It has been a joy to note the growth in mind and spirit of some of the people in the SCM since a year ago. In Cracow a whole group faced the need for re-organisation, and decided on the following concrete steps:

1   To stand together in the face of the grumbling to be heard all around;

2 To set themselves a time every day, when they would unite in intercession for the cause, wherever they were;

3 To undertake that each member would recruit a new member before the close of the term;

4 To assess themselves one per cent of their income for the general treasury.

This spirit animated their resolve not to fall down in their undertaking to be hosts to the SE European Conference announced to be held in Zakopane. I counselled strongly against this, but was overruled. There is nothing these people cannot do if they only *will*.

True, the Warsaw union had been severely upset by the graduation of some of its leaders, as well as by the 'secession' after Sandomierz. Two groups were meeting, and a fine young leader had appeared in the person of Miss N. (She was later to marry one of our senior members from Poznań, and together they were to do good work as mayor and mayoress of one of the new industrial towns of Central Poland.) But things were not going well, one reason being the general state of the nation. Late in 1923 the first resolute effort was made by the government to deal with the nightmare of inflation that had been growing for more than a year. A major surgical operation was necessary, and it left the patient for a time almost flat. The vast quantities of paper money were called in, and 'real money' – the guilder (złoty) with the value of one franc – put in its place. There was now not enough money to go around, and when the incidence of taxation was also raised, much discontent as well as some privation resulted. The 'scissors,' as it was called, was bound to make many short-sighted and selfish people rebellious and it took some faith and courage to express the longer view.

All this made itself felt in student circles; but there was no disposition among our members to succumb to pessimism, or to do what not a few youth of those days did – decide to let others worry while they set out to have 'a good time,' too often with alcohol to help them along. From the outset the tone of the movement had been buoyant. Looking back I recall the amount of laughter that we indulged in – the real kind that heals both body and spirit. And why not? The aspirations of a century had been fulfilled, and an opportunity given that had been denied to their fathers. Even if there was still a good deal of poverty on all sides, the way to meet it was not that of a long face and a martyred grimace. More than once I was reminded of the name given to the student clubs of the University of Wilno just a hundred years earlier – the days of the Romantic awakening in literature in Eastern Europe. They were known as 'the men with the radiant faces,' and the description was a just one. This same kind of medicine was needed in 1923.

In a spirit of positive faith, then, the Polish SCM faced the task of welcoming the Southeast European Conference in Zakopane in May, and for geographical reasons most of the work devolved on the Cracow union. H.L. Henriod, the Swiss student leader who was general secretary of the federation, was in charge, and delegates from fifteen countries were expected. All together we numbered over fifty, one-third of them from Poland. Among them were students of the Orthodox faith, of course Russians in exile; and one of the most helpful senior people was Pastor Fischer of Graz. At the time I felt that too much attention at the meeting was devoted to matters of religious belief; but this may have been a blessing, for adherents of all three branches of Christendom were present. For our Polish delegates this meeting with fellow-students from abroad was most salutary, since only a few had been able to attend conferences outside the country. To the general atmosphere of goodwill and seeking after truth a great deal was contributed by 'George' Cockin from London, later bishop of Bristol.[9]

To my keen regret Pastor Siegmund-Schultze of Berlin, who was to have led a discussion group, was refused a visa by the Polish authorities – a left-over from older days. One other sign of things that should have been buried was seen when a police officer appeared and asked to be allowed to sit in at the meetings. Henriod was at a loss to know how to handle this, but I urged him to make no objections; and I invited the government 'delegate' to sit in at the sessions I conducted on the Parables. He did so for two days, and then disappeared. At one of the evening meetings, I recalled the days of prewar Austria, when the police expected to be invited to all gatherings; and I spoke of the 'freer' atmosphere of ten years later. I did this in order to administer a mild rebuke to the Polish authorities; but some of those present did not see the point. All in all the conference was a success, to which the superb surroundings of this little town nestling under the rocky Tatras certainly contributed. One trouble was that people wanted to go climbing when they should have been at meetings.

Partly because of the effort required for this meeting, it was decided to organise in July a 'retreat' in place of the national conference. It was held at a small place near Warsaw called Radość – the Polish word for gladness. My report on this said: 'There was none of the exaltation of Goleszów, but also none of the dissonances of Sandomierz ... I shall never forget those hours, especially when we came to witness what the movement meant to each of us personally.' The morning hours were spent on thinking about 'preparedness,' 'inner growth,' and 'dealing with people.' The Committee on Methods of Work decided to revoke a

9 Frederick Arthur Cockin

ruling made the previous year permitting the creation of denominational study circles. Finally, a new venture was launched – the publishing of a modest quarterly, to be called 'Our Paths.' Senior members, already graduated, undertook the task of editing this. When the first number appeared clerical criticism followed under the caption 'Mistaken Paths,' but no one paid any attention. The Polish SCM published a *Report* for 1921-2, a second for 1922-3; and then *Our Paths* (Nasze Drogi) – two numbers in 1925, three in 1926, four in 1927 – in all some 450 pages of notes, articles, and news.

Space limitations do not permit me to tell of the spirited debates that were going on in the National Council of Polish Students during the session 1924-5. One of them grew out of the fact that the annual congress of the *Confédération Internationale des Étudiants* had been held in Warsaw, and that Jan Baliński-Jundziłł had been elected president. This organisation had included up to now only students from Allied countries, but under British pressure a move was on foot to admit the Germans. Much tension was aroused on this account; but even more was caused when at its Wilno meeting the National Council decided that for the future Jewish students at Polish universities should not be allowed to live in residences maintained by the Fraternal Aid Association. In actual practice the Jews had their own 'hostels,' the first one being (I think) in Warsaw; but this official stand in a very delicate matter was not accepted by all universities, or by all students anywhere. It marked an emergence of extreme nationalism that was to lead to excesses ten years later, and harm the Polish name in the outside world.

In the SCM there were from the outset students of Jewish blood – converts, of course, to the Christian faith. Some of them were active leaders in thought, and never did their presence cause any friction. It was notable, however, that two of the ablest left us with the 'secession' following the Sandomierz conference. They became leaders in the society that gathered around Father Korniłłowicz. Whether they should ever have left the faith of their fathers and become Christians is a question I have never dared to face.

For the summer conference of 1925 we went to one of the distinctive spots in Poland, the little 'resort' of Ojców a few miles north of Cracow, of which more will be said later. We had only forty present; but among them were the beloved professor of English literature from Cracow, Roman Dyboski, and a Catholic Father, Jan Ciemniewski, from Lwów, famous for his fine work as teacher of religion in high schools. He had all the devotion of Father K and even more wisdom. While not necessarily approving of all we were doing, he gave us his blessing, and helped us with wise counsel. Among the things he advised was the use in our study groups of the version of the New Testament approved by the Mother Church – that of Wujek of the year 1599. He added that if we could have an ordained priest as adviser in each group things would be better; to which we replied that nothing would please us more provided they were men with the wisdom and love of mankind he himself showed. What struck us all was his dislike of any kind of 'tyranny over souls,' which has, alas, been too common as a weapon of priestcraft since the days of ancient Egypt.

At an evening session, held around the supper-table on an open verandah, we heard a former member, who had been acting mayor of his home town in the mining area of the southwest, tell of the work he was engaged in of turning a dirty, unsanitary, and ill-managed community into a place of health, beauty, and happiness. As one of our group remarked, it sounded like a tale from the Arabian Nights. Actually, it was only one of many such enterprises going on in what had been Russian Poland, where neglect and graft had made any kind of self-help an almost hopeless business in prewar times. The story meant the more to us since it was prefaced with an account of how the teller had come into the movement as a senior student in Poznań a few years before, and had there decided on social work as his life vocation.

During my two final years in Poland I was able to give less and less time to the SCM. Its older members were now out in the world, some of them in responsible positions; but the task of recruiting new people, necessary every year if an organization is to live in a fast changing community, had not been done as faithfully as it should have been and activities were desultory. It was possible for me to lead a study circle in Warsaw on the 'Life and Work of St Paul.' These meetings were memorable owing to the attendance of Father Joseph, a young German priest from the Silesian world, whose family had been Polish but had become quite Germanized. He had been in the cavalry regiment that helped to drive the Russians from Warsaw ten years before, and was now here in order to learn Polish for home mission work, where the emphasis was on preaching. It was an inspiration to have so devoted a spirit in our midst. He may have learned something from us; we certainly learned much from him. Not even the knowledge that he had been stolen from his own nation by the assimilation methods of other times hindered us from rejoicing in the fellowship that rose above human differences.

It might be added here that more than once in these years I had the privilege of meeting with and speaking to the Protestant Students' Association of Warsaw University, a more homogeneous group in a way than the SCM could be, and one that had a distinct mission to perform. Here I found a couple of people whom I had first met at our own conferences. Two reflections have forced themselves on me as a consequence of the contacts made with university people from my Leipzig days until we returned to the New World:

1 Because of the constantly changing character of its constituency, no student organisation is likely to live for a longer time unless someone can be set free, as a paid officer, to give all his time and strength to nurture and promote it. He can

serve as a link between centres, and as a sort of adviser who can also do some of the spade-work necessary for the smooth running of things.

2 It is difficult for an interdenominational student society to prosper and continue without living contact with the church or churches of the nation concerned. Students emerge from communities and then return to them. What they do during their academic days is of little concern to the communities from which they come. Where no links exist each student generation will go its own way, but permanence is not to be expected.

Under the circumstances our Polish SCM was bound to run into these difficulties. Perhaps it could not do other than fade out, but it was a great adventure for all while it lasted.

5
Liberated Poland 2

3 THE RED TRIANGLE

The American YMCA's War Service had done a notable piece of work, not only for the Allied Expeditionary Force, but also with its *foyers du soldat* for many units of the French army. Its men were to be found with Haller's Army[1] from the start, and I had seen them in the camps of Lorraine. They accompanied that army to Poland in April 1919, and had their place in the 'march past' of those grey-blue uniformed men during the celebration of 3rd May[2] in Warsaw, with the sign on their sleeves that stood for the cultivation of body, mind, and spirit – the Red Triangle.

The official call to serve the Polish army as a whole was not actually published until the autumn, although by that time there were canteens and clubrooms for troops in operation in Lublin, Modlin, Żabkowice, Dąbrowa, Częstochowa, Rembartów, Płock, Włocławek, Kutno, Będziń, Sosnowiec, Lwów, Brzczany, Stanisławów, Oświęcim, Brześć-litewski, Cracow, and Wilno. Some of them were small, and some temporary, but all were doing needy work. Of course the biggest task lay in the capital; but this list shows the measure already realised of a large-scale enterprise that was to continue right through the year 1920. Then, with the coming of peace, most of it was liquidated. Army Order 9716, pro-

---

1 'The story of the later phases of this "mission" and of the Polish Association that grew out of it will be found in Paul Super's *Twenty-Five Years with the Poles* (New York, nd),' [WJR]. Actually, New Jersey 1947 [DS]
2 Pre-World War II Polish national holiday honouring the constitution of 3 May 1791.

claimed on Armistice Day 1919, made the Red Triangle an auxiliary of the Polish army, and gave all its workers free travel facilities in the way of duty, as well as the right to draw special rations.

What follows is not even a sketch of this service, though important stages will be noted; it gives an account of one man's share in the whole, together with some explanation of methods, purposes, and obstacles encountered. Weaknesses will not be glossed over, nor any claim made to the working of miracles. For the performance of any task three things are necessary − people, quarters, and means. At bottom these resolve themselves into one − the first. Where the right men are available, places to work can usually be had, and means will be found. Actually, for the postwar work of the Red Triangle the last-named were at hand; a good part of the large sum raised just before the end of the war in the United States was not needed as expected, and at least part of it could be used for deserving causes. People too were at hand (although some of them were of inferior calibre) among those who had served in France or Italy and were willing to continue for another six months. Some had to be brought from the New World, and, of course, many were soon found in Poland itself.

Roughly speaking, the personnel consisted of the following categories: a number of executives, each of them in charge of a department, such as management, transport, finance, physical education, or of a local centre; a few American women for special jobs; a much larger number of assistants, chiefly Polish-Americans, some of whom were interpreters; and, last but not least, a large group of Polish women who did all kinds of work. Young men were also recruited on the spot, chiefly from the services, most of whom had already been or hoped to become university students the moment peace was restored, but some of whom remained in our work and became leaders in the Polish association that came into being late in 1923. This company represented a wide variety of background and competence. The young Polish-Americans had in many cases only elementary schooling, but the resources and skill they showed in handling practical tasks was reassuring, and some of them developed into real leaders.

Here I want to pay a tribute to those in charge of this enterprise − the Americans with whom I was now to be working for eight full years. They too were a mixed group, and some of them unfit for any but routine duties. Dr Mott had long since described the war effort of the YMCA as a 'scramble,' and in spite of the care taken in selecting workers men got in who were unsuitable. Some simply wanted a safe field in which to do war service, others had a hobby they wanted to follow. I recall one man who did his work faithfully, but spent all his spare time taking pictures to be used for lantern-slides in lecturing when he got home! We had another who showed great zeal in buying valuables of all kinds from people forced to part with them − chiefly silver or precious stones, what we called 'loot.' Two men got onto the slippery path of intimacy with Polish women, and had to be sent home. There was one, not serious, case of misappropriation of funds. But these were exceptions, and rare – a tiny percentage of the whole mission.

Almost every profession was represented – ministers, teachers, lawyers, journalists, social workers, business men – some of them with little book-learning, though competent in affairs. Some were rather crude of speech and manners, though with hearts of gold. This crudeness, characteristic of much of the New World, was not understood at first in a country where formalities counted for more than even in France. Such men did not realise that on entering a shop or a bank, or on any errand, one should take off one's hat; or that on making a business call, one should first spend a moment or two in polite trivialities before getting to the issue at hand. Only once, however, did I feel it necessary to apologise for the manners of a colleague, and that was in Paris. I was acting as interpreter, and the purpose of our visit to a Polish official was to secure free transport for supplies. My well-meaning colleague thought he could help things on by tossing the official a package of the special cigarettes he carried; but it was quietly returned to him with the remark, 'Thank you, I have my own!'

The majority of the workers were stronger on the side of getting things done than on that of quiet example. Perhaps this had to be, since in war-time, what one does counts for more than what one is. Nevertheless, the most loved among all our Americans, seen from the point of view of their Polish colleagues, was singularly ineffective as an executive. As I saw it, there was room for every kind, so long as they were genuine. What disturbed me very much was to hear one of the best of them describing an acquaintance (obviously in the sense of admiring him) as a man 'who at any time can write his cheque for five figures.'

One thing I learned, which I did not realise before. There is no 'American type'; there are a dozen. My colleagues came from all over the great union, and the differences of temperament and taste were startling. More than once I found myself having to pour oil on the troubled waters of disagreement. The New Englander was as different from the Southerner as chalk from cheese; the Easterner from the native of the Middle West no less so. It is the glory of America that people are brought up 'to be themselves'; but they can be united by the power of a great purpose and then you have a dynamic that can move mountains.

Some of these men made warm friends in Poland, but only if they took time to do this. Working day and night on common tasks is one of the surest schools of friendship, but sometimes things go the other way. At times one should 'go apart' and commune with people. This was difficult for most, who knew no Polish, and the few who spoke fair French were lucky. Yet many Poles had a command of English, and all were eager to learn. One thing is certain – the Red

Triangle people won the confidence and gratitude of nearly all with whom they had to do, and on leaving they took away many proofs of this fact.

The Polish women workers, without whose help little could have been done to make the canteens and clubs attractive to the troops, were almost without exception a boon to the enterprise. Most of them came of better-class families, had real educational backgrounds, and rejoiced in the opportunity thus given them to do useful work in the service of their nation. Many belonged to families which had been beggared by war conditions – those brought up in Russia, for instance, who had come 'home' destitute. Much the same could be said of the native-born men, of whom a few were still with the Polish Association when it was dissolved by the Communist government after the Second World War.

My relationships with these young people were cordial, and in nearly every case happy. With only one did I have a sharp difference, and I was within an ace of being challenged to a duel! But the hot-blooded youth was talked out of his anger by his mates, and nothing came of it. Knowing something about their country, its past and its hopes for the future, I was able to spend many a profitable hour in discussions, and to make many friends. Our head office used me for liaison work and called me in as adviser on policy; in particular I made myself useful when the need for training personnel became imperative. Working together, we learned – each from the other, the teacher from his pupils as much as the latter from him. The courses organized were an invaluable school of *esprit de corps*, and only the dullest of workers did not see that the running of a canteen or the arranging of outdoor games was a means to an end as well as an end in itself.

As noted already, I spent a year in more or less broken activities before being posted to Cracow in the critical summer months of 1920. Of that first year a few incidents deserve mention since they bear directly on war work. At the end of September, A.S. Taylor, who had been in charge of the Red Triangle centre in Brest during the latter war years, arrived to take up the post of general secretary in Poland. English born but American trained, he spoke French well and so was able to deal with many national leaders directly. He proved to be a man of vision and courage, though not always able to co-ordinate all phases of the work. A few months later there also arrived in Warsaw an older man, accompanied by his charming wife, long experienced in school management, to act as adviser on educational questions. William Orr was an Ulsterman by birth, but had been educated at Amherst, had taught for years in Springfield high schools, and then became deputy minister for education in Massachusetts. During a longer stay in Poland, after which he went on to help in Bulgaria, he won the confidence both of his fellow-workers and of the Polish Ministry of Education, and was (I think) the first among us to be given a decoration by the government. It was chiefly thanks to him that we were able to make a start with a training programme for social workers.

Shortly after the New Year 1920 Taylor asked me to accompany him on a tour of inspection of the outpost areas in the northeast – what of old was known as Lithuania. He needed someone as interpreter, and also as counsellor in case of special problems arising. The prospect looked good, for I had long wanted to see this part of Europe – and for special reasons. The first stage of the journey took us to Wilno, where the romantic movement in Polish literature had its birth; the second to Mińsk, capital of what was being even then called Belorussia; while the third would bring us to the Berezina River, where Napoleon lost the larger remnants of the Grand Army in the winter of 1812-13. Amid Russian snows, an ill-clad and ill-equipped Polish army was holding a line against what most of Europe feared as the menace of Bolshevism.

Taylor had secured an upper berth in the one sleeping-car attached to the Warsaw-Wilno express, thanks to the courtesy of General Stanisław Szeptycki, then in command of the whole front. The general, with his wife, occupied the lower. The prospect of sitting up all night in a crowded compartment was facing me until one of the Food Mission officers took me under his wing. The result was a comfortable place to sleep and congenial company. My host had worked for months in Vienna, and was alive with sympathy for the half-starved inhabitants. In my view, however, those people were paying (perhaps unjustly) for the sins of the Habsburg monarchy through the ages, and could hardly expect to get off scot-free. We had thus plenty of room for an exchange of sentiments.

Arriving in Wilno about noon (the trains of those days travelled at a snail's pace), we were met by the general's adjutant and taken to the Hotel Bristol where our Red Triangle workers, with W.M. Berry of Montclair, New Jersey, at the head, gave us a warm welcome. A full programme had been set up, more than Taylor, who was far from well, could cope with. After dinner we were to see the military hospital, then visit the canteens, and then make some courtesy calls. At the hospital I met the commander of the Women's Batallion, widow and mother, who had been through incredible things during five years; and we were only half way through our tasks when a messenger arrived to say that the general would like to see us as soon as possible. A change of plans was effected, and we went at once to the High Command. The interview, carried on in French, was most cordial. The commander-in-chief knew all about our work, and welcomed the chief warmly to his area. Directions were given for the tour to the front, which was delayed a day so that Taylor could get a little rest. This suited me better, since I could now hope to visit the university, recently reopened after being closed by Tsar Nicholas I after the uprising of 1830-1.

During our visit to the canteens speeches were in order, with interpretation, and we could then settle down for a quieter evening. After a night's sleep some hours were set apart for sight-seeing – the cathedral, the ruins just above it of an ancient Lithuanian castle, the charming river Wilejka (a branch of the Niemen), and the astonishing baroque church of St Peter and St Paul in the suburb of Antokol. The St Casimir chapel in the cathedral is a gem of high Renaissance art, revealing the fact that only from the sixteenth century did this part of Europe come under the effective influence of the West. As for St Peter and St Paul, the whole interior is a lace-work of bas-relief figures and imagery, the equal of which I have never seen elsewhere.

We were guests of the general at lunch. On both sides of me were staff officers who had served in the tsar's armies right through the war, against the Germans and the Turks. One of them had been wealthy but Bolshevism had robbed him of everything, and his present salary was worth just nine dollars per month. Among the brief speeches made was one by the chairman of the medical faculty of the university, who pleaded for help of any kind in the rehabilitation of his department. Two years later this man was to help us set up valuable services for the state railway workers in the whole northeast. Later in the afternoon we made some of the visits planned for the day before; in particular to the senior professors of literature and philosophy – Marian Zdziechowski and Wincenty Lutosławski.

The next day saw Taylor restored to strength, so I could leave him to matters of organisation while I went to the university. As I soon discovered, lectures had been suspended for the morning in order that both staff and students could attend the funeral of a brilliant younger professor of philosophy, Dr Horodyski. While serving at the front, he had given his overcoat to a picket without one, and caught a fatal chill in consequence. Pneumonia followed, and nothing could save him. By sheer good fortune, for me, Professor Zdziechowski had come late for the requiem in St John's Church, and the procession had already gone. He acted as guide, and we were soon on the way to the lovely cemetery of Rossi, on a hill outside the city. The coffin was being laid away in a vault as we arrived, and I was then shown the tombs of poets, teachers, and patriot leaders of other days. In the course of this visit I met the head of the Department of Fine Arts, Ferdynand Ruszczyc, who walked back with us to town. Many years later I was to admire his symbolic painting 'Nec Mergitur,' which hung on the staircase of the Wilno museum.

After a late dinner, I rested and then slipped over to the university to hear Professor Józef Kallenbach on the poetry of the late romantics – that day the subject was Wincenty Pol. After his return to Cracow, I was to know him personally – an authority on the life and work of Mickiewicz, but in the older tradition. (From him Monica Gardner took her main theses for her biography of the poet.³) After supper we got to the station, where the general had put his coach at the disposal of our party of five. We reached Mińsk, after a quiet journey, the next morning at ten.

For the first time I was in a truly Russian city, and in the middle of winter. Rooms were waiting for us at the Hotel Paris, and we were soon in touch with our people – the chief of whom was a middle-westerner, Waggoner. Having just recovered from the 'flu,' he was wrapped up in a huge coat – fur both outside and in. Everyone was busy, for the canteen and club centring on the main square was to be opened in two days. We delivered mail to the Grey Samaritans working in the district, and then went to visit a base hospital. Here, indeed, I saw the primitive conditions in which sick and wounded men were being cared for. But the striking thing was that when asked what they needed most, the answer was uniformly, 'Something to read!'

During the afternoon, which was short, I strolled about the town and saw with astonishment what fine furs were to be had, and at bargain prices. The dealers, all Jewish, were eager to do business on any terms. After dinner we had only an hour before getting the train to Borysław – the real front. Arriving at five in the morning, we were placed on a siding until day broke. When we could see, we found ourselves in the midst of a snow-storm that could match a Manitoba blizzard. And now, almost verbatim, from my diary.⁴

Snow everywhere – Russia! We are sitting in the office of the brigadier. The road past the door leads to Moscow, while a path turning off into the woods goes to a neighbouring village. Figures are moving about, in intermittent flurries of snow. Our sleighs are delayed, so we decide to walk up the road to look at some one-time Russian barracks. We found a huge ruin, with what had been the chapel of the artillery school, a vast hall nearly three-hundred feet long which was now to be put in order for a Red Triangle canteen and club. On our return we found Colonel Z, a bearded man with a businesslike manner. Waggoner had met him before, and the canteen plans were reviewed.

Then our horses appeared – for Taylor and myself they had 'the finest pair in the brigade.' We started off sharply, crossing the wide reaches of the Berezina into Old Boryslav, and thence up to the front, as the Poles were holding a 'bridgehead' at this point. We halted at the regimental HQ, where a third sleigh joined

3 Monica Gardner, *Adam Mickiewicz: The National Poet of Poland* (London and New York 1911)
4 Rose left his papers to the University of British Columbia library. Some diaries are included among them but no sources as valuable as the ones he refers to here and elsewhere appear.

us, and then on we went. A blizzard was in progress, fortunately at our backs. I had a rug about my shoulders and a woollen helmet (balaclava) on my head. Fields, then forests – absolute silence. Now we approached the first positions – we saw dug-outs.

In one of the larger ones a class was going on for illiterate men, and we were shown specimens of their work. In one company there were thirty students, keen to learn. But again they were short of suitable reading materials. On foot we made our way along the trench, which reached for miles. A hundred yards out in front was a six-fold barbed-wire screen, in the forest beyond every few rods had its look-out. The men had two hours duty and then a change; but in very cold weather they were relieved every half-hour. Too few pairs of good boots, too few overcoats; so they have to be exchanged also. We were shown one of the 'look-outs' and a machine-gun nest.

We said 'Au revoir!' to the captain, who spoke French, and went on to the 2nd regiment. This was in charge of an engineer, and he told us that dinner was just ready; would we go along and join the group? A long hour was well spent, drinking tea and eating our biscuits. One of our party took a couple of snapshots, but the snow was getting thicker, so we asked for our teams. Berry and his colleague had been spilled out of their sleigh on the way out, and now they had as driver a real *muzhik* – beard, cap and all. So off we went across wide fields, following the barbed-wire screen toward our right. Then we got down, mounted a slight rise and were in a 'look-out' where the picket was just coming off duty. His mate was splitting wood in the dug-out and was barefoot. They had only one pair of boots between them, and the temperature was nearly thirty below.

Giving the men some cigarettes, we followed the path back to an artillery post, set on a rise and commanding a view for five miles. Little could be seen, however, in such a storm, so we moved on. In a village nearby the sleighs were waiting, so we had only time to pop into a cottage, where the reserves were housed. Two rooms, over-crowded. A big stove in the centre, on which people sleep. A woman sitting in front of it, spinning wool, with children around her. Yet everybody was cheerful, including a lean porker running about the yard outside.

Again we were off through the woods, in which wolves and bears can be seen at times. One trooper had been pulled down and half-eaten, we were told. And now we were on our way back to the casino where I said 'Thank you' to the officer who had lent me his sheepskin coat. Soon we were crossing the river again on the ice, and at six we were eating sandwiches in our coach. An hour later HQ sent us some 'bully' and beans – the best they had. We settled down for the night just as the engine began to move us off. No coal in this area, so wood sparks were flying merrily as we moved ...

Such was the record. We got back to Mińsk, were present at the opening of the new canteen, and watched a theatrical performance put on by the troops. In between we got away for half-an-hour to visit the big Orthodox church on the square and hear the responses sung at vespers. Male voices singing without organ accompaniment leave an impression different from that of our western choirs – for Taylor and myself it was something new.

So much for my first and only trip to the eastern front. It should be added that our mobile canteens accompanied the Polish army, and that of Semon Petlura the Ukrainian leader, in their advance to Kiev, and shared their headlong retreat.[5] Formidable Red Army concentrations north of the Pripet River made this necessary, and now it was a case of defending the Vistula. The Peasant party leader, Wincenty Witos, became prime minister and a call went out for volunteers for special services. Among the first to offer themselves were the students, and a rendezvous was set up a few miles east of the capital at Rembertów.

I made one visit with Taylor to this camp – if such it was – to see in what way the Red Triangle could help. Hundreds of young men were improvising a bivouac in wooded country, with almost no shelters; and we found them busy preparing dinner over open fires with the help of women volunteers. Anything looking less like a military unit would be hard to imagine! We made arrangements to set up a canteen, and promised supplies. The care of this centre would have devolved on me, had I not been sent off two days later to Cracow in order to help our executive there prepare for the reception of our women workers, evacuated from the capital. I therefore saw no more of the war. It ended with a defeat of the invaders, whose front had become too far extended, and a general retreat. Peace negotiations began in October and were completed six months later.

Meanwhile Dr Mott's first visit to Poland had come in June. This meant my being put on the Red Triangle budget, with the understanding that I was to continue to give most of my time to work in the student field. For the whole enterprise it meant a stock-taking of what had been done, a survey of the field and, not least important, a good deal of publicity for the mission. The presence of a second distinguished American (counting Hoover as the first) gave the Poles a chance to declare their sentiments for the Allies and for the New World in particular; but it also gave those who had doubts about this 'invasion' a chance to express them by way of restoring the balance. In effect, these were devoted Roman Catholics, a few laymen but mostly clergy, and they looked on with con-

---

5 A Polish offensive together with Ukrainian troops headed by Semon Petlura captured Kiev in May 1920 but were forced to retreat by a Soviet offensive. The Polish counteroffensive began only at the outskirts of Warsaw.

cern at the popularity of non-Catholic agencies whose influence might hurt the church, or even the cause of religion as such. In the forefront were the Jesuit Fathers.

It was no surprise to some of us that the addresses given by Dr Mott, listened to with interest by large audiences, provoked a series of replies. In a letter to him, dated 30 July, I wrote:

Enclosed you will find a translation of the first serious paper that has appeared on the YMCA and its future in Poland. As you see it was called forth by the appearance you made in the university here – the writer, Father Morawski, has just returned from Rome where he has been finishing his studies; and he will now have a place in the publications department of the Jesuits in Cracow ... I had the pleasure of a long talk yesterday with one of his colleagues ... I found a man who is thoroughly in sympathy with the ends we have in view, but who disagreed when I insisted that both the YMCA and the YWCA are really handmaids of the Christian Church, serving her ends. He is doubtful about this, seeing in them agencies likely to take people away from the church rather than lead them to it ...

With regard to the article of Father M's, I went on: 'It has much of true criticism in it. We have men with us who scarcely conceal their disapproval and scorn of everything Catholic. That is not the way to work, nor is it the kind of thing you set out in your address. It is mostly due to ignorance, but it can do harm.'

Owing, no doubt, to the national crisis, little attention was paid to the matter at the time, but the whole issue flared up afresh in the autumn. For this I was in part to blame. On the invitation of a well-known society, I prepared three lectures and they were listened to by a large gathering in the Copernicus Hall of the university. Professor Chrzanowski was good enough to take the chair. The first evening many high school pupils were present, who had to stand; but they did not appear a second time – rumour had it that they were warned not to come. These addresses were repeated a month later in Warsaw, and they appeared the next summer in print.

After explaining how and why the rise of industrial cities in Britain and elsewhere had created a situation for which the churches seemed to have no answer, I set out the major facts as to the rise of the association, its fundamental principles, and its methods of work. The fact was not hidden that the promoters of this movement were members of the evangelical churches, and that the Portland basis of 1879 limited membership to men belonging to those churches. However, I did show that the guiding principle had always been to help young men to a fuller life, rooted in the teachings of the Gospels, and that no denominational purposes were involved of any kind.

Among those who came to hear me was the veteran Jesuit Father Urban, who had worked for many years in Russia. In the discussion periods that followed the talks, he expressed his anxieties about certain matters, taking the view that for Poles to accept guidance in such things from outside was dangerous. The audience listened politely, but did not seem to share his fears. However, friends came to me later to say that Father Urban reflected the feelings of many people, both clergy and laity. It was therefore needful for us, not to discontinue our work, but to act wisely; above all to use every opportunity to explain frankly what we were and what we were trying to do. To this, of course, we had no objection.

Within a few weeks the whole issue was thrown wide open by the appearance of a message from the Holy See itself. This famous document, though since forgotten, is of sufficient importance to justify reprinting in the official English version:

THE VATICAN LETTER of November 1920
The Supreme Congregation of the Holy Office has addressed to the Bishops of the Catholic world a LETTER dealing with a certain class of Societies which menace with the gravest dangers the faith of their flocks; and pointing out the necessity of protective measures being taken on behalf of the Catholic people. One well-known and wide-spread Society, the Young Men's Christian Association, was mentioned by name, its operations exposed, and its principles stated and condemned.

We offer herewith the official English translation of this letter. M.F. Fallon D.D. Bishop of London

LETTER to Local Ordinaries in Which Their Attention is Called to Certain Recent Attempts of Non-Catholics Against the Faith.

The most eminent and most reverend Cardinals who, together with the undersigned, are Inquisitors General in matters of faith and morals, desire the Bishops to note with vigilant attention the activity of certain newly-formed non-Catholic organisations which, aided by their adherents in every country, have for a long time been laying snares of a most dangerous sort for our Catholic people and especially for our Catholic youth. While they provide facilities of every kind under the guise of physical training and intellectual and moral culture, in reality they shatter the integrity of Catholic faith and wrest her children from the arms of Mother Church.

Considering indeed that these associations are supported by the goodwill, the resources and the co-operation of highly influential persons, and that they render efficient service in various kinds of beneficence, it is not surprising that they deceive inexperienced minds who fail to detect their inward nature and purpose. But their true character can no longer be a matter of doubt for anyone who is well-informed; their aims, hitherto but gradually revealed, are now openly declared in pamphlets, newspapers and periodicals which serve as their means of publicity. Their avowed object is the intellectual and moral culture of young men through educative processes, and this culture which for them is religion, they define as unlimited freedom of thought quite apart from any form of religion or denomination whatsoever. Thus, under the pretext of enlightening youthful minds, they turn them away from the teaching authority of the church, the divinely established beacon of truth, and persuade them to seek in the depths of their own consciousness, and hence within the narrow range of human reason, the light which is to guide them.

DANGERS TO YOUTH

It is chiefly students – young men and women, who are drawn into such snares. They, above all others, need help and direction in order to learn Christian Truth and to preserve the faith handed down from their forefathers. Instead, they fall into the hands of men by whom they are robbed of their great inheritance and gradually led away until they hesitate between opposing opinions, then come to doubt about everything, and finally content themselves with a vague indefinite form of religion which is altogether different from the religion preached by Jesus Christ.

Far greater, however, is the harm done to those – too many, alas! who, through the neglect or ignorance of their parents, have not received at home that earliest instruction in the truths of faith which above all else the Christian needs. In consequence they forsake the sacraments, give up the practice of piety, grow accustomed to pass judgment with absolute freedom upon all things even the most sacred, and finally sink into religious indifferentism so-called which, repeatedly condemned by the Church, involves the denial of all religion.

Thus in the flower of their youth, groping without a guide amid the darkness and distress of doubt, they wither away; the rejection of a single dogma is sufficient to make shipwreck of faith. If, indeed, they still retain some vestige of piety – a word upon their lips or a fading trace in their hearts; if they show no little eagerness for doing good – this is readily explained; it is the result of inveterate habit, of kind and tender dispositions, or of a purely human and natural virtue which of itself does not avail to the gaining of eternal life.

YMCA

Among these organisations it will suffice to mention one, the parent of many others, and the most widely known of all (owing specially to its work in relieving large numbers of those upon whom the war brought suffering) and the most fully equipped with means; the organisation known as the Young Men's Christian Association, or in briefer form YMCA. To this society non-Catholics, acting in good faith, have given unwittingly their co-operation, regarding it as beneficial to all, or at any rate as harmful to none; while some Catholics of the more easy-going kind, lend it their support without knowing what it really is. This Association, it is true, professes a genuine love for young men as though it had nothing more deeply at heart than to further their physical and spiritual welfare. But at the same time it undermines their faith inasmuch as it claims to purify that faith and to impart a better knowledge of true living 'above every church and independently of all denominational belief whatsoever' (see the pamphlet published by the Central Agency of the YMCA in Rome, 'What the YMCA is, what it proposes to do,' etc). And yet, what good can be looked for from those who fling away their faith and, after resting securely in the fold of Jesus Christ, wander afar whithersoever desire or temper may lead them?

You therefore, one and all, whom the Lord has charged in a special manner with the government of his flock, are urged by this Sacred Congregation to exert your utmost zeal in preserving Catholic young men from the contagion spread abroad by these organisations, whose very benefactors extended in Christ's name endanger the Christian's most priceless possession, the grace of Christ. Warn the unwary, steady those who are wavering in faith! Arm with Christian spirit and vigor the Societies of young men and young women which are already established, and organise others of the same kind. And in order that they may have the means to counteract their opponents, appeal for aid to those among the faithful who can and will give of their abundance. Exhort also the pastors and directors of your Young Men's Associations to an energetic performance of their duties. In particular, through books and pamphlets, let them check the spread of error, lay bare the schemes and wiles of their enemies and furnish suitable aid to those who are zealous for the truth.

NEWSPAPERS AND REVIEWS

It will be your duty, then, in your episcopal conference to deal with this matter as its seriousness demands and adopt such measures as your united counsels may demand. In this connection, the Sacred Congregation judges it opportune that the Bishops in each country should state publicly that the newspapers, periodicals, and other writings of the Association in question which aim at spreading among our Catholic people the errors of rationalism and religious indifferentism, are expressly forbidden by the law of the Church. (See the Code of Canon Law, Can. 1364, p. 2. 1399, PE.) Such publications are, among others, *Fede e Vita* (Faith and Life), a monthly review of religious culture, organ of the Italian Federation of Students for Religious Culture; *Bilychnis*, a monthly review of religious studies; *Il Testimonio*, review of the Italian Baptist Church.

Metropolitans will see to it that whatever is decided upon and put into effect in each diocese, as conditions require, shall be reported to the Apostolic See within six months.

Given at the Palace of the Holy Office in Rome on the fifth day of November 1920.

R. Card. Merry del Val. Secretary

This document, thought by many to have special reference to the Italian situation, was bound to have some effect on the attitude of the clergy everywhere. It could easily lead to pronouncements in other countries which would provoke unnecessary controversy. In any case it was clear that certain things should be made clear to our Polish friends:

1 That the Red Triangle Mission was in the country for a specific task; and when this was completed it would withdraw.

2 That it was for them to decide whether anything should remain behind as a lasting consequence, apart from the gratitude felt in wider circles for the service rendered.

3 That, nevertheless, in our opinion, based on long experience, a vitally important piece of work for youth was waiting to be done, in which the laymen of the nation were morally bound to take more than a platonic interest.

Partly because the Polish nation had been subject to aliens during the nineteenth century, a tradition had grown up of dealing with many issues through voluntary associations, and the idea we represented found many sympathisers. In addition, six long years of war had left the best people weary, and any help from a trustworthy source was welcome. Finally, the fact was not forgotten that most of these associations set up by the native-born had been party-political in character, the most active being leftist in tendency and even hostile to religious convictions in any form. Few who knew us had any suspicions that we were interested in stealing the youth away from their church; and those who considered the matter seriously at once said what was obvious – that the religious affiliations of people could not be worth much if the presence of a group of foreigners, no matter how clever they were, was likely to prove a genuine threat.

A movement led by laymen, the basis of which was that humanity can only attain the best things in this world if it is aware of the existence of God and of the implications of this fact for society, made a strong appeal to people who watched what was going on on their eastern borders. They could not call it disloyalty to their church, in whose teachings their forefathers had been grounded for centuries, if they welcomed the co-operation even of non-Catholic forces as soon as they were convinced as to the honesty of their intentions. I leave on one side the fact that the number of 'intellectuals' in Poland, whose attitude was one of agnosticism, if not of atheism, was considerable. As we well knew these people rejoiced at any embarrassment caused to clerical circles anywhere, in any form; but it would have been folly on our part to league ourselves with them. Being believers ourselves, we simply could not do it without losing our own souls. Fortunately, with few exceptions, they refrained from thrusting themselves under our tent, so we could go our way with a clear conscience.

But the Jesuit Fathers formed the spearhead of an opposition to our work which could not be ignored. For them it was an axiom that *extra ecclesiam nulla salus* – only organisations controlled by the clergy were safe agencies for influencing the youth. The clergy were bound to be on the alert for signs of 'indifferentism,' in particular where the rising generation was at stake. Some of their critics, with whom the Jesuit Fathers were never popular, remarked that the order was concerned for its own prestige, but that was not my impression. Writing and speaking against the YMCA, they protested that the Triangle meant Free Masonry, which on the continent of Europe had always been hostile to revealed and organised religion. For us there was nothing to be done except get on with our work, making it clear that everything we did was open at any time for inspection. From the start we had found a good few friends among the local 'shepherds of souls,' and more than one of our canteens and clubs had been 'consecrated' by the curé.

I have given some time and space to this issue at the risk of wearying the reader, since it could not be avoided. With the conclusion of peace in March 1921 rumours got about that the Red Triangle people were packing up to go home, and a cry of dismay was raised on all sides. The press had letters, and witness was outspoken as to the help given both in the armed forces and for railway personnel. The alarm was unnecessary, and was caused by the fact that the American workers were indeed reduced substantially. But Father Morawski took advantage of the situation to raise again a voice of warning, this time in Poznań whither he had been transferred, and in a public lecture.

Under Prussian rule the order had not been permitted to work in Poznania, but the devout Catholicism of this province had long been proverbial – it had served to stem the tide even of Bismarck's fury forty years before. Our war work there was now wound up, but we had many friends, so I heard of the proposed public meeting and made it my business to be present. In advance I called on Father M and found that he had received part of his training in Hastings – his English was as good as my Polish. He expressed the hope that I would come to his meeting, the more so as he was going to deal with some of the points I put forward in my (now printed) Cracow lectures. I found a large gathering when I arrived, among them many university people.

The lecturer followed the traditional pattern of saying many nice things about the service rendered by the Red Triangle workers, before going over to an attack, both on the principles we stood for and on the workers themselves. In closing he noted the fact that I was in the audience, and invited me to open the discussion.

None of us had any intention of entering into debate with critics like Father Morawski. I knew how easy it would have been for an outsider to say the wrong thing, and contented myself with thanking the lecturer for his recognition of our services to the youth and the nation, and telling the audience that the presence of one or two Free Masons in the war work of the Red Triangle in no way meant any kind of connection between the two agencies. A few desultory questions followed, and this was all that happened. Father M, as I heard later, was disappointed.

Nothing would have better suited the book of those opposed to all non-Catholic assistance in Poland than to get the issue shifted to the denominational plane. They could then have rallied a good deal of popular opinion, and our task would have been more complicated. As things turned out, the real issue remained something quite different; whether in this vital matter of youth guidance laymen should or should not have an important part to play. In effect this question had been settled long before, when the efforts of the church to get control of popular education had failed. With the decision that the school system of the new Poland was to be controlled by the state, with full provision for the teaching of the faith in the classroom, the main battle had been won.

All the same, the apostles of clerical leadership would not let things rest. In November 1923, just as the Polish YMCA was being constituted, a lengthy article appeared in the Warsaw *Catholic Review*. The keynote was struck in the first paragraph with the famous line from Vergil: 'Timeo Danaos et dona ferentes.' The issue had by now become clearer, as the writer pointed out. It was bad enough to have an American mission winning many friends in a Catholic country; it was quite another thing to have a Polish Young Men's Christian Association being formed, in which youth of all denominations would work together. Some nice things were said about the work done in war-time, and a fair account was given of a booklet I had helped to prepare before going on furlough, *Report and Progress*, in which the point was made that the Polish association wished to buttress the church, not itself 'to be a church.' But the rock of offence was the bringing together of the youth of different churches as Christians in a common cause, and the fear that this would destroy the purity of faith. The Vatican was thus bound to intervene, and all loyal churchmen should listen!

In May 1924 still another, and even longer, analysis and attack appeared in the *Universal Review* (organ of the Jesuit Order) from the pen of Father Podoleński. The history of the association was set out, and the fact noted that at the Jubilee Convention in Paris in 1905 a rider had been added to the original YMCA statute to say that the basis was 'not at all a theological formula, but the expression of a fundamental religious experience.' The conclusion reached by Father Garesch, who had studied the association's work in the United States was quoted: 'The YMCA in its fundamental purpose is a distinctly religious organisation, Protestant in principles and administration.' No one denied that in many cities there were Catholics among the members, but the controls were in the hands of non-Catholic leaders, and this alone justified the warnings given by the Holy Father in 1920. Specific cases were known of young men and women led away from the Mother Church by the SCM and/or the YMCA.

This forthright pronouncement failed to reach the wider public, and did nothing to change the minds of those who had helped to create the Polish association. The latter could say that they were watching for any signs of proselytism on the part of the few Americans remaining in Poland, but had seen none. What is more, no less a person that the Cardinal Archbishop of Cracow, the saintly and honoured Adam Sapieha, was known to have dissented from the Jesuit position. In a pastoral letter he had quoted the warning of St John about false prophets, and spoken of the presence in Poland of 'sects' such as Methodists, Baptists, Adventists, whose activities were, to say the least, equivocal. As for the YMCA he noted the fact that in prevailingly Protestant countries it was Protestant in character, and could not admit that any one church should regard itself as the sole interpreter of the faith. This gave grounds for concern, but not for fear that such activities in Poland would draw loyal Catholics away from their faith. 'The Catholic faith has already passed through more than one testing' was his conclusion, and he had no doubt that it would survive happily now.

As some of us felt from the outset, the Red Triangle had more to fear from some of its over-zealous friends than from its critics. Already in 1921, when the rumours got about that we were to leave Poland, a much read Cracow daily came out with a slashing article, 'Shall Stupidity or Culture Triumph?' In it Father Urban was accused of appealing to Rome against the 'crimes' of American workers; and of having found a ready helper in the priest-brother of the world-renowned philosopher, Wincenty Lutosławski, known for his efforts in Warsaw to get the schools of the country under church control.

Prince Bishop Sapieha knew what he was doing, in speaking as he did in his pastoral letter. He had taken care to inform himself as to what we were doing, and how. Three eminent members of the senate of the university, all later to be active in the Polish association, had gone to him (without our knowledge) to set out the whole matter as they saw it. He thus knew that pictures of Our Lord, and of Our Lady of Częstochowa, were to be found in all our club-rooms, and that wherever possible the latter were opened formally by the clergy of the parish. Conversely, nothing was said or done (unless by some unauthorized person) that could wound the sensibilities of the most devout Catholic.

It should be noted that the Archbishop of Warsaw, Cardinal Aleksander Kakowski, was less friendly. Had he become primate of Poland instead of (the later) Cardinal August Hlond, there would have been difficulties. But Kakowski, for other reasons, wielded far less influence in the country than he could have; and our work was so firmly entrenched in popular favour that he could only have made trouble for himself by being unfriendly. One sample of this entrenchment became known, and deserves mention.

Before the Red Triangle war work had been largely curtailed, our women workers to the number of nearly fifty held a conference in Warsaw. All Poles, and nearly all Catholics, they were a fair cross-section of the nation. They ran the whole meeting themselves, and one consequence of their get-together was a longish resolution, embodying six points relative in one or another way to the subject-matter of these pages. In the first two they stated roundly that none of them at any time had encountered anything 'that would in any way wound our national or religious feelings.' They went on: 'The organisation releases us from work during the time of mass and of recollections, keeps Lent in mind, and accepts our Catholic practice of consecrating new premises. It also encourages any religious work carried on by the clergy.' Paragraph 6 read as follows: 'Desiring to back up our words with actions, we are setting ourselves to acquaint the Polish people as well as may be with the activities of the YMCA. We shall answer all objections raised by presenting the facts; and we shall assist in every way in establishing a Polish Association, supported by Polish funds.'

So far as I know this document was never given to the press; but copies of it were passed around, and one is beside me as I write. Those women had no axe to grind; they meant what they said; and we were to have many proofs of their loyalty in years to come. But they were by no means alone in their stand. It is possible now to reveal what happened about a year later, in Cracow; which shows what a lady in high position was prepared to do in order that toleration and fair play should prevail in her mother country.

By this time plans for the creation of a Polish association were taking shape, though the opposition of the Jesuit Fathers remained as before. More than once

I had suggested to Taylor that we try for a conference with someone in high position in the order, and he finally put the matter to Dr A.D. Davis, who from the Geneva office exercised oversight of what was left of the Red Triangle service in Europe. Davis was soon to visit Poland, and he agreed to take part in a meeting in Cracow, if one could be arranged. His elegant French removed any possible language difficulty, and it fell to me to arrange a meeting, on neutral ground, and where complete discretion was assured.

Thanks to August Cieszkowski, I had been privileged to meet in her townhouse Countess Róża Raczyński (destined in a few years to be mother of two ambassadors of the Polish republic), whose interest in all good causes was a matter of common knowledge. She had been present at one of my lectures, and told me that I was to consult her at any time if I needed help. Now, if ever, seemed to be the time; so I went to her with my problem. Her response was characteristic: 'Let me arrange a small tea-party. I shall ask Father R (she named one of the high-ranking members of the order) and one of his colleagues. You bring Dr Davis and Mr Taylor, and after tea we shall talk.'

Everything went as planned. For half-an-hour there was chatting about everyday matters over cups of tea. Then at a sign from our hostess the cups were cleared away, and the business of the day began. The countess explained her motives in asking us to her home, and requested Dr Davis to express the regrets of association leaders at what we thought to be needless fears of certain Catholic circles. Father R was a little taken aback, but he did not flinch. For fifteen minutes he listened while Davis explained why the position taken by Fathers Urban and Morawski was unjustified. A discussion of various points followed, with the argument running strongly against the clerical position. Suddenly Father R stood up, made a stiff bow, and left the room.

We looked at each other in dismay, and began to apologise to our hostess. But with a wave of the hand she dismissed us, got up at once, and followed Father R. We could hear the sound of voices in the larger room – clearly there was a difference of opinion; then the countess came back, leading her guest with her. Father R apologised handsomely for his *gaucherie*, and the conversation went on as before, though rather less on controversial lines. When we took our leave, without, of course, knowing at all whether any good had come of it, the countess said to me in Polish: 'Tell your colleagues that I never allow anyone to be rude to guests in my house!'

4 TRAINING WORKERS: OSADA

From our first experiment in a training course for club-workers, conducted in the early summer of 1920 in the fortress of Modlin, we learned many things.

Chief among them was that good results in this field could be obtained only if we had a place of our own for such work, somewhat apart from the bustle of daily life. It therefore seemed imperative to look about for a suitable building or buildings, preferably away from any city, but not too inaccessible. If we could rent such at a reasonable rate, we should want to house and feed thirty or more people at a time. To find such a place in Poland in those days, even a shed with a roof on it, which was not already occupied, was almost impossible. Feeling a certain responsibility I did not give up hope, however, and suddenly something very near to what we wanted was found.

In the spring of 1921 one of our Cracow workers drew my attention to some red-brick barracks which stood ten miles north of the city on the old Russian frontier, on the neglected country road leading to a tiny summer resort in the hills, known as Ojców. Two oblong buildings, set in a large garden with a hedge around it, with a cottage adjoining already being used as a village school, had been deserted by the Russians on the outbreak of war. Standing miles from anywhere, they soon became derelict. The doors and windows were stolen, the roofs nearly gone, the floors rotted – in short, there was little left in one case save ninefoot brick walls, though the other was in better condition. Standing on rising ground, the site afforded a charming view of the city of Cracow; while on clear days the High Tatras could be seen fifty miles away to the south.

I got my colleague, Oberholzer, to look at the ruins, and he estimated that we could make them habitable with an expenditure of about a thousand dollars. The worst snag would be that of transporting the necessary materials, but there was hope of getting the army to help us. We put the matter to our head office in Warsaw and got leave to go ahead. Of course, I had to get the permission of the Polish authorities to restore the ruins, and this took me to the little town of Ołkusz, famous in history as the home of lead mining, and to the larger city of Kielce. No objections were raised, since all such work was welcomed as a part of general reconstruction. We learned that seven acres of fields belonged to the place (to which I gave the simple name Osada – Polish for 'settlement'). We also learned that, though some land was needed for the schoolteacher's support, the rest could be reserved for our use.

Operations began without delay. Local workmen from the nearby village were only too glad to get work, and a timber dealer undertook to provide us with material. The commander of the Cracow region, General Czikiel, put in a word for us in the capital, and got a sympathetic response from Colonel (soon to be General Władysław Sikorski[6] of the War Office. A heavy truck with driver was

---

6 Władysław Sikorski, soldier and politician, premier of the Polish Government-in-Exile and commander-in-chief during the Second World War, died in an airplane crash in 1943.

Liberated Poland 2   155

provided for our use, with the right to use army fuel. Our first job was to get the long-befouled well in shape, and to make habitable the smaller of the two barracks, so that someone 'in charge' could live there. By the end of the summer this was achieved, a matron installed, and one of my friends from Teschen, a young engineer who had just finished in Vienna, was secured to supervise further work. Out of the ruins of the former stable, there was soon to arise a two-storey outbuilding, and an old root-house was made into a cold-storage chamber for keeping food. Two of the twenty-foot-long iron frontier posts, with the Russian eagle on them, which had stood at intervals all along the former boundary, were recovered, repainted, and set up as gate-posts at the entrance to the property. By the spring of 1922 things began to look respectable.

At once we began to organise shorter and longer training courses for social workers, which proved to be of first-rate importance for the whole future. These courses went on during five years, and before they had ceased (chiefly owing to the demand made by our boys' camps, which took the attention of our workers during the summer months) they had given us close to a score of men fitted to occupy important posts in the work of both the Red Triangle and the Polish association which followed it, as well as many other helpers.

In doing this work, I could not have got far without the backing of William Orr. The moment he saw the place he recognized its possibilities, and decided to recommend that New York give us a special grant of ten thousand dollars for its development. We could then raise the larger of the two buildings to a second storey, and thus secure the ground-floor for a diningroom and a classroom. On this larger task we were engaged through the summer of 1922, while the courses were in progress. Clay was found on the spot for making bricks, so we built our own kiln and thus saved both money and transport. The task was not completed when the snow came, but we did get it finished the following spring and Osada now looked like a plain but serviceable mansion. Early that spring I even managed to have a tree moved a hundred yards to fill a gap in the row that stood along the high road. It was nine inches thick at the base and forty feet high; but it did live, and in two years had a leafage equal to its neighbour. By levelling the space between the smaller building and the road, we secured a usable tennis court; while at the back between this building and our kitchen-garden we had a space for basket-ball and volley-ball.

The first gathering of workers met in the spring of 1922. It was arranged by the branch of the Red Triangle that had care of Russian POWs, and it lasted only ten days. But from the summer our own regular courses began, usually going on for four weeks. The programme was simple: an early morning period for meditation and discussion, a second period on methods and principles of social work, and a third dealing with general questions of education or even with Polish history and institutions. In the early days the leadership of the first period fell to me, while Paul Super, who had come from America to succeed Taylor as general director, took the second. Various competent visitors handled the third period, some of them Americans, others Poles. The afternoons were given to outdoor games and discussions, the evening to entertainment or study.

It is a slight overstatement to say that the Osada experiment brought Super to Poland, but the prospect of helping to train workers did more than anything else to influence his decision, when Dr Mott asked him to come. The responsibility was shared by Orr; and so the man was secured who, until his death more than twenty-five years later, was identified with Poland and the Polish association more than anyone else. Just before his arrival he had published a useful book, *The Training of a Staff*, and now he had a chance to try out some of his principles. For years Super made what I considered a mistake in not setting out to learn Polish, and so had to work through interpreters; but he never pretended to be a linguist, and what was lacking on this score was more than made up in other ways.

Among the Polish scholars who were good enough to give us up to a week each of their time for these courses were the eminent sociologist, Florian Znaniecki,[7] whose lectures on the elements of social science were devoured (no other word fits) by the mature ones of our students, and were more than once mentioned to me in after-years; Aleksander Janowski of Warsaw, founder of the Geographical Society, who was deeply versed in national folklore; Roman Dyboski, professor of English literature in Cracow.[8] The last-named had recently returned from seven years absence as a prisoner-of-war, spent chiefly in Siberia, and when he asked me to suggest a theme for his periods I replied at once, 'The Fight for a Man's Soul in Captivity.' He accepted the suggestion, and told me long afterwards that it provided him with the thread out of which grew one of his most interesting books. Another helpful visitor was the younger brother of Father Korniłowicz, who had been concerned about the SCM; a man with a keen mind, rare purity of spirit, and an unbounded interest in the social changes which had marked Western Europe in the nineteenth century. A convinced socialist, he saw clearly how little could be done to achieve a healthy social order until men and women had undergone a 'change of heart.' During one summer Tadeusz Mitana, who had already got his doctorate, also helped us.

From time to time we had visitors from the New World, some of them association men, others friends or merely interested travellers. The experiment in

---

7 Florian Znaniecki, sociologist, well-known to English readers for his work (with E. Thomas), *The Polish Peasant in Europe and America*, 2 vols. (New York 1927).
8 Roman Dyboski, author of *Outlines of Polish History* (London 1925).

training workers attracted outside attention, and on one red-letter day in 1923 we had as a guest Professor Paul Munroe of Teachers' College, Columbia University. He could only stay a few hours, but he recalled his visit with interest when I saw him six months later in New York. The oldest of our visitors, who stayed for nearly a week, was the eighty-three-year-old Richard Morse – for half-a-century a founding father of the YMCA in the New World. These summer courses had a value for the cause which went far beyond what was done in the classroom. Attended chiefly by our own workers, but also by interested outsiders, they gave our men a chance to get to know one another at work and at play, and so develop an otherwise unobtainable *esprit de corps*. They provided a chance for discussion of all kinds of problems, without any inhibition on the part either of student or teacher. It is not too much to say that both our own workers and those from outside became acquainted for the first time with the underlying principles of social service, something of real importance in the history of the new republic.

But we were also doing a bit of local reconstruction as well. In the winter of 1922-3 Engineer H made a beginning of a boys' club for the youth of the nearby villages. There were three of these, two of them on the Austrian side of the old frontier, and one on the Russian. We had long since discovered that animosities arising from the fact of the frontier had left shadows behind them which only time could erase. These boys, however, soon got to know one another, and enjoyed the parties at which no vodka was served, the rather primitive films we were able to show, and the elementary dramatic productions they themselves staged. When one of the village priests told his flock that the Red Triangle had been condemned by the Holy Father, the peasants shook their heads and said that 'He could not be referring to our YMCA.' Seeing the possibilities and the need, we even considered a plan to organise an experiment in rural community work, for nothing was more needed in the new Poland. The project, however, had to be abandoned, partly because we had no trained worker in this field.

Only in 1925 did the authorities get around to making the rather primitive road which went past our door to Ojców into something like a decent highway. Up to then the place had been difficult of access, especially in bad weather. From now on things were much better since we had everything needed for vacationing except a swimming pool. One attraction was the picturesque valley, almost a canyon, in which lay the ancient village of Ojców (already before 1914 becoming known as a summer resort); while a further mile away stood an ancient castle ruin, Piaskowa Skala. Beyond this lay some of the wildest country, and the most backward, in southern Poland. The soil was poor, it lay remote from the railway, and had been cut off by the frontier from its natural contacts with Cracow. I found villages in this area without a decent well, and until the first years of this century there were still wooden ploughs in use on some holdings. All this provided for Osada an environment with plenty of interest to the social worker, while the garden and orchard at home gave us many a pleasant hour of lounging in off-hours.

By the autumn of 1924, however, it was becoming clear that the Polish association could not any longer make adequate use of the property. What was to be done? It seemed advisable to follow up a lead from the National Association of Elementary School Teachers whose secretary, Dr E. Nowicki, was urging a plan to found a second Peasants' High School on the Danish model in Poland. This association was strongly leftish in its political views, and was well aware of how much needed to be done for the young men and women of the villages beyond what they got in school. They were looking about for a place to begin with this work, and it seemed clear that Osada would serve the purpose. One of our own national council members, Aleksander Janowski, knew the situation well and supported the plan for turning over Osada to the teachers as soon as the Polish association was through with it. He even proposed that joint use could be made, the Polish High School being accommodated during the winter months.

We sounded out the Ministry of Education, and found that there was no objection to such a merger, and early in 1925 the arrangements for a transfer of Osada were completed. The whole plant was handed over, with the exception of a few furnishings, and the occupants were to use it rent-free. From a letter received from William Orr, who had long since been busy in Salonika but never ceased to keep in touch with our Polish work, I quote the following: 'The news about the new enterprise at Osada has been a source of unalloyed satisfaction. The pictures you sent of the familiar scenes revealed to me what a firm hold Osada has on my interest and affection. You deserve the greatest credit for saving this plant for the second time ... Please convey to Dr Nowicki my warmest congratulations on what he has accomplished and on the happy prospects for the future.'

A number of reports of the work done by this Peasants' High School in subsequent years are beside me as I write. From them one can see that no mistake was made in the transfer, and that the choice as principal of a Cracow graduate in engineering, Ignacy Solarz (who had been a member of the student executive in the early twenties), was a happy one. After the Congress of Historians, held in Warsaw in the summer of 1933, I was able to make a flying visit to Osada with a young American university professor and, though we found the place empty of students, it was easy to see that the best of traditions were being maintained. Only the long tennis court had not been kept up; but in its centre stood a mighty stone on the flat side of which was engraved the name of the village genius from the foothills of the Carpathians who had become one of the most celebrated prose and novel writers of his generation – Władysław Orkan. His name had been given to the school and his spirit pervaded it. No better choice could have been made.

5 CRACOW CITY

The work of the Red Triangle in the historic city of Cracow had been opened in the autumn of 1919 by E.J. Oberholzer of New England. As he later put it: 'I had one room, a box for a chair, and a shelf for a desk.' From a modest beginning in the Old Arsenal on Castle Street, right under Wawel Hill, where a canteen for the troops were set up, it grew inside of a year to imposing dimensions. A one-time riding school in the heart of the city was turned into a cinema and concert hall, and regular work in games and gymnastics organised. Finally, when the threat of invasion from the east matured, Cracow became more important as a base of operations, and a spacious Officers' Club was opened in the Hunters' Club beyond the railway station. Though engaged to the limit with military work, Oberholzer made not a few friends among civilians, and a new phase began after the visit of Dr Mott in June 1920.

Earlier that year H.W. Long had arrived from the United States to help with sports and games, and before the fall he and his wife were settled in Cracow with the express purpose of promoting physical training for young people. We were able to get the use of the Sokół Hall, one of the few indoor gymnasiums in the country, and before Christmas a full-scale programme was under way. I lent a hand with the club work, in particular with organising our library and reading-room. As adjutant, Oberholzer had a fine young Polish lieutenant, Tadeusz Michalik, who handled all routine matters while at the same time making himself familiar with our basic principles and methods. We were already a team.

Our first Christmas in Cracow was marked by a warm invitation to the Oberholzers, the Longs, and ourselves to spend the hours of Christmas Eve (known in Polish as *Wigilia*) at supper in the hostel and club of the Welfare Society for Apprentices on Krupnica Street. A keen interest in this formerly neglected group of youth had long been taken by Michał Dziewicki and his wife (the man who was translating Reymont's *The Peasants*); but the moving spirit of the whole enterprise was the frail but tireless servant of God and society, the Jesuit Father Kuśnowicz. Starting long before the war, when living conditions of apprentices in the city were primitive, he had by his courage and faith cajoled and shamed the people of Cracow into providing a real, though far from adequate, home for these ex-village lads; and he welcomed such help as relief agencies could give him in improving this service. Madame Dziewicki used to tell of days when few apprentices knew what a handkerchief was; and when the majority, their day's work done, would clean the floor of the shop, throw down a straw mattress or two, and sleep there – often in their working clothes.

We sat down that evening to a real supper, a company of some sixty in all, and enjoyed afterwards a programme of songs, speeches, and good fellowship. Two volunteer workers from this society, themselves one-time apprentices, had been present at our Workers' Training Course in Modlin, and this link was now the stronger since Long was busy two evenings a week with the boys at games. Two years later the society acquired its own sports field on the Blonie Plain outside town, and here the Red Triangle workers helped to set up an all-round programme of physical education.

Rarely have I met a man who lived and worked with such devotion as did Father Kuśnowicz. He loved boys, and had a keen sense of the right and wrong ways of helping them. Not without incurring censure from some members of his order, he insisted on training the youth as they grew up, not only to look after themselves as workmen but also to organize their own cultural and spiritual activities. With this end in view he stuck to his guns until he was able to send off to the United States for study and observation one of his promising assistants, who came back in due course and took up responsible work at home. By that time, thanks in part to the shaking-up given to the city of Cracow by the fund-raising campaign for the new YMCA building, the father was able to launch a scheme for a fine new home for his society, in which it entered on a quite new phase of its history. What had been a grain of mustard-seed was now become a mighty tree, and 'the fowls of the air came and lodged there.' But I am far ahead of my story. Returning, let me say that one of the things encouraged by Father K from the start was amateur theatricals; and the first performance I saw of Rydel's Christmas Play (*Jaselko*) was done by the boys and older men of his society.

And now a diversion. If Father K had been busy for years removing one of the reproaches of Cracow, an older man, also a churchman, had set us all a grand example in the general field of dealing with the homeless and outcast. I refer, of course, to the celebrated Brother Albert, whom I did indeed see but never got to know. Son of a well-known family, he had lost a leg as a mere boy in the rising of 1863-4, but in time settled down in Cracow as a promising painter. Suddenly, for some unknown reason, he discovered the bodily and spiritual hopelessness of the down-and-outs who frequented the doss-houses of the city, and he threw up everything to go and live among these tramps and beggars. From now on he gave his life to their rehabilitation. In a monk's habit he could be seen at the task, and in time he was joined by others – a sort of Brotherhood. Not without justice was he called 'one of the greatest Poles of our time.' True, it is open to question whether his was the best way of dealing with this phase of the social evil – something to which the YMCA has not (to my knowledge) given special attention. As one leader put it: 'We are concerned less with the "down-and-outs" and more with the "starting-outs."' But, as will appear, we did tackle this issue in Cracow in a small way, and the Warsaw association was later on to make it one of their major concerns.

By the early summer of 1921 the war work of the Red Triangle in Poland was completed, and voices were being raised in favour of launching a civilian programme. If a Polish association was one day to come into being, preparatory work was necessary, and Cracow seemed to be a suitable place. In May word came from Taylor, who was abroad for a European conference, that I was to get ready to take over the Cracow centre with a view to experimental work in the civilian field. At first I recoiled from the idea, as nothing in my training had fitted me for this enterprise and the prospect of administrative duties did not attract me. But it did make sense. My predecessor knew no Polish, and he had been identified officially with the American mission as I never was. His success in the war work was unquestioned, but this was now over and a new approach had to be made. Scouting had to be done among influential people, and some assurance gained of moral and material backing for the new venture. Cracow was not a wealthy place, but support could be found for any worthy project.

We arranged for Taylor to come to Cracow to speak at a gathering of invited guests, to whom we served tea in the diningroom of the Grand Hotel. His address met with such approval that, for lack of discussion, the meeting threatened to fall flat. I therefore grasped the nettle, and turned it into a 'farewell' to the Oberholzers. At once tongues were loosened – people would speak on a concrete theme who did not care to talk on generalities. Warm tributes were paid by representative people, among them the vice-mayor, to the work done by the American mission, and the hope expressed that its departure would not mean an end of work still going on. From that day the way opened up, and we could get down to our task.

From a report made to headquarters in December I note the following items of progress:
1 Changes in staff with a view to getting more balance and improved quality.
2 The creation of sections, with men or women of university level in charge of each.
3 The setting up of a Vocational Guidance Bureau, which could give more personal attention than was usual with the city agencies.
4 The launching in November of special work for 'street arabs,' most of whom were orphans and homeless.
5 The extension of our physical training programme, in particular the September Swimming Course conducted by Long and his helpers for which 900 tickets had been sold.

Before leaving for home Oberholzer had effected the closing down of the Officers' Club. The riding school programme had long since become unnecessary. Almost all our activities were centred around the Castle Street building, where our library attracted attention and discussion clubs were formed. Out of one of them came a man who before 1939 was nationally known as a poet and thinker. Nearby we secured a room big enough to set up a brush-making shop in which boys could start learning a trade. From August onward fortnightly staff meetings (we were twenty in number) were inaugurated for exchange of views on theory and practice. Finally, Michalik was able to get the use of the hall in the Industrial Museum and begin the showing of educational films of various types – nothing startling, but at least a variant from the kind of stuff to be seen in most cinemas.

By April 1922 we had made some headway with our projects, though not without set-backs. An epidemic that broke out in the Orphans' Home, where some of the boys slept, dislocated the workshop for a time, but the service done to the 'street Arabs' as a group went on. From the start the cost was borne from gifts from outside our regular budget. An American Polish visitor started the fund, then Mrs Taylor gave us something; then the women workers contributed their Christmas bonuses. Of this last, part was used to set up a Christmas party, the boys decorating their own tree. Arnold of the Russian POW Branch of the Red Triangle gave us clothes and shoes. Two unexpected gifts in March ensured the continuation of the effort into the summer.

The beginning of this piece of service had been almost like a fairy tale. All of us had noticed these lads dodging about the street corners, living by their wits. On a cold morning in November one of our workers told three of them, who were selling matches, to come along to Auntie Imka[9] at ten o'clock and get a mug of cocoa. They were to bring any of their 'pals' as well. Twenty turned up, half-starved and shivering, of course without overcoats. We started with that number, turning away older boys who wanted to join in. The rule was that they should come from the shelter (where they slept) first thing each morning, wash with hot water and soap, say their prayers, and then get cocoa and buns. Then followed some games and even lessons, lasting until noon; after which they were free for the day. By Christmas we had them doing some sort of handicraft – crude, of course, and some of them would stay the afternoons. Intractable at first, they soon entered into the spirit of the thing, and after New Year's Day the smarter ones joined the brush-making course. From February we got a food allowance from the ARA, and were able to give the fifteen 'reliables' a hot dinner each day.

9 IMKA, Polish sounds for YMCA, a Polish song was written with the title 'Auntie YMCA.'

We were under no illusions as to the gamble involved in all this – as long as the lads were living in a public shelter where adults of both sexes went in and out nothing really constructive could be accomplished. A home was needed, and the American Red Cross assured us of cots and bedding for this, but no place could be found to house them. Nevertheless, some good was done, and I know that the odd boy was saved for a life of usefulness.

In the summer of 1922 our general outlook was favourable. Preliminary negotiations with the ministry in regard to the forming of a Polish association were going forward, and we had secured a good many new friends for the idea in Cracow. A fresh step was to be taken by putting Michalik in charge of our activities (Long was still director of sports and games), so that I could be free to give all my time to preparing the way for a civilian organisation, when out of the blue came disaster – we lost him. The tragic blow thus sustained taught me more than one lesson, so I must explain what happened.

A year earlier he had married one of our women workers, Helena T. I had first met her as a helper in our Wilno centre, and she had later been moved (during the war threat) first to the capital and then to Cracow. The young couple were living not a block from our flat, and I was called out of bed one May morning by our servant with the word that an accident had happened and I was wanted at once. The maid from the family where the Michaliks lived was at the door; she knew only that a shot had been heard and that the lieutenant was hurt. I got there quickly to find him lying on his bed, with a bullet hole under his right eye, and a service revolver on the coverlet about the height of his navel. His wife was dressed, sitting in the other room with a fellow-worker who lived in the same flat; both of them were weeping. Before long the police arrived, and the story Helena told was that they were planning to go out for an early walk, that her husband always carried his revolver when out at unusual hours, and that, while trying it after he sat up in bed, he had accidentally touched the trigger – and shot himself.

The police held a council around the bed, behind closed doors, and seemed ready to accept the verdict 'accidental death'; though a stupid rumour got about that it was suicide, which nearly prevented us from getting him a Christian burial. I was so upset by it all and, in general, tired by the winter's work, that I did not sit down and analyze the story bit by bit. Had I done so I should have seen (what I saw long afterwards) that the whole thing was a fabrication. The course of the bullet was downward through the pillow, which was soaked with blood. This would not have been the case if what the wife told was true. Nor could the weapon have lain where it did, without any finger-prints on it. Too late I saw that murder had been done – as subsequent events were to show.

Our work went on as before, and I made a second mistake in allowing the widow to continue in a responsible position. One day a sum of money from our Student Relief Fund was missing from my desk, and she threw the blame on a youth whom we had been helping to find work. There were also other mysterious things occurring, but it was only during our summer course at Osada in early August that things broke open. A messenger arrived from town to say that there had been a fire in the office; it had been put out, but someone should come in. That evening Mrs M disappeared. Investigation showed that she must have tried to put things on fire, including new banknotes. These had refused to burn, and she got in a panic. Too late, we examined the stores in another building to find that sugar, flour, and other things were missing. Then we knew the truth.

Two of our workers followed her and found her in Danzig (Gdańsk). She would not admit anything, and when her father (who lived in Pomerania) came at the invitation of our head office to Warsaw, he told us that he had warned Berry in Wilno never to trust the girl with money. In the confusion of moving this warning was forgotten, and with the consequences here set out. She had always dressed beyond her means, explaining this by the fact that she had some private income from a farm. To pay these bills she sold things from our stores, and the controller's check-up in Cracow, made while I was away on furlough, was not thorough enough. The result was a broken-hearted mother, a sorrowing sister and two brothers – and the loss of one of our most promising younger workers. The fault was in part at least mine, as I should have kept a closer watch on routine matters. But I learned this lesson – never to have on my staff both a husband and wife. Suspicious as I had been of Mrs M, I did not act with despatch in order not to embarrass the husband. An old Polish proverb, a variant of our own, tells of the man who is wise after the harm has been done.

Before assuming the task of preparing the ground for a Polish association in Cracow, I had consulted a number of trusted friends. The outburst of opinion against our critics in 1921 was embarrassing in that it went too far; but great as was the gratitude of the public for the war service, prudence told me that this alone was no safe basis on which to build a structure that would last. Almost to a man my counsellors said, 'Go ahead!' They saw the need, and were ready to lend a hand in meeting it. One of them said, 'Get the backing of university people, and the thing will not fail!'

My first concern was to have some financial support assured for our present activities. Less and less was available from the Warsaw office, and already our members were paying small dues. But another thing was no less vital – the securing of a group of sponsors out of which might emerge the future board of directors of the association. Acting in an advisory capacity, it could in time assume full responsibility for what was done.

One step of importance had to be taken at once. The lease on our quarters in Castle Street was bound to end any time, and others had to be found. In a civilian club-room we should be our own masters, and could watch things grow. Our group of sponsors would have a place to meet, when necessary, free from any obligations toward the army. As the group took shape it was seen to include professors, business and professional people, civil servants and journalists. The large majority were Catholics, but three were members of the Protestant faith. In an old notebook I find the record kept of contributions made during the early months of 1923. From fifteen friends I had received 300,000 marks in December; in January the number of givers was twenty-four and the total doubled. No one declined to help, and when our head office heard of what was going on they wrote me a letter of congratulations. These sums were not as large as they might look, for inflation was already out of hand; but they did help us substantially with our monthly expenditure.

Meanwhile the search for a new home was rewarded. A corner 'locum' was found on Retoryka Street opposite the Sokół building which had been a dramshop and 'pub,' and had living quarters behind it. The rooms were small, but the largest at a pinch could accommodate up to fifty people. The former tenant got a premium for vacating the place, and the major share of costs of renovating were gladly paid by headquarters. The work done in this place during the next three years was enormous.

Super had assurance from New York that the master-plan initiated by Dr Mott, for securing bigger gifts from American industrialists to construct association buildings abroad, designed at first for China, was also being extended to include Europe. This meant that, wherever evidence was forthcoming of maturity on the part of a local association, there was a good chance of securing money for construction. The condition was that the costs of equipment and furnishing were to be borne by those on the spot.

All this presented me with a serious issue. I was willing to do the spade-work needful for such an undertaking, perhaps I had more fitness for it than some others; but I had neither the experience nor the courage necessary for superintending an important piece of construction and managing a city association. We knew that, when things were ready, master plans would be provided by New York, which the chosen architect would adapt to his needs; but a large sum of money was involved, and the raising of a substantial sum locally for furnishing the new quarters was to be guaranteed. For such a task only a man 'who knew his onions' was competent, and such a man should now be sought for. When I put the matter to Super he agreed with me, and the search was begun.

Fortune favoured us. E.O. Jacob of Illinois had been for years an association worker in the Near East, and had just been through the Smyrna debacle.[10] He spoke French well, and when approached expressed willingness to come and look over the possibilities. His brief visit ended happily, and the matter was settled. Early in the summer of 1923 he arrived with his wife and son and, joining us all at Osada, he began to learn the rudiments of Polish. Before leaving for my six months' furlough, I was able to hand over to him the work I had been doing, including the supervision of our summer school site.

Few more competent men could have been found for the job than Jacob. He was given a cordial welcome by the group of sponsors, one of whom remarked afterwards that he made everybody work like dogs, and himself set a tireless example. Among his advisers was the older man, whom I had met on my first visit in Cracow in February 1919, Tadeusz Żuk-Skarszewski. A veteran journalist and the author of several books, he had lived early in the century in St Petersburg and had for a time served his liberated country as a press man in New York. Possessed of classical features and a mane of greying hair, he looked curiously like the portraits of Franz Liszt. Now he was to throw all his wisdom and energy into something quite new; and was to be given, in due course, the honour of turning the first sod when excavations began on Krowoderska Street.

Shortly after my return to Poland in January 1924 news arrived that Mott was coming to Europe. We had good grounds for believing that something would be done for Cracow, and so it turned out. When he arrived, a formal reception was arranged in which city and university officials took part. In the evening he met the sponsors' group and senior workers at a dinner and business session in the Hotel Poller. When Professor Marchlewski saw the composition of the party, he remarked to me that it was made up almost to a man of whose who had worked in war time on the Prince Bishop's Relief Committee. The fact was auspicious, for these men knew and trusted one another. They could be depended on to see through to a finish whatever they took in hand. We heard later that our visitor got the best of impressions from what he saw and heard; he said that this group was one of the best of its kind he had ever encountered.

In his address of thanks to Dr Mott for his presence, the chairman recalled occasions as far back as 1365 when Cracow had welcomed distinguished guests (among them five crowned heads), and contrasted the modesty of the present reception with the splendour and extravagance of other days. But, he went on, 'even those kings lacked the power which is behind the man being honoured today - that of a noble and lofty ideal':

In Europe ideals and business do not rhyme. We hold still the old conception of the idealist as an unpractical dreamer, and of the business man as a shrewd fellow

---

10 Recapture of Smyrna (Izmir) in 1921 marked Turkey's victory in a war with Greece. Many civilians perished in the first days of Turkish reoccupation.

whose eyes are directed earthwards ... Thus we were surprised when an American business man offered a fortune for the erection of a YMCA building in Cracow ... And now you, Sir, come to us as the standard-bearer of these ideals, to help us with your counsel. We are not used to this, and are obliged to revise our ideas ... Has not the money of business men been behind all the idealistic enterprises of the American nation; behind the religious communities which have sent expeditions to Poland to feed the hungry, clothe the naked, nurse the sick? Were they not inspired by the words of Scripture, 'Cast thy bread upon the waters, for thou shalt find it after many days?'

The story of the Cracow building project, in particular of how Jacob organised a city-wide campaign, the first of its kind in this part of Europe, for the raising of twenty thousand dollars – real money! – for equipment, cannot be told here. The money came in from every quarter, in spite of some opposition from clerical circles; most of it was in small sums, and the number of donors who paid in tiny monthly amounts was enormous. This sum represented at least three times the value it would mean in the New World, and sufficed to meet the need. The formal opening and consecration of the building was a milestone in Polish association history, and representatives were present from all over the country. First among the 'heroes' were the architect, Wacław Krzyżanowski, and the general secretary, E.O. Jacob.

6
Liberated Poland 3

6 THE POLISH ASSOCIATION

In his first workers' meetings in Warsaw and elsewhere, before he had committed himself to stay in Europe, Super took up the questions later to be set out in his book *What is the YMCA?*[1] From the angle of social psychology he would ask what is meant by 'association' and help his group to realise how many kinds of this phenomenon can be met with, though one central concept quickens them all. He would then show how out of an association grows an institution, as its visible expression; but how, behind and underneath it, giving it content and form, was a movement. With the maturing of associations into institutions, which operate through buildings and machinery of all sorts, there is a danger that 'togetherness' may be crowded into the background, that the visible thing may come to take the place of the invisible force. This last must be constantly regenerating its life or the whole structure will topple.

The word 'movement' has an interesting history. Doubtless this goes far back, but in modern times it has been with us since what began in Oxford in 1833. It is, of course, a metaphor – taken from physical life; but it has been reinforced by all that has happened in the field of modern machines, and is associated in our minds today above all with power. And so we come back to the much overworked term we owe to the Greeks, 'dynamic' as opposed to 'static'; two terms used in our time of societies, of ages, indeed of individual personalities. On the analogy of the human organism they are said to be conceived, born, grow, flour-

[1] Paul Super, *What is the YMCA?* (1922)

ish, and then fail and die. Whether this last need be the fate of movements and institutions is debatable; history shows how true it has often been, but *need* it be so? Can institutions renew their life; not become 'white elephants,' but adapt themselves, live afresh with each new age, and serve as well as they did in the beginning?

These questions, together with the further one, 'Is not every movement at bottom a fellowship?' were in our minds for many months as the prospects grew of the birth of a Polish Young Men's Christian Association. There was little doubt as to the answer we hoped to give; but could we count on the projection of the forces inherent in a movement into the succeeding institution? And could all this be set out in a constitution, in such a way as to safeguard what was relevant to the cause while at the same time meeting the peculiar conditions of a traditionally Roman Catholic society? The more we studied the situation, the more our conviction grew that the answer to all these queries was a confident 'Yes!' As noted already, the general atmosphere in the country was favourable to an association of laymen of all social groups and religious affiliations, although there were people distinctly hostile.

On going through the seven-page draft report, which I helped to draw up, I find that we stressed the following points:

1 Desire to put into service for the new Polish republic the fruits of three generations of experience gained by the YMCA in other lands.
2 Recognition of the fact that these must be adapted to existing conditions, and brought into line with the best Polish tradition in education.
3 Desirability of lay control, while welcoming the collaboration of the clergy.
4 The wish of the association always to serve the church in every possible way.
5 Need for the type of lay leadership that would command the confidence of the public.
6 Need for carefully chosen and trained workers, whose one thought would be the service of God and their fellows.
7 Necessity for close collaboration with primary institutions such as the home the school, the community, and other voluntary agencies.

As our plans matured, and it became clear that the man behind this projec would be asking for the help of American specialists over a period of years, w concluded that a relatively small-scale action was wiser. Three city association would be our first objective, created in centres where the work of the Red Tr angle had been known and prized. These were Cracow, the most visited of a Polish cities, home of national traditions since the end of the Middle Ages; Wa saw, largest of Polish cities and national capital; and Łódź, the chief industri city of this part of the continent. Such help as might come from outside for tł erection of buildings was to be used in these places, in the hope of giving a d monstration of what could be achieved. Success won in them, together with the witness of boys' camps and other auxiliaries, would suffice as a pledge for the future. Expansion into other cities, or even into rural life, would only be a matter of time.

Yet not quite. The determining factor would be the emergence of young men, some of them growing up through our boys' departments, who proved themselves as willing, devoted, and competent leaders. There was no lack of human material; but as the economic and administrative life of the nation recovered from the shocks and disorders of war the opportunities beckoning would be legion, and many of these would offer rewards of a material kind far in excess of anything to be had from association work. Some of the men who had served under the Red Triangle were promising, and as things turned out they were to be the first executives of the Polish association. But their number was not large, and they needed much more experience. Some of this training could be expected as the result of courses such as those held at Osada; but most of it had to be won from the daily routine of association work, from watching their seniors in action, just as the apprentices of old learned 'by doing' under the eyes of a master. By way of parenthesis let it be said that Super was criticized by some for not having realized in fact more of his fine ideas about 'the training of a staff.' At times I myself felt that more could have been done. We made mistakes in regard to men, expecting of some more than they could deliver; and we lost some of our ablest men to industry and to government service – how could it be otherwise? But in most cases these men remained staunch supporters, members of boards of directors, and valuable champions of all the association stood for. They were not really 'lost.'

The Constituent Convention met in Warsaw in December 1923, during my absence from the country. A splendid, though difficult job was done. Much debate had been held as to the name of the new organisation, and a brilliant compromise was reached. A double name was agreed on: The Union of Christian Youth – Polish YMCA. The first part defined its character, the second indicated its tradition. A new creature had been born, but the link with the past was maintained. No honest person could be in doubt as to the nature of the enterprise. What is more, in spite of the fears widely mooted about the 'Triangle,' the convention insisted that it be retained. Thus was the emphasis on the three-fold nature of the human being, whether scientific or not, commended as something justified in practice.

The delegates met on a Saturday morning, and attended mass in the Church of the Capucines. Then followed a long business session, the closing minutes of which were honoured by a brief visit from the president of the republic.[2] In the

---

2 Stanisław Wójciechowski, second president of Poland, succeeded Gabrial Narutowicz who had been assassinated after only two days in office.

afternoon and again on Sunday morning discussions went on, devoted to principles and methods of work; and the gathering ended with a formal luncheon, attended by representatives of the city and the province. Thus was set in motion a venture of faith, involving people of more than one national background, of at least three religious affiliations, and of wide differences of tradition and experience.

Enough has been said already about objections taken by some of the clergy, and a few lay people, to any such undertaking. They were smothered by the enthusiasm and resolve of those who took the opposite view. The principle of lay responsibility for leadership in youth guidance triumphed. It had already been accepted in 1911 when the Boy Scout movement made its beginning in Poland; it was now to be entrenched and extended, this time without the need to ask for any favours from an alien power.

One reasoned argument against all this had appeared a few months before the association was constituted, and I quote a single paragraph from it:

When General Haller accepted the help of the YMCA for the Polish Army in France, he at once made the condition that the organisation was to bring to the soldier moral and material aid, but to keep itself altogether from every political and religious agitation. Otherwise the general would not have agreed either to the YMCA working in the army under his charge or to its coming with him to Poland. All the same the YMCA has now begun so-called 'peace-time work,' i.e. planting on our savage soil the true religion of Christ! The Polish land is in darkness and demands, according to these people, the work of missionaries! The YMCA provides these and is finding a large number of Poles whose wish it is also to plant (sic) Christianity in a land that was Christian before Columbus was born.

With this somewhat sarcastic introduction the writer went on to say that Poland had in Catholicism the surest bulwark against both inner weaknesses and outer dangers - for example, Bolshevism. He also expressed grave fears as to the way the Polish association, if and when it became a fact, might become subject to an international board, on which sat Free Masons, or even Jews. The moral, therefore, was 'Beware in time!'

The people who took this line were very much in earnest, but those to whom they appealed could not take them seriously. It was expressly set out that the national council, and under it the local boards of directors, were in complete control - even the actions of the American helpers remaining in the country were scrutinized with care. On those boards the majority were Catholic in convictions, men of whose integrity there could be no doubt. Among them differences of opinion did at times arise with regard to tactics, but never on a matter of principle.

To me, who knew the whole field, it soon became clear that the spirit and atmosphere prevailing in the three city associations were distinctive, that of Cracow more devout, that of Warsaw more free-thinking and 'ethical,' that of Łódź more social and practical. Yet the blending of the three emphases was remarkable. When it came to dealing with young lives on the workaday level there was no difference to be seen. Frank Eyman had done years of splendid work as director of sports and games in Warsaw before he was asked to set up the first regular season programme in the new Cracow gymnasium. He became as much loved by the boys and young men there as he had been in the capital. The same thing would have been the case had he remained in Poland long enough to launch the wider programme possible in the new building in Łódź.

One word more. The concern mentioned by the writer of the paragraph quoted above was quite uncalled for. In the sense in which he used the word 'religious agitation,' the hands of the Polish YMCA were completely clean. However, if the term is understood in the wider sense – that used by the noted Polish nineteenth-century thinker, August Cieszkowski, 'Religion is everything for all!'– then the association must plead guilty, but with a clear conscience. On this ground it would have behind it not only the great body of Polish laymen, but also the witness of Polish history. No people in Europe is more unfortunately situated on the map than Poland; only then can the nation hope to maintain itself as a free society if it unites all its powers, seen and unseen, temporal and spiritual, in a single resolve to survive. One of those powers, perhaps the most effective of all, is faith in God and man, undisturbed by theological differences or dissensions.

And the consequences of all this for me personally? Having been absent for six months, it might look as though I was 'out of work' on my return. Where was I to fit into the 'machine?' I was no longer needed in Cracow, where Jacob had a first-rate assistant in the person of Jan Stanisławski, later to become lecturer in English in the university. My relations with the SCM continued, but could not be called a full-time job. I wanted to get down to study, but that was only possible in my free time.

For a few weeks I was told to 'look around' in order to become acquainted again. Then I was given the task of preparing a short pamphlet on the Polish YMCA, 'Facts for Friends in America,' a copy of which is before me as I write. Then a new project was suggested, the publishing of a regular news sheet, indeed a periodical, to be called *Wiadomości*, to appear at least six times a year, the aim of which would be to keep the various branches of the association in touch with each other and to get news of what was going on to friends outside our membership. From now on, though we lived in Cracow until the summer of 1925, I was given a desk in the head office, and spent much of my time there.

In taking on editorial responsibilities for something in a language other than my own, I was asking for trouble – and it soon appeared. The materials that came in were in either Polish or English, and, of course, I got help in preparing them all for the printer. But I should have realized that there had been no Poland during the nineteenth century, and therefore no central, accepted authority (such as France has had in her Academy) to settle many a moot question as to style, grammatical usage, or even spelling. Polish colleagues coming from opposite ends of the country often differed radically as to what was correct or elegant; a fact that was made worse by their being educated, in many cases, in German or Russian schools, their own being denied them. Their feeling for their mother tongue was as varied as instincts usually are. If ever a man needed to walk delicately, and even when things seemed safe to take still another look, it was I.

For the first number, one of our senior Polish workers had been asked to write a front page, introducing both the association and its organ; and this he did, quite nicely. Using my connections, I made arrangements for printing in Cracow with a well-known firm, but again I saw too late that this was a mistake. The manager of the firm was not Polish-born but a Czech, who was indeed educated but was as capable of errors as myself. We got our proofs, and they were duly 'corrected.' I trusted the firm's proof-reader to do the rest. The day came when I could bring to our financial secretary, E.R. Cummings, in the head office, the finished product. I laid it before him with a sense of relief.

Alas for my sentiments! At noon the next day I was called into Super's room, to find him and Cummings looking worried. The number of *Wiadomości* had been seen the night before by a member of the national council, and pronounced unusable! On the front page were a number of blemishes, including misspelling of proper names; objection was taken to various phrases elsewhere, and the punctuation was faulty. To publish it would bring down a host of criticisms that would hurt the cause. It had to be 'killed.'

Cummings was very long-suffering, and did not ask me to pay the bill. We changed our printer, the whole thing was sent back for resetting, and it reappeared ten days late. It was a lesson to me; in future I saw that someone of unimpeachable reputation proof-read each number in page-proof before passing it for publication. But one bit of smartness I never reported. The writer of the introductory article had heard of the trouble before I did, and saved his own skin. Finding in the drawer of my desk all the 'copy' of the number, he filched his own production and destroyed it! When I checked things I saw at once what had happened, but decided not to let him run the risk of losing his job. He has long since been gathered to his fathers and 'taken his wages.'

An experience of quite a different kind, though no less challenging, came my way at least twice a year, when the general secretary called at one of the local associations a workers' conference at which all helpers from all centres (so far as possible) were in attendance. It would last as a rule a day-and-a-half, and at least three longish sessions were held, mostly with discussion, in which everyone was expected to say just what he thought. Super was particularly good at this kind of thing, but he laboured under a severe language disability. The meetings had to be in Polish, and he knew very little in those days. That is where I came in, for it fell to me not only to interpret what he had to say but to keep him posted every minute as to what was going on. Nothing disturbed him more than to be in a gathering with something under discussion without his following it.

Of course we went carefully over the proposed agenda before the conference, but even this did not prepare us for surprises. If something needed translating word for word, I made notes in advance. Others would prompt me where a word or phrase would not come, and we got on without too much loss of time. During discussion I sat next to the chief and made notes in English for him to follow, so that he was never out of touch with the trend of things. It was a wearing business before the day was over, but none-the-less good fun. At times I had to act as 'skipper' in spite of myself. Super would be watching the clock, and whisper, 'Drive ahead, Bill!' or 'We must push on faster!' for he knew how much there was to be done. Having the sense of the meeting better than he, I had on occasion to say 'No!' for we did not want any difficult matter to be left hanging in the air. This kind of experience did much to convince him in time that he must leave other things and devote some attention to the Polish language.

The autumn of 1925 brought me a task that could only be called formidable. For the World's Convention of YMCAs to be held the following summer in Helsinki, a long and comprehensive questionnaire had been prepared, covering not only the work of the various associations, but many other matters, like the attitudes of youth toward social, religious, and educational issues. Materials were needed on historical points – in short, every field of human interest seemed to be there. These questionnaires reached us in November, and we were given three months to get them circulated, answered, and co-ordinated into something like a readable document. The whole thing was laid on my desk, and I did little else in the next weeks than push the undertaking. Both staff and members were laid under contribution, and every department had its specific set of questions. People responded magnificently, and I was snowed under from New Year's Day on with documents – mostly, of course, in Polish.

To digest this material, to sort out what was characteristic of the whole from what diverged sharply, to draft a résumé (often quoting at length) of each section, and then to make a reasoned 'report' of the whole that would not be one-sided or tendentious – that was a labour of Hercules. But here my work in the student field stood me in good stead, and I could call in helpers of experience wherever necessary. Our report was a little behind time, and enquiries from Geneva kept coming, which told us that other countries had sent theirs in, so 'Why not you?' When we finally got it off, the document amounted to sixty pages of typescript – close to 25,000 words. Within ten days word came to Super to say that at last they had got something worth while. Other people had done the thing casually, putting little care or thought into it. Our report from Poland, though our association did not belong to the world's alliance, was recognised as one of the best.

Super has told little about the Helsinki convention in his book. It meant more to some of the rest of us, in particular to our Polish colleagues who had never attended such a meeting, than it did to an old war-horse like him. Both the journey into an unknown world and the gathering itself meant a lot to me, and I count myself lucky to have been a member of the delegation. For one thing I met many old friends; for another, I saw with my own eyes the pattern of living created by the Finns – one of the most gallant and competent nations of Europe. The brief glance we had en route of what was going on in Latvia and Esthonia, only seven years after liberation, was no less cheering. Then we had close on a hundred people with us on the way home, mostly Americans whom Super persuaded to change their plans and see something of Central Europe; and though I had a trying time making the travelling arrangements and was nearly a wreck at the end, this too was worth doing. Among our guests was the stately and cordial Metropolitan Archbishop of Greece, Athenagoras, and the press in Warsaw and Cracow said some nice things about this distinguished company of visitors.

7 POLAND'S MANCHESTER

Few more incongruous or uglier sights can have existed in the civilised world in the early years of this century than the city, if city it was, that stood on the open plains in the very heart of Poland, called 'the Polish Manchester,' Łódź. In it lived at least 400,000 souls, most of them engaged in spinning, weaving, and dyeing cotton wares; but there was little sense of community, there was no proper municipal authority, and there were neither sewers nor a central water supply. The controls were really in Russian hands; the owners and managers of the cotton mills were mostly of German or Jewish blood, while the workers were chiefly Poles from the surrounding rural area, or again the poorest and most ignorant type of Jew. Not for nothing did Reymont choose this 'monstrum' as the scene for his two-volume tale *The Promised Land* – which indeed it was, whether for the youth seeking employment or the ambitious, often gambling, entrepreneur in industry. In the hey-day of *laisser faire* fortunes could be made quickly, and lost just as readily.

Before 1820 there was here only a tiny village, surrounded by forests. Then came parties of adventurous weavers from Saxony, attracted by the markets of the east and by the presence of clear water in a chain of small lakes. By the forties they had secured power machinery, mostly from Belgium; in the sixties gas lighting was introduced and banking established; a few years later the railway connection with Warsaw and the west was completed. From now on growth was assured, but everyone thought of himself or his firm, and few had any concern for the social or cultural interests of this faraway place. The traveller who approached it by rail or road (if the trails through the open country could be called roads) saw in front of him a forest of chimneys, belching smoke when times were good; then he entered built-up areas through which ran a single long street (the Piotrków Road), at the end of which was a small square with some ugly buildings around it — one of which was known as the town hall. But there was neither a park nor a monument of any kind, the lighting was primitive, and most of the 'streets' had ditches beside them to carry off drainage in wet weather. In dry spells the dust was unbearable.

When I first saw Łódź it was not pretty to look at. Of course it never had been. People were interested in utility but not in beauty. Like Topsy, it had just 'growed.' Periods of prosperity had alternated with those of depression; but for the immediate prewar years the story was one of expansion. Everybody had a chance to earn, and those who could stand the pace got on well. Around each of the dozen or more larger mills clustered an industrial slum, and the artesian wells which provided water for the works served the workers from pumps worked by hand. Only in the homes of the wealthy was there indoor plumbing. A slow-moving stream ran across the middle of the whole, into which flowed the drain-water from the mills, much of it coloured according to the dye being used; and this stream afforded the only drainage to the whole community. What amazed me was that, in spite of these primitive conditions, no serious epidemic occurred either in wartime or in the years that followed.

These conditions had been made worse by the course of the war. Already in the first months, and again in 1915, the whole region was in the firing line, and from August Łódź passed into the hands of the Germans. With the outbreak of hostilities the importing of raw cotton had ceased, and now the Russian market was also lost. True the Germans were ready to buy everything, but they paid in paper money or 'obligations,' which before long were worth little. Of what use was money, anyway, when little or nothing of value could be bought with it? Such stocks of materials or half-manufactured wares as the mill companies possessed were soon dissipated, and things came to a standstill. Scores of thousands of people were out of work, and remained that way unless they were ready to migrate to the Reich. The population of the 'city' fell by one-third and thousands of living-quarters were soon derelict.

Ten years after the event, I heard from the veteran editor of one of the city dailies, published even then in German, of what happened late in 1915 when the 'All-Highest' himself came from Berlin and honoured Łódź with a visit. He came with his usual pomp, with a mind to persuade the captains of industry that they had a great future if they would declare themselves loyal Germans. My informant felt that this meeting was something no good journalist should miss (even though he was not allowed to write a word about it), so he used his personal friendship with the manager of the Grand Hotel to get smuggled into the large room where it was held. I made a mistake in not keeping notes of his story. The emperor did his best, but he made little impression on these *Lodzhermenschen* ('men of Łódź' - so-called because they recognized no national affinities of any sort). Though German of speech, they were Saxon in sentiment, and Saxony has never been in love with its Prussian overlords. In any case, the visitor had little to offer and the visit was a failure.

Actually the mill-owners were to experience to the full the war-time yoke laid upon them. As the war-machine of the Reich began to suffer under shortage of every kind of equipment, there began a systematic requisitioning of everything that could be used - first of all electrical apparatus (motors and accessories), then of fixtures and wiring. Whatever had copper or brass in its make-up was taken, even the furnishings of private homes like bells and door-knobs or the mortars and pestles used in the kitchen for pounding spices. Mill and home were left bare, substitute articles made of iron being furnished as and when possible, but not always. On reliable authority I had it that the value of property thus stolen (for it was never paid for) from the city was well over sixty million gold dollars. As one industrialist said to me in the middle twenties, 'If we had back what we were robbed of by the German armies we should soon be on easy street and ask no favours of anyone.' It should be added that nothing was done after the war to provide any kind of indemnity.

But this was only part of the story. When the Russian overlords pulled out in 1915, they had taken with them 'for safety' all the city's accounts and assets, leaving the treasury empty. This of itself was a crippling blow, for a project had been under way since the nineties for the installation of municipal sewers and waterworks. I was later to see the plans drawn up by the eminent English engineer, Sir Henry Lindley, which would have transformed the whole place. But no efforts on the part of citizens' committees or others could prevail on the tsarist authorities to let the work proceed. Only in the thirties, when the worst days of the depression were over, did the Poles get to work on an overall plan, some of which had been completed when war broke out in 1939. Part of this was the creation of a magnificent park, including a small but charming lake. For this the water was found in the dirty creek described above, with the difference that the creek was put under ground, the open space where it had meandered turned into a boulevard, and the foul-smelling water purified chemically before being discharged in a tiny waterfall into the centre of the parkland.

The immediate postwar years were a grim time for all. Thousands of makeshift living quarters on the outskirts of the built-up areas had been torn down by people in need of fuel, and the desolation was complete. Slowly, however, as peace conditions returned, the less devastated blocks were restored, and new homes of a sort were built. Even before peace was signed with the Bolsheviks, raw cotton began to come in, and the wheels of industry turned again. Some of the 'thousand chimneys' began to smoke, and a resolute city council was busy straightening out the tangle of ruin and confusion. One of its chief cares, of course, were the children, and the first new schools to be opened in the country were those of Łódź. Train services, though far from adequate or reliable, did operate; food came in from the open country to the markets, and small businesses were again in motion. Nevertheless, the visitor got the impression of incredible dirt and ugliness. Arriving at either of the two stations, he would be met by a mob of ill-looking idlers, chiefly Jews, anxious to earn a few cents by carrying his bag, by acting as a guide, or by selling him some trinket. If he was lucky, he secured a tumble-down droshky to take him where he wanted to go, and equally lucky if he arrived without an accident. It took years before this state of things was entirely transformed. When this did come, Łódź was a new place.

Almost from the start the Red Triangle was serving the troops in and around the city, and the American secretary in charge was the only man among us who had a fine car at his disposal. The reason for this was that a wealthy mill-owner, who had succeeded in hiding his car from the Germans, was now anxious that it should not be requisitioned for use in the war with the USSR. Along with our work for the army, some programme of sports and games for school youth was soon under way, and out of this grew the demand for the first local boys' camp. When the change-over to civilian work came, a new director arrived for Łódź in the person of A.K. Griffin[3] of Trinity College, Toronto, who had just finished his studies as a Rhodes Scholar in Oxford. During a term of three years he succeeded in renting temporary quarters in the heart of the city for our mens' work (the boys' department had found a home on the edge of town), of which two storeys were used for club purposes and two more for classrooms. Night-school facilities were much in demand, particularly on the side of practical training in mathematics and business skills, and the association won laurels in helping many young men to improve their earning capacities. It was, again, thanks to Griffin's organising abilities that a keen advisory committee took shape, the first step toward what became in time the board of directors of the Łódź association. The

---

3 'Later head of classics at Dalhousie University, Nova Scotia.' [WJR]

chairman of this group, Dr Alfred Grohman, belonged to the family which controlled one of the biggest enterprises in the city; but he gave most of his time and strength to social and civic services and became the most generous giver to the Polish YMCA of my generation.

When Griffin left to return to teaching, Super was able to get an experienced worker in the person of A.A. Ebersole, whose fair knowledge of German (though it caused some head-shakings among a few of our members) was a distinct help in a task of this kind. Being well on in his fifties, he could give only three years to the work, but his energy and devotion were exemplary. In particular he knew how to stir up his younger colleagues in a worthy cause, and he added not a few friends to the list of those contributing time and money. The yearly campaign for funds which he instituted set an example for other associations; Łódź became the first centre in Poland to become virtually self-supporting.

At Ebersole's request I was able to render a service to the association, and indeed to the city, which was badly needed. It began, I think, in January 1924. In talking about things that were needed in Łódź we noted the fact that, though it was second in size of Polish cities, Łódź was virtually unknown to the nation. Not even its economic importance seemed to be realized by people in high places. The reason was not hard to find. By contrast with Cracow or even Warsaw, the place was new; it had no charms of any kind such as other cities possessed; it had no historic past, nor had it any place in religious or artistic life. We therefore decided to get the board to sanction the offering of two series of public lectures, one before Christmas, one after New Year, each eight in number, to be delivered on subjects of interest by the best men we could induce to come. Each man would stay two days and give two lectures. We should offer hospitality and a modest honorarium. The board agreed to the idea, and my task was to find the lecturers.

This proved less easy than I expected. For one thing, the best people, whether in the universities, in public service, or in the business world, were loaded with work, and some of them declined to add an extra few pounds to their load. No one could blame them, in a way; yet there was no denying either the opportunity or the responsibility. I did not hesitate to tell them, as some needed telling, that Łódź had developed during the years when there was no Poland, and that no one need be surprised if it was not Polish! The rest of the country needed this metropolis of industry not a bit less than it needed a Cracow or a Częstochowa - of course for quite different reasons, but to leave Łódź to find its way without sympathetic guidance from all concerned would be a mistake.

It is only right to say that most of the men I went after needed no persuading. If they were in a position to help they did so, and gladly. Themes suggested were discussed, the level of intelligence of the audiences kept in mind, and the first course announced in good faith. The response was gratifying, both from our own membership and from outside. Social and scientific subjects were among those best received, but history and letters were not forgotten. Only party politics and theology were not wanted. These courses went on for at least four years, and could be called an unequivocal success. Not a few of the visitors admitted that this was their first visit to the city, and some of them asked to be invited again. By 1927 other agencies were at work, including university extension services. In the thirties regular studies on a university level were in progress; and it was a natural consequence that in 1945 a state university should be founded in Łódź – the more so as for the time being Warsaw was a heap of rubble. In all this the Polish association can claim to have been one of the pioneers.

In 1926 Ebersole was due to retire, and the question arose as to his succession. Search was being made for a man with experience from the New World, but for the time being no one was available. Super asked me whether I would serve as a stop-gap until the right man was found. Thinking it would be a matter of a few weeks only, I accepted.

For a year already E and I had been living in Milanówek, an outpost of Warsaw, some fifteen miles away, on the main line running from the south. Here we had a flat in the midst of woods and gardens, very different from our crowded quarters in Cracow. I could spend five days each week in Łódź, which was only fifty miles away, and even look in if needed at the head office in Warsaw. As things turned out I spent most of my last year in Europe on this new undertaking, doing much the same thing as I had been engaged on five years earlier in Cracow. The difference was that the association had its board of directors and at least the nucleus of a trained staff, and that instead of an ancient, university atmosphere, Łódź was – what I have described.

The spirit was splendid. Two of the workers were Polish Americans who had been with Haller's Army, and had helped set up the Red Triangle work in Poland – first in Lublin and then in Łódź. Tom K was maturing into a fine boys' work leader, and Stanley C had become a good business manager. Sports and games were in the hands of Aloise T, a Silesian, who had been at Osada for all the early courses and was the first physical director to have his own boys' camp. The evening classes of all kinds, which had attracted much attention, were well organised by Edgar S, who was studying law at the University of Poznań. Finally, the association had something unique in the country at that time – a school for the teaching of driving. As yet cars were a rarity, but Łódź was prospering, and many hoped to have them soon.

As already noted, the Łódź association was on the way to becoming self-supporting, thanks in good part to a well-organized annual fund-raising campaign, during which members, staff, and board all went out to lay their cause before the public. Their faith was often put to severe tests, for many people did not like the direct method used. The public was accustomed to having beggars ask for pennies, but not to being approached for larger and regular amounts for an institution. Fortunately, inside our own ranks we had business people who set a fine example, and we had a cause, the worthiness of which not even the hardest head could deny. In the campaign I supervised in the winter of 1926-7 we raised something over $10,000, of which Dr Grohman gave $1000 and his firm a like sum.

Right here emerged one of the few grounds for contention in the ranks of the Polish YMCA. It was understood that help from the United States in getting buildings could be expected by the associations more or less in proportion to their own givings. In other words, Łódź had a claim that surpassed even Cracow, though the first beginnings toward self-support had been made in the latter. Now, however, the Łódź people looked on while Cracow was getting the gift from Mr S.P. Fenn of Cleveland; and even Warsaw was said to be in line while for them nothing was done. The answer, of course, was that for Cracow a much smaller building sufficed, and the task was consequently easier, while the case for Warsaw rested on its importance as the capital. Murmurs were heard at times about this, but the day came when a magnificent gift for a Łódź building did materialize, and the thirties saw its construction. The Nazis were to make good use of it for their own purposes during the war!

But I am far from my story. During the ten months of my sojourn in Łódź a good deal was accomplished. The weekly routine of activities in the men's section was strengthened, many new supporters found in the city for our cause, and something done to improve the quality of our staff. I myself learned a great deal in the course of the winter.

In a city of this kind wholesome entertainment was badly needed. There were too few places where young men could find social amenities in the evening without going to a beer-shop. To meet this we had a regular 'social' every week with dancing, to which members could bring their wives, sweethearts, and sisters. The large room on the ground-floor served fairly well, and coffee with sandwiches and cake were available at cost. It was a principle with the association from the outset that no alcohol should be brought into buildings where the Red Triangle hung, and some people shook their heads at this. How could you have a good time without cocktails and beer? Well, we proved that it *was* possible, thus making a dent in an ancient custom. After all, our 'line' was the same as that of the Boy Scouts and Girl Guides, and commonsense was on our side. The 'socials' were a distinct success, and when all three city associations secured their new quarters they came to be very important features of our service to the communities concerned.

Card-playing was not forbidden, though we discouraged it as a regular practice. It seemed to me then that the Polish people (not unlike others I have known) could not get along without their bridge; but we insisted on moderation, and everyone agreed that no money should be involved. Other games, including chess, were promoted with zeal. On one evening we had as our guest the nationally known chess master, Regedziński, who faced twenty of our own players simultaneously in a tournament. He won most of the games.

Regular staff meetings were held every week, usually on a Monday morning, for the discussion both of principles and of methods of social work. These were handled by the staff with interest, in particular when they could be related to specific problems. Each worker would report on what he felt to be a new development worth following up, or a difficulty encountered in the course of his duties. Differences of opinion were welcomed, and where necessary expert advice called in. The reading of good books was encouraged, and each man was asked to put together his ideas in writing. Our meetings were always conducted in Polish, unless we had a visitor from outside who could not understand what was going on. Apart from this we managed at least once a week to get over to the boys' department and strip for a round of basket-ball or volley-ball, designed especially for the staff.

By Easter 1927, when we were still without the promise of a new director, Super was raising with me the question as to whether I would not remain permanently in charge. Already we knew that Dr Mott was at work on his 'second mile' in regard to new buildings in Europe, and Warsaw and Łódź were on his list. This prospect presented me with the same problem that I had faced years before, only in a more acute form. I was now past forty, and the decision had to be made as to my future. Administrative work was not my 'cup of tea,' as I well knew; in particular the task of superintending the construction of an association building seemed to be beyond my powers. My heart was in teaching and with the study that must go with it.

Somewhere in my papers is a letter from Dr Davis, in which he urged me not to desert the ship, but to accept the task of guiding the Łódź association for some years. It was not easy to decline this offer, but I felt that I must say 'No,' while at the same time thanking him warmly for the compliment. E agreed with me, and the matter was settled. I should quit in June, and return to the New World.

8 FURTHER STUDY

Committed from the outset in 1919 to work among students, I had the conviction that few things could serve better than to be a student myself. My interest in the past of the Polish people, and in the thinking that had prompted its actions, strengthened that conviction. In order to be of most use to those studying in what were difficult times, I too should share the experiences of the classroom; in their terminology be a 'colleague.'

It was clear that any continuation of classical studies was out of the question. At best I should have attained second-rate scholarship, and the pressure of events pointed to my turning to modern themes. During the war I had made a beginning with an understanding of the European situation; now peoples had been set free which had long been in chains, and the face of a continent had changed as a consequence. What is more, few people in the English-speaking world had paid any attention to Central Europe, and even now few grasped the significance of what had happened since 1914. Anything I could do, and I knew that regular studies were out of the question while so much work was in hand, was bound to be of some use. Why not make the best of every opportunity?

By now my knowledge of Polish was substantial. I could read it almost as freely as my mother-tongue, and could discuss intelligently all matters of general interest. Even as a help in my daily work, some acquaintance with the things intelligent Poles had learned in school and university would be an asset. To avoid being 'illiterate' in social circles, I had to know what the poets and novelists had been telling their fellows, just as I had to keep in touch with what was being said in the daily press. Polish literature had always been more closely related to the doings and the destiny of the nation than that of, let us say, England.

So I registered as a student in the humanities in the early restored University of Warsaw in October 1919. The certificate of admission bore the name of a man whose work I was later to appreciate – Stanisław Thugutt. A self-made man, he was the leader of the radical peasant group known as 'Liberation,' and he held the portfolio of home affairs in the coalition cabinet formed in the previous January under Paderewski. Attendance at lectures was bound to be irregular, but I did get to hear much of value from men like Juliusz Kleiner and Józef Ujejski in literature, the veteran Władysław Smoleński in history, and the still older philologist Adam Kryński, author of a notable *Grammar* of the Polish language. From time to time I went with Theodore Abel (then a Red Triangle worker) to a course on the Sociology of Law, given by the celebrated Leon Petrażycki, for long years professor in St Petersburg, whose Polish had the musical tone so easily borrowed from the Russian. Only later did I meet the equally famous Tadeusz Zieliński, dean of classical scholars, whose book *Ciceron im Wandel der Jahrhunderte* was known the world over, and who was later to be given an honorary degree by the University of Oxford.

Then came, at the end of the winter term, February 1920, an interruption. It devolved on me to accompany a young and wide-awake priest of the Mother

Church, Father O,[4] on a visit to America, and my Warsaw studies came to an inglorious end. My return to Poland coincided with the first visit of Dr Mott, out of which came the decision that we were to live and work in Cracow. By the end of June we settled down to a residence of five years in one of the most interesting corners of Europe.

Life in Cracow was less exhausting than the nomad existence of the past year. The city was small, by comparison. One was freer from political controversies; the century-long tradition of learning, not wholly broken in wartime, appealed to me. Outstanding scholars were to be found there, and it was the seat of the Academy of Sciences. Busy as we all were, I knew that something could be learned if only I set myself to definite tasks. The Warsaw University people gave me a 'release' and I registered at once for courses in literature – above all that of Professor Chrzanowski.

'Dla Polakow ojciec Kraków, A Warszawa matka!' says the ancient proverb,[5] but it has always seemed to me that it should be the other way around. Warsaw, at least in modern times, has fulfilled rather the functions of a father, while for many reasons Cracow is more like a mother. Warsaw had been the 'head,' Cracow the 'heart.' The former had grown since 1815 into a mighty metropolis, while the latter had preferred to stand quietly by, concerned rather with the things of the mind and the spirit. Its charms call for a volume in English (it should have found a place long ago in Dent's Mediæval Towns Series!), the more so as the fine book by Lepszy, published in 1912, is long since unobtainable.[6] The walled town, more Gothic in style than any other city in this part of Europe, was shaped – as were many ancient places – like an egg, with the point resting on the Vistula. Here towered Wawel Hill, on which stood a thousand years ago a tiny romanesque church. About it was built the ancient castle, part of which was the Cathedral of St Stanisław, patron saint of Poland and famous for a tragedy like that of Becket in Canterbury. Then there rose, in the sixteenth century, an imposing renaissance castle-palace built by Italian masters, to which were added by the Austrians in later days some ugly red-brick barracks.

The 'yolk' of the 'egg' represents the Town Square, its centre occupied by one of the famous Cloth Halls of Europe, near which stands a lofty tower – all that remains of an older town hall. Facing the Cloth Hall is the parish Church of St Mary, one of the lofty Dutch Gothic edifices that are found from Gdańsk [Danzig] through Toruń [Thorn] and Wrocław [Breslau] to the Polish city. From

---

4 Father Oraczewski, see note for page 117.
5 'For Poles, Cracow is the father and Warsaw the mother.'
6 Probably Leonard Lepszy and Stanisław Tomkiewicz, *Kraków, kościół i klasztor* (Cracow 1924).

its tower sounds out hourly the time signal of the 'heynal' - a broken line of trumpeted notes, recalling the last Tartar raid of the mid-thirteenth century. All around are townhouses of well-to-do burghers, each with its three windows facing the square, while here and there a five-windowed front betrays the palace of a landed nobleman.

Castle Street connects the Square with the Wawel, close on half-a-mile away, crossing as it goes the smaller All Saints' Square, on one side of which towers the Church of the Dominicans, on the other the lowlier Church of the Franciscans. As in Florence, the two orders of friars kept watch on one another! In the open space between them, the artisans of Cracow have met on a Sunday morning since time immemorial to pass the time of day and to hear the latest news.

At right angles to this axis runs St Anne's Street, in which stands the university library - once the university itself - with a lovely courtyard recalling northern Italy, set off by a statue of Copernicus. Becoming a teaching institution in 1400 (its charter was given by Rome a generation earlier), this Jagellonian university celebrated its 500th anniversary in 1900, welcoming scholars from all over the world.

To the north of the Town Square ran two streets, each at a corner; the one led to the Academy of Sciences, the other (at its passage through the city wall) was straddled by the Gate of St Florian - one of the best preserved samples of a city approach on the continent. Just outside the gate, serving of old as a defence but now surrounded by gardens, stood the Barbican - a pleasing structure, though of red brick. Like mediæval Norwich, Cracow had inside its walls more churches almost than business places! Truly a wealth of cultural associations for one coming from the 'wild west' of the New World!

My relations with Cracow, whether with its citizens or its officials, were never other than cordial. More than once I had to go to the quaint, though unimposing, Town Hall with this or that problem or request, and never did I come away empty-handed. True, in some respects the city had lagged behind the times; even the Town Square, on which weekly markets took place - a scene of many colours and of some confusion - was not properly paved and so could not be kept very clean. True, the shops in Castle Street still had in the twenties small windows with iron gratings and shutters that could be closed up at a moment's notice. But the view from Wawel Hill, still more from Kościuszko's Mound[7] a mile-and-a-half away to the west, was something one could not forget.

My subject however is study. During the winter of 1920-1 there was little time for it; and owing to the Osada project the next season was little better.

---

7 Kościuszko Mound (Kopiec Kościuszkowski), built in honour of the Polish general, leader of the patriotic insurrection of 1794.

Something was accomplished in the summer of 1923, but I really got down to work only after my return from furlough in Canada. By this time my choice of field and subject had become crystallized. I was to work under Professor Stanisław Kot[8] in the history of culture, and to give special attention to the history of education.

Literature had always interested me more for its content than for its form. I would look for what men had been concerned about in a given age in the books they wrote, but could not get exercised much about their style, or manner of telling. Among the less known prose writers of Poland's past was the man who had revolutionized the schools of the country at the middle of the eighteenth century – the Piarist Father, Stanisław Konarski. Occupation with the great romanticists of succeeding generations had meant that these earlier thinkers were neglected in Poland, but in 1923 the 150th anniversary of Konarski's death was celebrated – while I was away. Missing this, I was the more curious to make a serious study of a neglected educationist, and Professor Kot agreed to guide me. I had also missed a term's lectures on Konarski by the well-known historian, Władysław Konopczyński, whose book on the reformer was in the printer's hands. As long as I got the major part of my work done before this book appeared, I could get the theme accepted by the university authorities; and so it turned out.

In electing to work in the field of the history of culture I escaped what for me would have been a grind, but was an unavoidable part of the work demanded for a higher degree in literature – serious attention to language study, including some acquaintance with Old Slavonic. Later on I was to regret not having done this, but it is doubtful whether at the time I could have found the strength and leisure for such a study. Even as things were, I had my hands full for the next eighteen months.

My supervisor was kindness itself. I recall my first impressions of his sturdy figure, with his broad-brimmed hat and pointed black beard. Of the last-mentioned he afterwards told me that he let it grow so that people would respect him more! Actually we were almost of an age; but the range and calibre of his scholarship were quite beyond anything I could aspire to. In his seminar on the Reformation period, in which he was already a European authority, I learned as much as time and reading permitted. However, he told me plainly that the task with Konarski would make serious demands on me, the more so as two of the major works to be read were in Latin!

---

8 University professor and political figure, in opposition to the Piłsudski government after 1926, dismissed from his professional chair in 1931, but minister during World War II for the government-in-exile.

By the spring of 1925 I had managed to acquire some knowledge of my author, whose chief work, *Effective Counsels in Government*, appeared in small octavo form (four volumes) in the years 1760-3. By good fortune I had been able to buy a first edition of this work in 1922 at an auction arranged in Cracow by the Society of Bibliophiles. As a background I read much on the eighteenth century, both in Europe as a whole and in Poland in particular. In this I got much help from Smoleński's four volumes of historical essays; his single volume, *The Intellectual Volte Face*, I still regard as one of the best books on what the Enlightenment meant to Central Europe. Books of this kind were, of course, secondary sources, and my thesis was later to be criticized by some for relying on them more than was advisable.

Even here I had a reason for what I was doing. By special permission I wrote my dissertation in English, having at the back of my mind the hope that I might be able to publish it in London. This fact influenced in some measure the form it took, not altogether for the worse, I hope. A précis of the whole in Polish was attached to the manuscript, this condition being set by the Faculty of Arts.

The actual writing was made possible by the procuring of a month's leave of absence from association work, after the summer training courses were over at Osada. I slaved long hours over it, and it was ready for presentation to the faculty in the late autumn. That done, I turned to the reading necessary for my oral examination - the *viva voce*. For this I had to prepare something in psychology, something in the general field of philosophy, and something from Polish literature. One special incident of this ordeal taught me a lesson as to the relation of mental alertness to physical effort. It happened on this wise.

After getting safely through, or over, the snags in other fields I had to face a grilling by Professor Kot in the whole field of the history of education. For lack of other quarters, the interview was conducted in the room of the dean of faculty, with the dean (whom I knew well) working at his desk not far away. On coming in I was motioned by Professor Kot to a settee in the corner, the length of whose legs was such that on sitting down I found my feet dangling. For the first half of that oral I found myself literally 'up in the air.' I could not collect my wits, and my supervisor observed this. Then I shifted my position so that I did get my feet on the ground, and at once things went better. Only years afterwards did I tell the professor about this, and he rated me for not complaining at once. In any case I got through, and the date for the degree ceremony was set for 22 May 1926.

Several others were being 'promoted' that day, and I was asked to wait till they had been dealt with. The news had got around, my friends were all in the great hall, and even photographers were in attendance. The first Anglo-Saxon to be given a doctor's degree since Reformation days was 'news,' and the press was not to be denied an inning. After the ceremony, with my association colleagues and a few professors, we had a little dinner at the Poller Hotel, and here I got even with Professor Kot. From my reading I had learned that of old a new 'doctor' was expected to present his sponsoring professor with six pairs of white gloves. So then, before we parted, I rose, walked around the table, said a few words of thanks to those present, and presented Kot with one pair of kid gloves. *More antiquo*! Most of those present did not know of the tradition, but their applause was the heartier on that account. I pleaded 'hard times' as the excuse for a single pair in place of half-a-dozen.

Thus ended another chapter of my years in Poland. But not quite. E.P. Kelly of Dartmouth College, who had been with the Red Triangle both in France and in Poland, and then gone home to teach English in his old college, was on leave of absence that winter in Cracow (with his charming wife) in order to do the groundwork for the first of his series of moving tales for youth set in a Polish scene.[9] That day he got the idea that a place could be found for me on the staff of Dartmouth, and a few months later I had a letter from the president asking me whether I would be interested in coming there to teach the history of civilization. How the way to this was to open up in the spring of 1927 has been told above.

Let it be added that no one knew as well as I how unsatisfactory my work done for the PHD degree actually was. I have always maintained that my examiners gave it to me rather on the ground of hopes for the future than of accomplishment in the present. My one source of comfort, humanly speaking, is that I have not disappointed them. The time came when I was able to go on and do further work in the field thus essayed. In any case my thesis did see the light of print - it was published in London by Jonathan Cape in 1929.

9 PLACES AND PEOPLE

It has been well said that the visitor to any country may be interested in places, people, or movements - perhaps in all three. The average tourist cares only about the first, those who stay a bit longer can get to know the second; while the real student gets beyond these to find out what places stand for, and what people are doing and thinking. This takes time, but it also demands that the traveller know a good deal before he sets out on his travels.

---

9 Eric Kelly, author of *The Trumpeter of Cracow* and other stories for children about Poland, taught a course in Polish literature in translation at Dartmouth College in the mid-1920s.

Few parts of Europe were a more completely sealed book in the first years of this century than Poland, partly because it was remote, partly because the controlling powers did not want strangers to see what things looked like. Liberation changed all this, but the ravages of war were such that travel conditions (by no means easy in any case) would discourage all but the boldest. Those of us whose duties took us into every corner of the land saw both the destitution and the remarkable way in which things improved as time went on. Much of the country was inaccessible by rail, and good roads simply did not exist. Locomotives and rolling-stock were old-fashioned, worn out and scarce. The arrival of the first American railway engines, coming from the Baldwin works in Philadelphia, marked a red-letter day for the nation. The same could be said of the time when the first machines of home manufacture were placed in service.

War damage to lines and bridges had been severe, and repairs took time. Yet we did get about; we had to. It was a triumph of patient organization that achieved the transporting in the year 1919 of hundreds of thousands of prisoners-of-war in two directions, as well as the bringing home of vast throngs of 'lost' civilians. By the spring of 1921 main-line services were fairly normal, with Warsaw as the hub of the state railway system. Eight separate slow trains would leave the capital early in the evening, with nearly as many expresses following later; and the same number would arrive in fair time in the morning. For a long time the condition of the coaches was bad – they were often without window-glass, the upholstery of first and second-class cars was in rags, little could be done to provide meals, and there was dirt everywhere. Nevertheless, from all my wanderings never once did I bring home any vermin, and never did I contract any epidemic. As things improved the state railway system came to equal the best on the continent.

We had too much to do to permit of leisure for extended sight-seeing. All the same, opportunity did come for getting to know much that was worth knowing, and in retrospect I regret not having taken chances that were at hand to revisit Gdańsk, to have a look at the historic fortress of Kamieniec Podolski on the Dniester, or to visit Zamość. In the same way I failed later on to make the trip by boat down the Vistula, seeing Kazimierz with its quaint grain elevators, or historic Płock and Włocławek. Opportunity seldom knocks twice at one's door.

The chance did come to have a look at what was left of Brest Litovsk (*Brześć-Litewski* in Polish) on the Bug River, scene of the famous Congress in 1596 which aimed to unite the churches of West and East, as well as of the meeting in January 1918 between the Germans and the Bolshevists out of which came the infamous Treaty of Brest. I was in the council-hall, on the wall of which Trotsky scratched his grim comment, 'Neither peace nor war!' And a scarcely less interesting visit was made possible a few years later to the imposing palace of the

Czartoryski family at Puławy on the middle Vistula. Professor Leon Marchlewski was in charge of the scientific station there for the production of serums, and he invited Jacob and myself there for a day's shooting. Memories of the great days of the Princess Izabella, when Puławy was a centre of arts and letters,[10] were mingled with joy at seeing work done which would safeguard the growing wealth of live-stock from scourges such as foot-and-mouth disease.

Among the shrines of Poland, sacred for their religious significance but also for national reasons, that of Our Lady of Częstochowa stands first, with that of Our Lady of Ostrabrama in Wilno coming close second. The latter I was to visit each time I went to Wilno, the former I first saw with E on a May Day excursion in 1923.

Jasna Góra (*mons clarus* in Latin) has been towering above the little town of Częstochowa, not far from the Silesian boundary, for centuries. A monastic foundation (Pauline Fathers), it was made into a fortress in years of invasion, the portrait of the Madonna being considered a treasure of priceless value. Legend had it that the picture had come to Poland via the Ukraine from Constantinople. In time of national stress tears would fall from the eyes, and miracles of healing were claimed through the ages. When we made our visit in May there were not many people about; but two years later, in high summer, when pilgrims were coming on foot in thousands from all parts of the country, I was able to make a second visit – as guide to a larger company.

Almost every year we had parties of American tourists in Poland, some of them university men and/or women, all of them interested in an out-of-the-way country. If and when I was able, I helped to show them things of interest, in particular places with cultural or national associations. In 1925 a group of thirty young college women spent a week in the country, two of their teachers being with them. They wanted to see 'the Lourdes of Poland,' so we spent the best part of a day there. First we saw the outside of the Shining Hill, and I told them something about the part played by the monastery and Prior Kordecki in the fateful year 1655, when the whole land was overrun by the Swedes under King Karl Gustav.[11] Then we went inside, and I planned our rounds so that we should be in the great hall just before noon, when the holy picture would probably be unveiled for the faithful to see. When we got in, the place was crowded to the doors.

All had been warned of the need for silence, and of due regard for those worshipping, but by some mischance our party got divided into two groups, and when the moment of adoration came not all kneeled down. One could feel the

---

10 That is, late eighteenth century.
11 The monastery at Częstochowa successfully resisted capture by the Swedes.

tenseness in the atmosphere – how could it be otherwise when hundreds of people were experiencing something they had looked forward to for years? When the assembly got to its feet again, I managed to pass word along to our people slowly to withdraw toward the door, and too late I realized that they had not been warned to keep their faces toward the picture. Two or three of them turned their backs, and the reaction of the peasant women around them was immediate. Rough hands were laid on them, and for a moment I expected them to receive bodily injury. Fortunately one of the teachers saw what was wrong, and intervened. But seldom have I been more relieved than when I got the whole group safely out of the building.

Years afterwards I came to know more about what this place had meant to Poles in the past – of how Reymont first won public attention as a writer by making a pilgrimage with a village party in the early nineties and putting down what he saw and heard; and still more of how, when just across the Silesian border the Germans frowned on all Polish sentiments, the people from the industrial areas would make their way in thousands to Jasna Góra to hear the preaching, and to buy devotional booklets in their own tongue.

I have written elsewhere of the Polish landscape: of the low areas facing the Baltic, the plainland that gave Poland its name, drained by the Vistula and the Warta; and the highlands to the south above which tower the Tatras – the Alps of Central Europe. From one end to the other the country was sprinkled with villages, most of them belonging in the old days to some manor, but many with spacious palaces, standing where fortresses had been before the days of gunpowder. In the villages of the west and south were lovely examples of Gothic churches built entirely of wood, and with masterly wood-carving to set off their chancels, of which not a few were burned down in modern times, to be rebuilt with care by the worshippers. Some of these I got to know well; but it was never my fortune to be a guest in one of the great country mansions where, I have been told, into our own day things went on much as they did in the eighteenth century. At least twice I had invitations, but pressure of work hindered me. Only after I had left Poland did the world hear of the startling prehistoric remains found, by one of my contemporaries at the University of Cracow, at Biskupin on Lake Gopło – famous in legend as the home of the mythical King Popiel.[12]

More interesting even than places are people. It was always my rule never to seek acquaintance with men of distinction unless I had a good reason; but in retrospect I feel that this was carried too far. Why did I never get to know Joseph Conrad, though I was in London at least three times while he was alive? And why

12 Biskupin, settlement from about 500 BC, discovered and excavated in the 1930s by Professor Zdzisław Rajewski.

did I not seek out in the twenties that astonishing 'Herald of Truth,' as he styled himself in the seventies and eighties, Aleksander Swiętochowski?[13] When I did try to see him ten years later his health was failing, and he could not see strangers. He lived to be ninety. The same applies to quite a different person, whom I did see once on the street in Warsaw, in his ninety-seventh year, but whom I never met. I refer, of course, to the 'Grand Old Man' of Polish Socialism, Bolesław Limanowski, whose *History of Polish Democracy* is hardly less important a document than the other veteran's *History of the Polish Peasants*. For once I was rude, and stared at a passerby, taking off my hat while staring.

But it was my fortune to see something of many eminent Poles, more of them thinkers than politicians, and I have something to say about them. Two were novelists of distinction – Władysław Reymont and Stefan Żeromski; two were teachers – Marian Zdziechowski and Wincenty Lutosławski (already mentioned in these pages); and last, not least, the son of Poland's greatest poet, Władysław Mickiewicz. Of these a word about each in turn.

In the late autumn of 1919 George Palmer Putnam came with his lady to Warsaw in the hope, among other things, of getting Madame Paderewski to write a book about her husband – then prime minister. That plan did not materialize, but other things did. When I met him at the Hotel Bristol, and found that he had no one to guide him in making some contacts, I offered my help. Meetings were arranged with Zofia Nałkowska, daughter of an ancient geographer, and with Władysław Reymont. The decision was soon taken to have the latter's famous story, *The Peasants* (known already to the world in a good German translation), put into English and published in New York. The question arose as to who would do the English version – a very difficult task since much of the original is in peasant speech. We took the best advice possible, and entrusted the work to Michał Dziewicki, respected *lector* in English in Cracow, whose parents had been exiles in England after the rising of 1863 and who was completely bilingual. The result was a masterpiece, but I fear that Dziewicki was but poorly paid for the time he put in at the task.

Then for some reason Putnam turned his attention to other things, losing interest in Poland. Only at the end of 1923 did the work see the light of day – from the firm of Knopf. A year later Reymont was given the Nobel prize, and his publisher reaped a harvest. This four-volume story is a grim picture of conditions as they existed in parts of 'Russian' Poland in the eighties, and presents scenes as true to the life of those ignorant people as the epic of Mickiewicz had presented them for the gentry of a century earlier. But when E read the book

---

13 Warsaw 'Positivist' of the 1870s, journalist and advocate of 'organic work' – economic progress – in order to keep the Polish nation fully modern.

her comment was, 'Those are not the peasants we knew in Silesia,' and she was right.

It was at Reymont's table that I met Żeromski. Hardly could one have found two men more unlike one another. Reymont was a believer; Żeromski an agnostic if not an atheist. Reymont pictured simple people going about their daily work; his contemporary saw them at war - either with enemies of the nation or with social oppressors. For years he had been a sick man, but his spirit was not broken. From beneath a towering forehead, sharp eyes looked at the world, seeing everything. He invited me to visit him in Konstancin, near Warsaw, and I am ashamed to say that I never went. How much I missed became clear as I got to know his moving tales (in later years); the epic two-volume *Ashes*, telling of how Napoleon had used and wasted the brave men of the Polish Legions in the mountains of Spain and the swamps of San Domingo, and his *Labours of Sisyphus*, which sets out his own experiences as a boy in a Russian high school in the heart of Poland. Everywhere a single overpowering passion - hatred of tyranny for its follies and its crimes. To Żeromski 'The simple nameless herd of humanity' had a right to something better than helotage; and who is to blame him if he went far in condemning both state and church for conniving at what went on?

The reader may remember that, on my first visit to Wilno with Taylor, we called on Professor Zdziechowski who had been expected as a speaker at our 1914 conference in Ligotka. Celebrated for his studies of religious thought, including that of the Eastern Church, he was a devout Catholic, and I knew that he could not be enthusiastic about some of the things his more famous colleague Lutosławski had done. Let me add here that he was the only Pole of distinction who ever expressed his regrets to me at the overturning of the old order in Central Europe; he felt that new forces had been let loose that could not be controlled, and said in effect, 'the old was better.'

But when I asked him to take us around to Lutosławski's home, he agreed at once. With Taylor he spoke French, and I let them enjoy their time together. But when we arrived at the other home the conversation turned to English. Lutosławski had lectured in England at the turn of the century and had also been invited to the New World. In both countries he could have done much more for the cause of his country, and for freedom in general, if he had not shown himself such a 'fire-eater.' This trait was now to reappear, for we had not been talking more than ten minutes before he turned on me with the proposition that the YMCA should provide him with an aeroplane at once, so that he could travel up and down the country and warn everyone of the dangers of Bolshevism! In vain did we try to tell him that we had no planes at our disposal and that the Red Triangle kept out of all political issues; he would not listen, and told us that as a Christian organization we should be alive to the dangers of this 'new religion' boiling up next door. Only later did I learn that one reason for his passion was that two of his brothers had been killed in the revolution.

Ten months later the professor turned up in Cracow at my third lecture on the YMCA in America. After the meeting he came up and spoke to me. In the meantime he had heard that I had published Cieszkowski's great work in an abridged form in English, and he set on me for 'mutilating' a masterpiece of Polish prose. As simply as possible I explained that no publisher would have accepted the work as it stood, but he would not agree. Then my chairman came to my rescue, and I escaped.

An interesting sequel to all this came fifteen years later, which must be told though it falls just outside the frame of this book. At work in Poland after my first year at the University of London, I called on Lutosławski, living in retirement in Cracow. He received me cordially, giving me slippers to put on at the door of his flat, and we sat down to talk. On hearing that I was setting out on an extended tour of the country to see how well the nation had survived the depression, he at once objected: 'It would be far better for you to stay here, and spend the time reading Słowacki's *King Spirit* with me.' To my assurance that I would be happy to avail myself of so great a teacher but that time did not permit, he turned a deaf ear. I was to discover later that he followed me to Warsaw, resolved to prove to me the wisdom of Mary's action as opposed to that of Martha! Who can say that he was not right? In any case Lutosławski fulfilled more adequately than anyone else I have known the injunction of St Paul to be 'instant in season and out of season.' Whether his brand of Messianism, however, was the right cure for human ills may well be doubted. He survived World War II and died at the age of ninety early in 1955.

My meeting with Władysław Mickiewicz, whose father died just a century ago while trying to raise a 'legion' to help in the Crimean War, was a sheer piece of luck owed to interested friends. He was paying his first and only visit to his father's homeland, by special invitation, in 1923, and I found him in Poznań. We chatted for three-quarters-of-an-hour while his portrait was being painted. The notes I made of our conversation got lost, so I have no proper record. Before me was a frail, bearded man, well on in his seventies. Being very young when his father died, he can hardly be said to have 'known' him, but he did recall a visit made in his home by the celebrated Italian patriot, Mazzini, with whom the Polish poet and leader had so much in common. He expressed satisfaction at meeting someone from the New World who took a sincere interest in his father's life and work, on which he himself had written at length. Since then we have all learned that much of his work was and is unreliable, since he seems to have wanted only one side of the life lived in exile to be handed on to posterity.

As for statesmen and political leaders, I saw little of them. In retrospect I regret keenly not having attended a session of the first Diet in 1919, and at least some sessions in later years. The record of parliamentary work done in the first seven years of independence, though not without blemishes, is one the nation need not be ashamed of. As the reader knows I did get to know Piłsudski, and I met him twice elsewhere after the first occasion in the Belvedere; but in spite of my efforts to arrange a meeting with his firm rival, Roman Dmowski, it never came off. Neither in Paris nor later in the homeland would he see me. On good authority I learned that he appreciated the help I had given him in connection with Teschen, but he was sure that I was a Free Mason and therefore not the kind of man to be trusted! For equally good reasons I should have got to know the peasant leader, Wincenty Witos, who was twice prime minister. I did see him once, and I knew some of his close associates, but that was all. Paderewski I saw once in the corridors of the provisional Foreign Office, and I heard him more than once 'resting' while playing his piano on the floor above me in the Bristol – but no more.

When Wickham Steed was in Warsaw in 1926, he asked me whether in my view Witos had any chance of recovering a first place in public life, and my answer was in the negative. My reason was that the peasant groups were still unable to achieve united action (actually they did come together four years later), so that their numerical preponderance was of little use to them. Had the farmers and the urban workers of Poland been able to compose their differences (and the same is true of other countries in Central Europe), the history of our time might have been very different.

Concluding this section I want to say a word about each of two experiences that have remained in memory, one from the summer of 1924, the other from the following spring.

On a never-to-be-forgotten day (I think it was in June), the mortal remains of one of Poland's greatest sons were brought home from Switzerland to be laid in the crypt of St John's Cathedral in Warsaw. Not only as a novelist, but also as the champion of human rights against the Bülow regime in 1906 in Poznania, Henryk Sienkiewicz had won the hearts of all patriots and his death abroad in 1917 was mourned by all. I had been in the home of his daughter more than once, wife of the second of the Korniłłowicz brothers, and made it my business to be in Warsaw for the great occasion. The coffin had rested all night in the railway station, with huge torches flaming each side of the entrance. Early in the morning a vast procession began to form, with delegations present from every corner of the country, state and church and university and school all taking part. To the strains of Chopin's 'Funeral March,' played by at least three military bands, thousands of people followed a course through the capital while scores of thousands looked on. I secured a place not far from the station, and then by hurrying across town got another on the steps of St Cross Church in Nowy Świat, in which reposes the heart of Chopin. Everything was dignified, everything full of emotional power. All the approaches to the cathedral were jammed, while the chosen few heard the last mass sung by the cardinal. A worthy tribute to a great soul, who wrote his incomparable *Trilogy* in the eighties 'for the cheering of men's spirits.' (Bulwer-Lytton was right when he said that the pen is mightier than the sword.)

Eight months later, all American workers in Central Europe were called together, with their wives where possible, to meet in conference with Dr Mott and other visitors in the picturesque town of Trencin in Slovakia. E.T. Colton was in charge of the sessions, in which weighty matters of policy were discussed, as well as the personal responsibilities of all concerned. Mott was at his best, and the most moving hour of the whole conference came when he had to face a birthday party – he had just finished his sixtieth year. Strong men from our physical education group seized him, and carried him on their shoulders across the lawn of the hotel where we were meeting, and I had the privilege of composing a little doggerel expressing our regard and affection. Usually dignified, even to the point of being stern, he did unbend and we saw the 'Big Chief' in a mood of cheerfulness approaching hilarity. Few of us could guess that, in spite of unceasing toil for his fellow-men, he would live on for close to thirty more years before being gathered to his fathers.

7
Silesian Research

Rose left Poland in 1927 to take up the position of assistant professor of sociology at Dartmouth College, Hanover, New Hampshire, and, with the exception of two years in Silesia, he spent the period 1927-35 there. At Dartmouth Rose set up an introductory course in western civilization which, since he lacked formal training, he had to prepare from scratch. He found time to study French at Middlebury College (Vermont) and to preach regularly to several New England communities which could not afford regular ministers. Canada maintained its appeal to him, although he rejected an offer from St Andrews College (Saskatoon, Saskatchewan) of a chair in church history and church missions on the grounds that he was not qualified. He spent several summers north of the border, however, serving in 1930 and 1931 as a judge in the community improvement contests sponsored by the Canadian National Railway in the western provinces. He observed with interest the process of acculturation of Central and East European-born new Canadians who inhabited the area.[1]

Living in New England did not reduce Rose's interest in Poland. He wrote a series of articles for the Warsaw-sponsored English language magazine, Poland, *which was published in New York; he also made translations from the Polish, especially the diary of a village mayor which was published ten years later in London. Rose launched a minor career of lecturing on Polish affairs. He took the Polish side in debates before the Foreign Policy Associations of New York and Springfield concerning the 'Polish Corridor,' while speeches to Polish-American*

1 'Old Wine in New Bottles,' *Canadian Journal of Religious Thought*, VIII, 3, May-June 1931, 177-90

communities in and around New England on occasions like Kościuszko and Pułaski days occupied much of his time. The lecture at Alliance College in Cambridge Springs, Pennsylvania, run by the Polish National Alliance, ended abruptly when the library burned to the ground. Rose later remarked that he gained a quite undeserved reputation around Dartmouth as a fiery speaker. [DS]

For years I had cherished the hope of doing a piece of research on something connected with the making of the new Poland. What attracted me most was the defence put up during the nineteenth century by the central provinces against Tsarist Russia. But when I approached the Guggenheim Foundation with this suggestion there was no response, and my first try with the Social Science Research Council also drew a blank. Then there came, out of the blue, a telegram from Professor James T. Shotwell, director of the International Studies Section of that council, asking me whether I should like to do a study of the Upper Silesian problem. For this, as he rightly felt, I had one special qualification – a competent knowledge of the two languages involved, German and Polish. He was prepared to find funds to assist me for a year, or even longer.

There was much to be said for closing with this offer, but for a time I hesitated. In the interests of scholarship, it would be better to attempt something less 'hot' (as the journalists call it); less the subject of controversy, or even wrangling. Steady pressure was being exerted by the Germans at Geneva, indeed the world over, 'to organise sympathy,' and not only for their own minority on the Polish side of the new frontier. In this matter my feelings were with the Poles, and the question arose whether I could preserve enough detachment for a sober appraisal of evidence. Shotwell felt that I could, and argued that someone would have to make a beginning with what was as yet an unknown field in historical writing in English. The matter was settled, and in June 1932 the authorities of Dartmouth College were good enough to grant me sabbatical leave, on half a salary, for one year, though actually I could not claim it until 1933.

On arrival in London I discovered that other people had the same feelings about things as Shotwell. The Royal Institute of International Affairs (Chatham House), of which I had the honour to be a founding member, had just arranged to make possible an enquiry into the whole subject of German-Polish relations, and Ian D. Morrow was to undertake the task. This choice rather surprised me, since Mr Morrow knew no Polish and, as he told me, was not expecting to learn it. Further, he possessed much wider acquaintance with the Southern German world than with things Prussian. In the sequel he devoted his whole attention to the northern sector of the frontier (the long chapter on Danzig is the best part of his rather unwieldy book), leaving to me the more complicated and thornier

Silesian research 199

region of Upper Silesia.² These adjectives, as the reader will see, are not ill-advised. German claims for a revision of the boundary line set up in 1921 were based chiefly on their need for industrial potential, while the Poles countered by drawing attention to the fact of an overwhelmingly Catholic and Polish-speaking population.

We arrived in Katowice, which was to be our headquarters for the next two years,³ on 19 September. With crowded conditions everywhere, the prospect of getting living quarters looked grim; but friends managed to let us have two rooms in a quiet street and here we spent the next six months. The world depression was now at its height, and was to continue for more than a year. I was reminded of this when I went to the railway-freight shed to get the two boxes of books and clothes we had sent on from London. The man in charge drew my attention to the empty halls and said, 'You should have seen them even a year ago; they were full to the rafters!'

If the outlook ahead was not too promising for the people of this crowded industrial region, the newcomer could look at it more cheerfully. I was not a stranger in any sense of the word; at every turn friends and acquaintances of other days were on hand. In public offices, particularly in education, but also in the professions and in industry were men and women I had known either in wartime (natives of the Duchy of Teschen to the south) or in the University of Cracow. What is more, from the outset everyone showed a readiness to assist me in my work. The governor (wojewoda) heard of my coming, and asked that I be brought to see him. From no side did I find any disposition to resent enquiry either as to what had been or as to the present. No one tried to hide from me the actuality – things were difficult, there was much unemployment, soup kitchens were to be found everywhere – but the situation was the same all over Europe, and no one doubted that the future would be better.

There were two major tasks ahead: to unearth the facts about the past of the Oderland, especially since its taking-over by Frederick II of Prussia at the middle of the eighteenth century; and to discover what people felt about the changes effected by the moving of the frontier in 1919-21, which gave a good part of the former Prussian province to Poland. The former involved long hours of study in libraries, pouring over books and periodicals, and an appraising of conflicting

2 Ian Morrow assisted by L.M. Sieveking, *The Peace Settlement in the German-Polish Borderlands* (London 1936).
3 Rose received one year's leave with half-pay from Dartmouth. A small grant from the American Social Science Research Council supplemented this. Finding that he could not complete his work within a year, Rose applied for and received a second year's leave without pay. The SSRC gave him somewhat more money and the Kościuszko Foundation also contributed.

records. The latter meant the reading of contemporary history as found in newspapers and journals, and endless discussions with all kinds of people who had been eyewitnesses of what had happened. The countryside, if a tangle of mines, foundries, and living areas could be called such, was new to me. I had been twice in and across it, but never to stay. Now by good fortune the weather was ideal, and I decided to get out and about as much as possible.

Before long it transpired that others had been there before me, and with similar ends in view. Most of them were from the New World, but no one was ready to stay for more than a few weeks. All got a shock when they realized the complexity of the problem, and at least one ended with a nervous breakdown. The sole exception had been the American geographer, Richard Hartshorne, who wrote sound and helpful things about the new frontier, as a frontier. He also left many friends behind on both sides of the line. Even while I was at work a scholar of some distinction arrived from the New World, who stayed only four days. His method was to leave with a few responsible people, of both nations, an exhaustive questionnaire, the answers to which he got posted to him in due course. Using these he wrote his book, and by no means a bad one!

That kind of thing did not appeal to me at all. It seemed to ignore the most important thing in history – the human factor. Those who had come and gone away empty-handed did so because they took too cavalier a view of social and economic relations: they were not ready to spend a year over five centuries of tortuous inter-connections and conflicts. Above all, no one had come with linguistic capacity to associate with the common people, whether German or Polish, whether Catholic, Lutheran, or Jewish. The field was in consequence a virgin one, and the opportunity unique.

In order that he might be in touch with what was going on, Shotwell asked me to write him monthly report letters, and he told me long afterwards that he found these most useful. On re-reading them twenty years after they were written, I feel that some of them are more interesting than parts, at least, of the 200,000 word manuscript I delivered in the high summer of 1934. What they give, of course, is the 'how' of my enquiry rather than the 'what' – the ways and means used rather than the results obtained. Still, there is a good deal in them that reveals the atmosphere of the country in 1932-3. Here are samples from letter 1:

... I was scouting about the parish of St Peter and St Paul here in Katowice, whose big church is being renovated. In the courtyard I noticed what looked like a queue of working people, and tables set out as if someone were eating. I suspected one of the soup-kitchens, so went in to observe. An officer was in charge of the sixty or more folk of all ages and both sexes, so I stepped up to ask him what was going on. He told me it was a 'city kitchen' and at once went on: 'But if you want to eat here you must go and get tickets at the office in x street.' I did not betray my surprise at the remark, but thanked him and went away. Telling this to a friend, I asked whether I looked lean and unemployed. He replied that of late the number of the intelligentsia out of work was such that no one could tell from clothes whether one is in need or not. Thus has the situation developed in recent months ...

... I have made three trips out of town by trolley – west, east, and north. It struck me that only half of the great chimneys were smoking ... Of course this means a lot of people out of work; but the news was announced with satisfaction three days ago that the Jupiter mine will reopen and 1200 men will go back.

Smaller and larger groups of men are to be seen sitting about the parks and squares, without employment but waiting for a chance. On the other hand I have found hundreds of men, women, and children busy in the fields, digging thousands of bushels of precious potatoes. Others are getting the land ready for the next crop. There is scarcely a bit of tillable soil lying waste – at the worst it is pastured by sheep and goats. All the same the big stretches ruined by the piling up of clay and slag from the mines make one wish that civilisation did not mess up the world as it does ...

One afternoon I went into one of the few cafes to be found in Królowa Huta to get a snack. I was answered promptly in Polish, and served by a neat 18-year-old waitress. Sitting down I watched people come and go. Alternately men and women, one with Polish, the next with German – all treated alike, and either tongue spoken. In an interval I spoke up in German: 'Do you mind, Miss, telling me how you know when to greet people in one tongue, when in the other?' 'Ach' was her reply, 'man kennt seine Leute!' To a further question she replied that she was born in Królowa Huta, had begun school in German, and finished it in Polish. Most people, she added, were ready to speak either language; but many who would like to use Polish could not, 'so one makes allowances for them.'

From my twenty minutes or so there I could conclude that in ordinary living there is no nationalist friction at all. I can see how there is when big firms come into collision, but that exists everywhere ... In every cafe where I have been both Polish and German papers are read ad lib. Nor have I found that any one group of cafes is thought of as Polish, or another as German. But on this I shall have more to say when I know conditions better ...

The event of our first week here for the Germans was their tenth annual Extension Lectures program, handled by guest professors from Germany. I have read the notices telling of three men coming to speak on Goethe – from Danzig, Halle, and Breslau. We were busy getting settled so I did not get the hours and place in time. When I did get to the office of the *Kulturbund* it was to learn that two were come and gone, and their lectures had been a success, but the third could not get a visa and his lectures had to be dropped. He was the famous Eugen Kuehnemann, whom we had at Dartmouth last year when he was on tour in America ...

By way of comment on this, it should be said that fifteen years earlier no such freedom of speech was possible in Silesian towns. The Poles had been hard put to get the right to their language in the churches. As for the extension lectures, I was to attend them a year later, and they were good. What one wished for was more of that kind of thing, on both sides of the frontier.

In my second letter I told of being taken to Senator K (retired), who as a young man had been forced to flee the country for political activities and had spent seven years in America. 'As president of the local chamber of commerce, he is still active in affairs; I am to get a copy of his *Memoirs*, as a guide to events of pre-war days.' I also wrote of meeting two younger men, one a lawyer and the son of a lawyer, the other a social worker who had come into the Polish YMCA (he was born not far from Warsaw) as a gangling youth and found there encouragement to go on and study under Znaniecki in Poznań. From the former I was to get much help in regard to the tangled relations existing in Polish party politics; the latter was to take me with him to all kinds of discussion meetings in and about Katowice, where I heard news and views 'straight from the horse's mouth.' He was also to help me with the section in Part Two of my book, dealing with the economic readjustments that grew out of the depression.

Much of the letter was about things people had to say on social and international affairs in general, in particular what was going on in the Reich, where Hitler was already a man to be reckoned with. There was little doubt that he would take up frontier issues when it suited him, though for the time being he was more concerned with 'the wrongs done at Versailles.'

For the essentials of the century-old struggle in the upper Oder basin between the Polish peasant and working class and the German landlord and (since 1800) industrialist, the reader must go to any good history or to my book, *The Drama of Upper Silesia*. Miss Wambaugh sums it up succinctly: 'To the Germans the industries of Upper Silesia have been built by German brains and capital, while to the Poles they are the fruits of Polish labour.' But it should be added that, with a Russian tyranny beginning a few miles to the east and with the Austrian empire adjacent on the south, there was nothing for these neglected and exploited people to 'tie on to' until their mother-nation became free in November 1918. As a consequence they put up with their lot, though separated from their rulers by religion, speech, social status, and as time went on by political self-consciousness. A fair proportion did succumb to assimilation: Who could deny that to do this

Silesian research 203

gave them and their children much better prospects for the future? But when the plebiscite of 1921 gave a vote of half-a-million for the new Poland, something had to be done: so a substantial part of this mining and foundry area was given to Poland, and an interim period of fifteen years fixed in which personal and economic adjustments could be worked out. To supervise these, two outstanding men, a Swiss and a Belgian, both of whom I got to know well, were sent to Silesia; and no better job of peace-making was ever done than that of these men and their colleagues.

As it turned out, roughly half of my book was devoted to tracing the social and material changes effected by Prussian rule from 1742 to 1922, while the other half sought to set out the consequences of the new frontier for the parts assigned to Poland. These were by no means simple, since the region presented a technical and economic whole – a common system of transport, of electric light and power, of water-works and drainage, of banking and exchange of goods at every stage of manufacturing; and, of course, of school, church, and community life. In all this the districts remaining with Germany were scarcely affected, so I gave them little attention. But the fact was that close on half-a-million people whose mother-tongue was Polish were left on the German side; just as a much smaller though far more influential number of Germans constituted a powerful minority on the Polish side. One of my German advisers urged me to add a third part to my report, dealing with the changes effected after 1921 on the German side, but this would have demanded at least another year of time, and made the resulting book too large.

During the first six months I was alternately occupied with serious study of documents and with 'field work' – seeing and interviewing all sorts of people. With the simple folk I could pass for an American Pole, and swap yarns about the new world and the old; with people of education the whole strategy was different, since they knew what I was after, and knew that unless they told me the truth I should find them out later on. A piece of good fortune came my way when I was asked to speak to the English Club which met regularly in Katowice, in which were Poles, Germans, and the 'third force' of people who called themselves Silesians: a neutral body in which politics was taboo and the one thing desired was to hear anyone telling a good story in English, or introducing a useful topic, which would then be discussed. Here I came across both cranks and wise men and women, some of whom invited me to their homes (with E as a no less welcome guest), all of whom helped me in one way or another. In the two years of residence I must have helped them out with some kind of an address (often improvised!) at least half-a-dozen times.

Before six months had passed, Hitler had taken over in Berlin, and everyone was apprehensive. But we took a month in the spring of 1933 to pay a long-planned visit to the new Yugoslavia – on which an interesting chapter could be written – including a week of complete rest on the shore of the Adriatic near Split (Spalato) and a short visit to the fabled plateau of Montenegro. Three days in Dubrovnik (Ragusa), picturesque outpost of Venice in her wars with the Turks, and three in Sarajevo (where the shots were fired that set off a world conflagration) were followed by a brief stay in Belgrade and a hasty return 'home.'

At once we moved with such of our effects as were necessary to the German side of the frontier, and settled down for two months in Beuthen (Bytom). I had long since visited this outpost of Germandom, chiefly in order to present the letter given me in Salzburg and to meet Dr Ernst Laslowski and his wife – he a specialist on Silesian affairs and a man of high idealism. Born of Polish-speaking parents, he had become a loyal German – as was natural enough; but as a Catholic he did not like many things Prussia stood for, and was from the start a convinced enemy of the Nazis. Thanks to his kindness we found living quarters in a Catholic convent-school, and I was admitted at once to read in the new library. Thanks also to him we were able to attend a couple of political rallies, by which the Nazis were seeking to convince a far from willing populace that they were called of God to save Germany, and even the world. As Laslowski said: 'I have to put in an appearance at some of these meetings (his post was an official one), but I always get away before the "Heil Hitler!" part begins.' In parenthesis I might add that we were only once in something of a quandary, when E did not want to stand up at the playing of 'Die Wacht am Rhein.' That would have caused some unpleasantness, and I reminded her that as guests we should not involve others in difficulties. This was only a sample of the open honesty she always cherished, sometimes to the anxiety of her friends.

It was soon clear to me that German Catholics were uniformly hostile to the Nazi regime. Knowing this, the agents of the new order sought to use the relatively small number of Lutheran pastors in this remote province as helpers in their task. Getting to know two of the best of these men, I watched the way they defended themselves and their work: but, as one of them said to me, 'On the one hand they stir up discord in my congregation from below, on the other hand they set about tying our hands from above. No one knows what the future will bring.' Of course the time soon came when this honest shepherd of souls had to resign, and a more amenable pastor was put in his place.

My letters to Shotwell from Beuthen tell of various types of Nazi action in Silesia, and of the reactions they met with. Uniformed 'workers' were using the sand-lots of the city to promote games of all kinds for the youth of the streets – a glorified 'boy scout' campaign all over again; or more properly the stuff we have been seeing in later years associated with Hopalong Cassidy or Davy Crockett. Every leader had his belt, and at least one knife was stuck in it. Field workers in uniform, with money in their pockets and a 'Hail-fellow-well met' smile, were busy in town and country long before the official 'taking over' of Silesia was announced. I ran into one of them serving as a guide to foreign visitors. He had in tow a couple of well-meaning American university women, whose ears he had filled with stories about 'the bleeding frontier' and the barbarisms to be found on the Polish side. I managed to get a couple of minutes with them alone, and asked them whether they had seen the other side of the frontier. The answer was 'No,' so I warned them to take all they were being told with a big grain of salt.

A delightful break in this two-months 'hard labour' came at Whitsuntide, when the Laslowskis took us off for three days hiking in the Grandfather Mountains that separate Silesia from Bohemia. The outing was most enjoyable, not the least because it gave me a chance to see the lovely Gothic treasures of Neisse – called 'the Athens of the north.' All of this territory was laid in ruins in the fighting of early 1945, and it has since become a part of the newest Poland. No one could have foreseen this ten years earlier.

Six months after our time in Beuthen, during which I was to have fresh proof that the German librarians had instructions not to place in the hands of visitors the best books written in the nineteenth century on Upper Silesia unless they had to, the whole 'line' hitherto taken by Berlin toward things Polish was suddenly changed. While on my way to the library in Katowice on Saturday morning, 26 January 1934, I was met by a friend who thrust into my hand the morning paper, exclaiming, 'What do you make of that?' Across the front page in big headlines was the news that a ten-year pact of non-aggression had been signed between Berlin and Warsaw. To say that we were surprised would be putting it mildly, although an astonishing change had come over some of the press in recent days, both that of the Reich and the minority in Silesia. From now on German-Polish neighbourly co-operation was held to be the manifest destiny of both peoples, and rivalries or differences were declared a thing of the forgotten past.

In my letters to Shotwell I had more than once expressed the hope that the threat of Nazi aggression would bring the governments of the two countries that bordered on the Reich – Czechoslovakia and Poland – to their senses, since any coolness or dissension between them was only grist to the German mill. The new turn of events, to the disappointment of many, not only did not help but made things worse – and the fault was with Warsaw. Almost at the moment of the pact there fell the fifteenth anniversary of the Czech 'invasion' of 1919; and the occasion was used by the mayor of Polish Teschen to make a needlessly provocative speech. I asked a well-informed journalist in Katowice why this happened, to which he replied: 'Under instructions from the capital; of that I am certain!'

Finishing up my all too short stay in Beuthen, I returned to Katowice with the wish to leave things for a while to simmer. The time had come when I needed to arrange the historical materials to Part One of my report, and this would take time.

Most of my attention had now to be given to the working out of the Geneva Convention of 1921: defining the tasks of the Mixed Commission presided over by M. Calonder and of the Tribunal of Arbitration under the presidency of Dr Georges Kaeckenbeck, and serving as a sort of constitution until 1937 for the areas ceded to Poland. The working of this machinery (the convention was longer than the Treaty of Versailles) was admirable, thanks in good part to the personalities of the two heads; but it was a thorn in the side of the active governor of Polish Silesia, Dr M. Grażyński. For me this meant seeing with my own eyes how adjustments had been made in respect of all phases of living; how special passes were available for people who lived on one side of the border but were employed on the other; how controls of water and electric power were regulated so that both sides would be fairly treated; how property adjustments were worked out; how disputes over citizenship were settled; and, for me the most interesting thing of all, how the school life of the youth was taken care of so that teaching could be given as far as humanly possible in the mother tongue.

The only way to get the facts was an endless round of visits and interviews. I spent many hours on the actual frontier, seeing things that were fantastic, such as places where people lived on one side and had their farm buildings on the other – a situation that lent itself readily to smuggling! I was in every kind of office, and sat in on every kind of school activity, whether in the classroom or on special occasions. Here is one passage from a letter to Shotwell, describing conditions on the Polish side of the border:

... Up to now I have visited three high schools, all of them state-controlled. I have sat in thirteen class periods, both of boys and girls, ranging from the second to the eighth grade. I have been in both Polish and German sections, and in the latter have listened to teaching both by Poles in Polish and by Germans in their mother-tongue. The atmosphere was cordial, and I saw no trace of friction either among teachers or pupils. This contrasts greatly with the conditions that existed ten years ago ...

... During the last three days I was guided by the German *Schulverein* people, who told me freely of their difficulties and showed me everything I asked to see. I was probably the first outsider in their class-rooms who could follow what they were doing in either language. So far as I could see their wish was loyally to keep the rules as Polish citizens, as much for material as for idealistic reasons. They understand the position of the Polish authorities, and maintain their own as far as they can. I'll admit to having an uncanny feeling when hearing a throng of German children singing the Polish national hymn on Piłsudski's name-day (19th March), assembled in the school hall in front of his portrait! But I comforted myself with the reflection that at least half of them were from families with Polish names – Germanised under the pre-1914 regime.

And here a diversion. On the advice of Professor Znaniecki I had set aside a hundred dollars to be paid to people of various walks in life for their 'life stories.' In view of the unemployment and consequent hard times, the securing of people, younger and older, for this task was fairly easy. But I had to screen those who applied rather carefully; or rather I had to get each one recommended by someone dependable, otherwise I should have been deluged with more fancy than fact. Here my former Cracow friendships stood me in good stead, and the results were highly satisfactory. In my collection I have materials both in Polish and in German, as well as some written in the Silesian dialect, by people who could not spell properly and had no idea of proper syntax. One of the most revealing of these 'creations' was the work of a school caretaker, who had known many hardships as a boy, had served in the German army, and was fully able to appreciate the prospects enjoyed by his children which were denied to him. That document deserves some day to be published as a contribution to the cultural history of his province.

The time spent in studying the school question saw me on fairly familiar ground. When I came to the technical and business side of 'the big heavies,' however, I had to start from scratch. I knew nothing about the technical processes of heavy industries – mining, smelting, steel-making, or subsidiary operations. When I got into the labyrinth of pit-heads, mills, and laboratories I was lost, knowing neither what certain types of structures were for, why certain things were done, nor the consequences for those involved. All I knew was that the work was hard, at times dangerous, and always highly specialised. In order to 'feel' the life of those engaged in such things, I needed to see them at work; and in order to be able 'to see' anything I needed to know something in advance. I was fortunate in that before leaving London I had come across a most informative little book by Lady Bell, *At the Works*, belonging to Nelsons' Blue Library. A careful study of its chapters relieved my total ignorance on mining and heavy industry. I also had the good fortune that among my friends were a number of mining engineers who made many things easier for me, in particular the head of the Anaconda Copper Co (which had bought out the Giesche Works in the heart of the Industrial Triangle), G.S. Brooks, who gave me some of his time and opened the way for me to see the zinc processing plant at Scharley. His little volume, *Critical Problems of the Upper Silesian Coal Industry*, which appeared in two languages in 1932, gave me needed guidance on many points.

A detailed account of our doings during the winter of 1933-4 would only weary the reader. The atmosphere was not congenial, but one had to make the best of it. There was still an acute measure of unemployment and, until the end of January brought the Non-Aggression Pact, political tension was severe. My time was divided between visits to institutions and interviews with leaders and officials (Polish and German) on the one hand, and long hours of study of documents on the other. In this latter E was giving me generous help, a sample of which was reading the two volumes of Gustav Stresemann's *Memoirs* in the original so that we could get at first-hand his views on German policy. Gradually the picture I was seeking became clearer in my mind: of how the Poles had handled things during a decade, and how a notable piece of collaboration with the League representatives and the German minority had achieved unexpected results. By Easter we were ready for a brief holiday, and we decided to have a look at the new Slovakia. Before telling of this, however, a number of other outings deserve mention, some of them inside, others outside, Silesia.

Thanks to the courtesy of the superintendent-in-charge, I was permitted to visit the huge underground reservoirs, built before the war by German engineers but now on the Polish side of the frontier, which provided the densely populated area of industry (both German and Polish) with an almost unlimited supply of drinking-water. The guaranteeing of this service, irrespective of boundary changes, had been one of the first cares of the authors of the Geneva Convention.

While on a visit to Myślowice, the last German station on the line leading to Cracow in prewar days, I took a couple of hours out to look at the 'corner of the three empires' – Austria-Hungary, Germany, and Russia. Here there had stood one of the three Bismarck Towers that signalled the majesty of the Reich in this part of Europe. The tower had been dismantled long since, and I brought away a small slab of granite as a souvenir. It has made a convenient paper-weight. The time spent here was given to musing on the way human ambitions have been turned to dust and ashes through the ages.

In the fall of 1933, on a borrowed bicycle and in the company of a one-time Cracow colleague who was teaching in the high school in Tarno-Góry, I rode for two days through the northern district of Polish Silesia, where one was quite out of reach of the smoke and bustle of industry. We had a look at points on the new frontier where roads, and even one railway, had been cut off rudely by the new frontier, causing no end of inconvenience to the local inhabitants. It was this kind of thing that made the Germans talk about the 'bleeding' frontier. We also saw points on the prewar frontier with Russia which had been notorious haunts of smugglers. But the most memorable sight of this trip was in the town of Tarno-Góry itself.

Silesian research

Here, in the guest-book of the inn on the town-square, one could see the bit of verse written and signed by Goethe when, in 1790, he stopped on his long journey by carriage from Weimar to Cracow to see the places associated with the legendary Faust. His staying in Tarno-Góry gave him a chance to look at the *Wundermaschine* just set up in a near-by mine – to pump water out of the shafts – the first steam engine to be used in this part of Europe.[4]

Over the New Year I took a few days of 'time out' to make a hurried trip to Vienna and also to visit old friends in Prague. Here I had hopes of getting an interview with the well-known leader of the German minority in Czechoslovakia, Dr Peters, author of *Der Neue Herr von Boehmen*. Fortunately, I found him at home, and we had a long talk. He spoke freely of what he felt were the injustices suffered by his people in the new republic, and one thing struck me forcibly. In Silesia many a German had said to me, 'Oh, if we only had the privileges here that our fellow-Germans have under Czech rule.' Now I heard what those folk had to say, and came to the conclusion that all things are indeed relative: Most of us think of distant fields as greener than our own.

But two journeys made during my time in Silesia stand out – the first at the end of February 1933, the other the Slovakian holiday just mentioned.

A Danish lady who had spent some time in Poland in the early twenties, adding Polish to an already uncanny mastery of languages, had been instrumental in creating a Danish-Polish society in Copenhagen, and I was invited to the Danish capital to give a lecture on Konarski. The prospect was the more pleasing since I was to be the guest there of Dr Michał Sokolnicki, the Polish minister whom I had got to know in Paris during the Peace Conference. The visit was most enjoyable. I tried hard not to be a dull lecturer, and I had a brief look at a People's High School. On the way back to Silesia, I reached Berlin on the morning of 28 February. When I came out of the station and made my way to the Friends' Service Headquarters, it seemed to me that the streets were curiously silent. After waiting some time I found an acquaintance of former years, who was late in arriving at work. Then I learned the news: the Reichstag had been set on fire during the night, and the city was under martial law. Everybody was wondering what would happen next.

---

4 'Since, as I discovered during the Goethe celebrations in London in 1949, this bit of verse is not known even to the savants, I append it here':
'Fern von gebildeten Menschen, am Ende des Reiches, were hilft euch
Schätze finden und sie flueklich zu bringen an's Licht?
Nur Verstand und Redlichkeit helfen; es führen die beiden
Schlüssel zu jeglichem Schatz, welchen die Erde verwahrt.'
[WJR]

After a chat I decided to stay over for one night in any case, and I got a room near by. Then I made my way out to Unter den Linden, where some traffic was to be seen, and as far as the university. Here pickets with rifles over their shoulders were on guard, and when I started to approach the entrance I was stopped. No one was allowed to enter! When I explained that I was from Canada and had been a student there in 1913, the answer was the same. When I asked whether I might in any case step inside the railing and have a look at the statue of Mommsen standing there, I got a grudging 'Yes,' but warning to go no further.

At noon I had an interview, arranged beforehand by mail, with a distinguished German historian (of the Left), and we talked for an hour about international relations. But he wouldn't be drawn to make any comment on what had happened. Late in the afternoon I got around by the canal alongside the Moabite prison, and from there could see the massive parliament building with smoke rising from the central dome. But everything was roped off and I could get no closer. I found one or two other acquaintances, including a British journalist of some reputation, but no one knew anything. Berlin had never attracted me, so I decided to clear out early the next morning.

Arriving in Breslau after noon, I discovered that Hitler was to be there that evening, and a great 'rally' was to be held in the Opera House. What was I to do: stay and try to get a ticket to hear him, or get the first train on to Beuthen and home? I debated the question for some time, and decided that discretion was the better part of valour. I arrived home after midnight. Perhaps it was a failure of nerve; in any case I missed my one and only chance of seeing 'der Fuehrer.'

And now for Slovakia. As the reader will remember, we had been across a good deal of it on foot in 1914, and I was anxious to see the improvements made since those days. Of course I had been in Trenčin in 1925, but no farther. Now we wanted to enjoy some of the lovely scenery, look at the cultural centre of Turčansky St Martin, and, perhaps, even get to Ružomberok, home of the veteran leader of the Slovak Catholics, Monsignor Andrej Hlinka. In St Martin I knew I should find some of the younger generation Slovak intellectuals, and so it turned out: but we were not disposed to spoil a holiday by discussing human affairs too much. We did, however, make the side-trip to Ružomberok, and I went along to ask whether the Father would receive me. His housekeeper explained that he was not well, and did not see visitors; but in a moment I heard steps and a tall figure came around the corner of the house.

Hearing that we were from the New World, Father Hlinka invited us in, and a pleasant hour of conversation about many things followed. As I was leaving, I ventured to say to our host that, since he was no longer young, the question arose as to who would succeed him. I added that Prague friends had described him to me as 'a backward idealist,' but that I could understand how as a churchman he was disturbed by the secularizing forces that threatened his people. He smiled, thanked me, and said that Father Tiso would probably be his 'Elisha,' but added, 'He is a friend of Dr Beneš.' Here was a man who at least did not hesitate to confess his fear of 'dollar-culture.'[5]

Back in Katowice we had six weeks of steady grind before packing up to start for home. The text of my report had to be completed, or nearly so; many courtesy visits had to be made; and some of our nearest friends called on unhurriedly – a time-consuming business. One unexpected invitation could not be ignored. The Polish consul in Oppeln, chief town of German Silesia, Michał Samborski, had helped me in various matters of fact, and he and his lady now asked us to spend Whitsuntide as their guests. They came for us with a car, so the trip was no burden. That we enjoyed it to the full goes without saying, but one feature of it deserves mention.

In the parish church there were tombs of ancient Piast princes, once masters of Silesia. I wanted to see them, but was told by the consul that they were closed to the public. It seemed that too many Polish visitors had been coming, wanting to take photographs, and even expressing their satisfaction at finding Polish notables buried in a German city. However, I decided to try, only to be told by the sacristan that special permission had to be got from the head pastor. To him I went, told him I was an historian from the New World, and asked for a pass. For a time he demurred, but finally gave in. I took with me E and Mme Samborski, who spoke English, and we were treated courteously, though without warmth. The tombs, standing in the lady chapel behind the high altar, were indeed worth a visit, and it would have been a pity to miss them.

Late in May we were ready to leave. The small box of books I brought with me had grown to five, no longer small, so I arranged to ship them by freight to London. Our own way took us to Prague, where I was to lecture to the American Institute on 'Frontier Problems of Central Europe,' and thence across Bavaria to the upper Rhine. For one thing we wanted to see the beauties of Strasbourg; for another I planned to have a good look at this 'border-land' that had been even more than Silesia a bone of contention for centuries; in particular I wanted to find an answer to a question that had long bothered me: Could a man be a good German without speaking German, or Frenchman or Pole though he could not speak the relevant language?

I was prepared to give a month to this fair but harried land of the upper Rhine, before going on to London where I had papers to give to the Institute of

---

5 Hlinka led the Slovak Catholic party which worked for autonomy within the Czechoslovak republic. Jozef Tiso became president of the Slovak republic established in 1939 after the Nazi invasion of Czechoslovakia. He was executed in 1947 for collaboration with the Nazis.

Sociology and to Chatham House. At the back of my mind there was also the hope that we might find Albert Schweitzer, for whose work in Lambaréné E had collected money for years. Reaching Strasbourg safely, we changed trains and went straight on south along the river to Kollmar. Here again we had to change, taking the branch line up the valley westwards to the little town of Münster. This was to be our headquarters.

Gunsbach is three miles down the road from Münster, on the way to Kollmar; and enquiries at the office of one of the local physicians brought the good news that Schweitzer was at home. I wrote him a brief note, saying that we should come along the next day in the afternoon, and hoped he would see us.

The story of the reception we got, of the visits we were permitted to make in the following days, including two delightful invitations to supper (along with other guests), can hardly be told here. Our host came right to the point, and asked me what I was doing. I explained what I was after, and he at once said: 'You will realise that I must not discuss politics with you or anyone else, and I hope you will undertake not to quote me in regard to such matters. My position could easily be exploited by visitors, and I have to be careful.' I gave him my word, and until now nothing has ever been published of what was said. But the time has come when a few of his pertinent comments can be made public.

At that time I knew little of his history, and almost nothing about his theological or philosophical works. But we knew the outlines of his life, and even then regarded him as one of the greatest living witnesses to the Christian faith. Approaching sixty, he had just a few grey hairs but admitted to me that his life was made up of work, work, work. Even then he was daily at his desk, in the little room that opened right on the road, and he let me take a snap-shot of his head and shoulders leaning out of the window on the ground floor. At supper the family spoke the Alsatian dialect which was his mother-tongue; but on being questioned he told me that he had been educated in German and written his theological works in that tongue. However, he always corresponded with his parents in French, and his book on Bach was first written in that language. English he could read, but did not speak.

One day he took me by a winding path to the little 'outpost' a hundred or more feet up the hill across the highway, where he loved to go and sit and meditate. From this vantage-point we had a view eastward across the Rhine valley, to the Black Forest on the other side. I ventured this question: 'Tell me, Sir, what is the difference between the people living here on this side of the Rhine and those living over there thirty-odd miles away?' With a smile he gave me this answer: 'When we stuff a goose at Christmas we do it with apples; when they stuff one they use chestnuts!' Not another word would he say, but it was easy to see that he regarded overdone nationalism as one of the chief menaces

Silesian research

to human happiness. In this I saw one of the reasons for his admiration for Goethe.

On the Sunday morning we were early at the village church, but the strains of Bach were already to be heard from the organ loft. Schweitzer had built the instrument, and only he was expected to play it when he was at home. His guiding of the hymns and in general of the service could be felt by any sensitive spirit. But I found myself for the first time in a church that had been used by the Roman Catholics three hours earlier, and was now echoing to the sound of Lutheran hymns! Of course there were two altars, and the one used for eight o'clock Mass was now screened off; but one would like to know why this sort of thing cannot be done also in the New World.

A good month was needed to deal with the things that demanded attention in England, and to get a week's rest before 'sailing' for home, Dartmouth College.

The most important task of all was still to be done - my report to Professor Shotwell. He heard with satisfaction that I had a virtually finished document; and we were invited to come to his summer home on the middle Hudson, to deliver it in person. The weekend we spent there was indeed a pleasant interlude, though I found myself facing the local Historical Society at a lawn party and telling them something of our experiences. Shotwell took the manuscript with him to New York, while I went home to work on the notes and bibliography. He wanted to get the thing in the hands of a publisher as soon as possible, though we had to admit that the dimensions were formidable and the subject rather special. To put it all shortly, we had no luck for some time; but then the Stephen Daye Press of Brattleboro agreed to take it on condition that a good fifty pages be scrapped. In the spring of 1935 they got to work, and six months later *The Drama of Upper Silesia* was published. When Williams and Norgate of London agreed to buy a substantial number of sheets for an English edition the financial side of the enterprise was cleared up. The book did much to secure my later status in the University of London.

Meanwhile, of course, I was hard at work on what (as things turned out) was to be my last year of teaching at Dartmouth. People were very kind, and the department fitted me in to the changed scheme of things. My old courses had been in the competent hands of Andrew Truxal, who was now head of the department, and this arrangement continued. I was given second-year students and a new course for seniors called 'The Sociology of the Great Society,' dealing with the tensions and problems of nations and classes in relation with one another. It was repeated in the second semester with a new group, and I found these fourth year men a good deal more mature than those who had been under me in previous years. This meant serious work, but it also gave me a chance for thought and reflection on the Silesian experience. My work with the village church in West Hartford was resumed, and a good few invitations to speak in nearer and remoter communities on European issues helped to keep me busy.

By the New Year a decision had taken shape in my mind that promised to occupy me for some years. There were two 'frontiers' in the New World where not dissimilar problems existed from those I had faced in Europe; the one was on the Rio Grande, the other at my door – the cultural tension to be found from the upper Ottawa down to the international boundary, and thence across the upper New England states to the ocean. The former was outside my beat, for I knew nothing of Spanish speech or culture; with the latter I could hope to come to terms more easily, though it would mean hard work at French. The fine book by Jean Bracq, *The Evolution of French Canada*, had come into my hands, giving me the historical background of the whole issue; and for years I had been conversant in a general way with the ecological issues involved. A fillip was given to these reflections in the spring when we were invited to Stanstead College, and spent three days with Principal Amaron and his lady in their home. My resolve was now taken to run up to Ottawa, as soon as the teaching year was over, to discuss the matter with Marius Barbeau, whom I had known since Oxford days. Dr Alan Foley of the history department was a student of the whole question, and he offered to take me in his car – I paying for the gasoline.

We had nearly three days in the Canadian capital, which was new to both of us. The Barbeaus were cordial in their hospitality, and at the Archives we found Professor Gustave Lanctôt. On the third day we were luncheon guests at the Rideau Club, where I had the good fortune to meet two men of whose work I had known for a long time: Professor O.D. Skelton of Queen's University and Senator Raoul Dandurand, whose services at Geneva had brought him much praise. On the previous evening, while at supper with the Barbeaus, I had been handed a telegram from E in Hanover. It repeated a cable, just received from London: 'Arrangements now completed; can you come?'

To understand what this meant we must go back a little. From the time when in 1926 I got my degree in Cracow, responsible people had been saying that I should be at work somewhere in the English-speaking world as a lecturer in Polish studies. The recently formed School of Slavonic Studies in the University of London, with Sir Bernard Pares as director and R.W. Seton-Watson (Scotus Viator) as Masaryk Professor of Central European history, seemed to be the proper place. But for this money was needed, and none was to be found. From 1925 a Polish scholar of distinction, Dr Julian Krzyżanowski, had been there, and in 1930 another had succeeded him – Dr Wacław Borowy; but their field was English literature, and they did not consider the work they were doing as more than temporary. We had seen the Borowys in London, and knew that they had hopes of getting back home soon. He was doing his best to get the Warsaw government to follow the example of Prague and Belgrade and offer a yearly grant to the University of London to make a Polish lectureship possible; but times were still so hard that this plan could not materialize. Now, at last, as the cable seemed to show, the way had been found; and Pares was asking me whether I would take the post.

Once more a serious decision had to be made, though less complicated than that of 1927. Then I was changing my whole field of activity; now I was changing only the place and the subject. To one who did not like big cities, a move from the charms of Hanover to the grime and bustle of London was not an attractive proposition. On the other hand, as one of my senior colleagues was to say when he heard of it the next week: 'There are plenty of people who can be found to do your work here; there are few who could tackle the post offered you in London.' Therein lay the crux of the matter, and from the start I had really no choice. We left Ottawa the next evening, washing out all we had come for.

Before leaving, however, I had spent some pleasant hours with very old friends like the Woodsworths and Dr W.J. Roche. The latter had been our family doctor forty years earlier in Manitoba, and was now high up in the Civil Service. We also visited the quarters of the National Research Council; and in Montreal on our way home we saw the magnificent site of the Catholic University on the slopes of Mount Royal. The next morning, after arrival in Hanover, I was received by President Hopkins, who graciously said that he would not stand in the way of my leaving if the head of the department was willing to release me. This was soon arranged, and the task was to be faced again of packing and travel.

As noted above, we took ten days in August for a first and last look at an unknown corner of the East – the historic Gaspé Peninsula; finding an hour to sit and meditate at the spot where, just four hundred years earlier, Jacques Cartier planted the flag of France and signalled the discovery of Canada. The rest of the summer was consumed with packing. Neither boxes nor crates could be bought, so I had to make them; and seldom have I been more relieved than when, early in September, a big van was loaded for forwarding to Boston. We were present at the opening of a college year in which we were to have no part, and sailed from Montreal on the *Empress of Australia* two days later. It was the end of August 1935.

In association circles it used to be said that no secretary had 'arrived' until he had done a world tour and had a nervous breakdown. That characteristic American combination of achievements may or may not appeal to one: in any case I could not qualify. More than once I knew that, desiring to help where there was so much to be done, I had worked harder than was wise and taken too little time for rest. In consequence there were times when body and mind were below par, and the job less well done than it should have been. With too many things awaiting attention, none was treated properly. Now, it seemed, at long last I was to be allowed to narrow my field of interests and responsibilities; at fifty I was to have a chance to work at one thing. Both the years in Poland and those at Dartmouth – each in a quite different way – could be said to be preparation for this. To fill the cup, I was once more to assume the role of a pioneer. Polish studies had never been thought of as a university discipline in the English-speaking world: the way would have to be trodden in the face of a good deal of indifference. Could I manage to bend the bow of Ulysses?

In the autumn of 1927, shortly after settling down at Dartmouth, I had received a note from a distinguished Canadian, welcoming us home to the New World, but adding: 'All the same, I'm sorry you are lost to us!' From London I wrote him eight years later, telling him of my new duties: 'The wheel has gone full turn: I'm back again.'

8
Epilogue:
London & the Return Home

THE LONDON SCHOOL OF SLAVONIC STUDIES

The decision taken in June 1935 to leave the beauty and quiet of New England and commit ourselves to the unknown - living in the huge city of London - was not easy. But there seemed to be no choice. How fateful it was to be and how soon, no one could foresee, although with Hitler running amok there were those who knew that trouble was ahead.

The School of Slavonic Studies was a small though lively institution. The idea of creating it had arisen during the First World War when in 1915 King's College invited Professor T.G. Masaryk of Prague, who had been living in exile in Switzerland (since December 1914), to come to London and deliver one or more series of lectures on Slavonic affairs. Although almost unknown in the English-speaking world, he had become famous as a political leader, a champion of democracy, in the old Austria-Hungary. In particular the appearance of his two volumes on Russia, published in German in 1913 (English edition, *The Spirit of Russia*), gained for him a wider public, and led of course to undertakings of national and even international significance. He got a world audience when he was asked to deliver the chief address on 6 July 1915 at the Swiss celebration of the martyrdom of Jan Hus, five hundred years earlier. Masaryk used this occasion for an eloquent indictment of the Habsburg dynasty for its age-long antagonism to national and religious liberty. In fact, he threw down the gauntlet and proclaimed in solemn prophecy the end of the Habsburg monarchy.

Nothing more could be done in the field of Slavonic studies until after the war. Then, however, King's College created a chair of Russian studies and asked

Sir Bernard Pares to leave his lectureship in the University of Liverpool and come to the new post in London. A Cambridge man, Pares had been knighted for his war work with the Russian Red Cross, but his claim to distinction lay rather in the fact that before the turn of the century he had begun to visit Russia and to learn Russian. He had been in St Petersburg during the whole period of the 1905 Revolution, and when no one else in the United Kingdom seemed to care about what was going on in the vast world, now known as the USSR, Pares did. Now at last he was to get a chance to develop, not only Russian studies, but those of smaller Slav peoples, and in the capital of the Commonwealth.

One of his first decisions was to ask that the Scottish scholar-gentleman, an Oxford man, who had become known years before the war broke out for his books on the Danube Lands, should be called by King's College as professor of Central European history. His pen-name, Scotus Viator, was well known but already by this time he had become a valiant fighter for the cause of national liberty under his own name, R.W. Seton-Watson, and had published for years a fighting journal called *The New Europe*. To complete the triangle, they got the philologist, N.B. Jopson, from Cambridge to join them and so provide for a balanced programme of studies.

Before long, it became clear that the kind of work these men wanted to do was not in step with other departments in King's College, and by mutual agreement in 1928 the University of London took over the whole enterprise and created an independent School of Slavonic Studies. For years this was housed in the Mabb Street barracks, but then moved to the house, 40 Torrington Square. Here I found a staff of at least ten men, four of whom dealt with Russian studies – one for social questions, one for literature, and two for language. There was also a fine native Serb, a graduate of Oxford, in charge of Yugoslav studies.[1] Into this sizable group I was welcomed as another collaborator and our chief regret was that, owing to unsuitable quarters and a weekly schedule that did not make sense, we could rarely get together or even get to know one another.

One reason for all this was the fact that our apartment house of four storeys had people on every floor, although the second was reserved for the library. Another reason was that teaching, or rather tutoring, went on from early forenoon till late evening in bits and pieces. Almost all our lectures had to be given in classrooms in King's College more than a mile away. These lectures were a major part of our work in literature and history, while the philology and language work was

---

[1] In the academic year 1936-7, there were fourteen professors, readers, and lecturers on the staff of the School of Slavonic Studies. A. Raffi and S. Boyanus taught Russian language, G. Struve taught Russian literature, B. Pares and S. Yakobson taught Russian history. The reader in Serbo-Croat language and literature was D. Subotić.

done at Number Forty. As was to be expected, more than half our students were interested in Russian matters, and the smaller nations followed sometimes far behind. But even in the field of Russian studies things were not easy. Few people in Britain were happy about the Stalin regime, and there was little chance of any cordial exchange of news and views between British and Russian scholars. Pages could be written about this and only later did we come to see what a misfortune it was both for politics and scholarship. I had to admire the way in which Sir Bernard, not liking at all the Soviet brand of communism, still maintained his interest in and loyalty to the essential Russia. I should add that for each of the three university 'terms' a broad sheet was printed announcing the lecture programme in literature, history, and languages, and it was made clear that to all these lectures the general public, if interested, would be welcome.

Every new-comer on the staff, if above the level of lecturer, was expected to offer an inaugural lecture, and mine was set for February 1936. On such occasions a distinguished outsider would be asked to take the chair and in my case we secured the former ambassador in Warsaw, Sir William Max-Muller, whom I knew well. My subject was 'The Polish Tradition,' and I had a sizeable audience to hear me.

Apart from one honours student in language and literature, I had in those prewar years a rather motley assortment of 'casuals' for language study. Some of them were bright but almost none had any academic interest. Each year there would be from three to six in a beginners' class, and we would meet late afternoons three times a week. Occasionally I was called on to help an academic student of some other language, who wanted to acquire some knowledge of Poland. Altogether a far from inspiring enterprise, even less so because we had no good text-book for the study of Polish until 1941. Then, with the coming of the Polish army and government to the United Kingdom after the collapse of France, everything changed. An old friend from the Polish Army Educational Service had been stationed in Paris for many years teaching Polish to French officers. He had a fair command of English and he set himself at once to prepare a decent text-book of Polish for English students. I had the honour of writing a brief introduction commending it to English-speaking students, and Dr J.A. Teslar's work went through three editions in the next ten years. I should add that a second text-book also appeared, a joint work by a competent Polish lady and the professor of Polish studies at Columbia in New York.[2] An additional pleasant and rather exacting duty that fell to me from 1936 on was to serve, at least once a year, as examiner in Polish for the British Civil Service.

2 M. Corbridge-Patkaniawska and A.P. Coleman, *Essentials of Polish Grammar for English Speaking Students* (London 1944)

From the outset I was honoured by the director of the school with a place on the Editorial Board of the *Slavonic and East European Review* – at first of course as a learner. Here I saw more of my British-born colleagues named above than anywhere else. Three numbers of the *Review* appeared each year, each comprising about 240 pages of papers, translations, and book reviews. Some of the contributors were Continental scholars of distinction. This *Review*, begun in 1922, was already well known on both sides of the Atlantic, and with time it has become a veritable encyclopaedia of Slavonic lore. With the outbreak of war in 1939 we had to hand it over to a willing group of American scholars, and Pares was afraid we should never get it back. But we did, in 1945, and for the succeeding five years I was the responsible editor.

For me in those first days the meetings of the Editorial Board were times of no small interest, often of keen and not seldom acrimonious conflict. Pares and Seton-Watson were warm friends, but they could fight like cats over various kinds of issues and I was soon Jopson's 'man Friday' in helping to keep the peace. Seton-Watson had come late into academic life and never cared much for teaching. In addition, he was a poor correspondent, and whether in regard to his own contributions or to papers he would procure from scholars abroad, he never realized the task that the editor of every journal faces to get the materials needed for each number through the various stages of preparation, including galley- and page-proof, so that the *Review* could appear on time. Every editor stands in cross-fire between his contributors and his printer-publisher and Pares did try to get the *Review* out as promised – in December, April, and June. In particular, he wanted to be free with the end of the Summer Term so that he could enjoy the two annual cricket games at Lord's that were for him a week of recreation – the Harrow-Eton match and the one between the two universities. Seton-Watson 'cared for none of these things,' nor did he appreciate enough the mountain of pains-taking work needed after articles were written and before they could appear in print.

In all these times of tension my sympathies were with the editor, although there were occasions when he was at fault. I still recall how, having offered to look for a publisher for my Cracow doctorate thesis of seven years earlier, he had left it in a cupboard in his home in the suburb where mice got at it and chewed away the corner of one whole chapter! But Pares did live up to his responsibility as director and editor-in-chief, and I learned much from him about the ticklish work of preparing all kinds of materials for the press. My personal debt to him grew as time went on. A year after I arrived in London an English edition of my book, *The Drama of Upper Silesia*, appeared, and he at once set out to use it as a pretext for getting me promoted to the status of professor. He also got me a seat on the Board of History of the university, for which I was little qualified since I had never been through the mill as an undergraduate.

From 1938, with Pares already seventy, the vital matter of his successor arose. Under normal conditions Seton-Watson would have taken over. He hated administrative work, never went to a meeting he could avoid, rarely answered letters, and in general was quite unfit for any headship. He knew this quite well; and we should have looked to Jopson as the next choice had he not been taken from us by Cambridge for the chair of Philology.

This left things wide open, and Pares asked me whether I would consent to stand if he nominated me to succeed him. This meant both as director and editor of the *Review*. He pointed out that I had not many students; he knew that I had done some administrative work elsewhere, and my status as professor made me eligible. There was nothing for it but to say 'Yes,' but only on condition that Seton-Watson was willing to accept a junior colleague. In due course, the latter invited me to his home for a Saturday lunch, after which we walked right across Wimbledon Common and back, going over the whole problem. He was quite ready that I should become his 'chief' once we saw eye to eye on policy, and the decks were cleared for what was to be an almost cloudless partnership. He reported our discussion to Pares, and the latter recommended me for the post he was vacating. This was confirmed by the university and announced in the daily press. Inside a week I had a letter from the manager of *Who's Who?* saying that my name was up for the next edition and asking for particulars of my life. I had arrived!

I attended discussions at Chatham House (The Royal Institute of International Affairs), of which I had the honour of being a founder member, but it was natural that I should be more concerned about the Central European scene than about other conflicts.[3] I recall vividly the private meeting, at which no guests were allowed, held in the smaller room at Chatham House with Konrad Henlein, who had set himself up as the spokesman of the Sudeten Germans. He certainly could orate, but he made out a very poor case for grievances, and the 'question and discussion' part of the meeting was in danger of getting us nowhere. Finally I got the eye of the chairman and asked the guest this question: 'Isn't it true that you and your colleagues are concerned far more with what is going on outside, just over the borders in Germany, than you are with the injustices you recall at home?' Almost without hesitation he replied, 'Now we are getting to the root of the matter,' and went on to admit that the sight of the resurgent world of Hitler's Germany just over the border was what animated the whole uproar in Bohemia.

I thought of this when, after the seizure of Prague at Easter 1939, one of my former American Red Triangle colleagues, who knew Europe well, brought to

---

3 Rose delivered three lectures at Chatham House: 'The New Poland' (1923), 'Progress in Poland' (1929), and 'A Talk on the Polish German Non-Aggression Treaty of 1934' (1934).

London a Nazi party map of the Continent in which, in large figures, the dates were set out on which all of Germany's neighbour countries would become part of Hitlerdom. The date splashed across the United Kingdom was 1948! Long before this I had got to know the refrain of the Nazi song, 'Today we are Lords of Germany, Tomorrow Lords of the World.'

Seton-Watson had been present in the House of Commons when Chamberlain assured a cheering and crowded audience that all was well. But he also heard, and we heard it from him, of how Jan Masaryk, Czechoslovak minister in London, had been asked by Chamberlain to come to a meeting at 10 Downing Street, where he found Lord Halifax and a few others discussing the ceding of whole provinces of his country to Germany, without even having a map in front of them to show what this meant. Of course he refused to take part until a map was brought in, and then showed the company how Munich spelt the end of independence. What worried us at the school was the knowledge that for years the Foreign Office people had been pushed aside while 10 Downing Street was making policy.

At a scarcely less revealing meeting in Chatham House than the Henlein one, we listened to a spokesman of the Germans living in the South Tyrol. His name was Reut-Nicolussi. He knew perfectly well that we knew what Mussolini was doing to his fellow-countrymen, but high policy forebade him to say a word until we pried it out of him piece by piece. He knew that to tell the truth would cause trouble for the Axis, and so played it dumb where possible. One of our own Britons, a man with a world reputation, told us one evening that this kind of thing looked to him to be the will of Heaven, and that there seemed to be little or nothing that one could do about it!

There were times when the atmosphere at the school was really depressing. Try as we might, we were unable to establish any real cultural links with the USSR, and the Central Europe set up by the Treaty of Versailles was dissolving before our eyes. The Soviet ambassador, Ivan Maiski, who had known England before 1914 as a refugee, was willing to come and have lunch as the guest of the principal of the university, at which Pares and I were present, but only as a private individual. He was a very charming conversationalist, and told us a story I had never heard. It was of one of the first 'stations' set up by the Moscow government on the Arctic shores of Siberia and was maintained for some years by air-service alone. However, in good time a road was put through and the first army trucks rolled in with food and other necessities. The native folk looked on with amazement, and shouted: 'Look, look! Here comes an aeroplane on wheels!'

From the outset I knew that part of my duty, as the one responsible for Polish studies in London, was to keep in touch with the land and people in question. Further, to acquire as much of an understanding as I could of Poland's

London and the return home

place in European affairs. To get a fair picture of this latter was not easy, for all relationships were dominated by Nazi Germany; and the Pact of Non-Aggression made in 1934 between Germany and Poland made many people set the latter country down as an ally of the Axis. Of course people forgot that Warsaw had made the same kind of a pact with the USSR, and was only trying to preserve the balance between greater powers. Personally I was most unhappy about the pact, that the two Slav peoples bordering on Germany, the Poles and the Czechs, who should have been marching together, were not on good terms with one another. To keep in touch with Poland I had, of course, the embassy in London and other Polish acquaintances as well as three periods of travel and study, two of them in the summers of 1936 and 1938, and the third, a shorter one with a single task to be done, at Easter 1937. The last had better come first.

For some time Cambridge University Press had been planning to publish a two-volume *History of Poland*, to which recognized authorities from both the homeland and abroad would contribute. I was asked to write a chapter on the eighteenth century, and this was already done. But after New Year's in 1937 an inquiry came as to whether I would attempt the chapter on the struggle of the Poles in Prussia against Bismark's ruthless policy toward all non-Germans and Catholics. I had some acquaintance with this from my Silesian studies, and I was tempted to accept. But for this I needed at least two weeks of hard work in the archives in Poznań. I therefore booked a return passage by sea, and was soon on the doorstep of an old friend, the librarian of the Raczyński Library in that city. Details of what happened either on this sojourn or on the longer summer study periods would be out of place here. Suffice it to say that I was given a warm welcome everywhere.

The summer study-travel periods were a more varied and exciting business. About half of each sojourn, six weeks or more, was spent in either Warsaw or Cracow with books and journals, while the rest was devoted to moving about, seeing again well-known places and people or discovering new ones. In 1936 I found the beginnings of recovery from five years of grim depression, during which the national income had sunk by half and nearly all the work of public construction already begun had been suspended. Now, however, the current was moving in the other direction – new buildings, new and better roads, improved conditions of living, and a general sense of buoyancy. Two examples, one material and the other spiritual, will show what I mean.

Thanks to an invitation from his charming wife, I was able to be a guest for some days in the country home of the Raczyński family in the lovely foothill of the Carpathians. The ambassador took me for a two-hour visit to one of two centres which Poland then possessed for extracting nitrates from the air for use as fertilizer in agriculture. This product, which was standing in sacks, ready for export, looked like coarse salt and is one of the most precious materials for fertilizing fields in the world. The wonders of this place, Mościce (which was quite new), would challenge alike the scientist, the artist, and the poet. It was proof of the way the government was busy with down-to-earth things, essential to the well-being of a chiefly agricultural economy.

The other incident is quite different, coming from the field of the mind and the spirit. I was a guest at an informal tea party, at which were gathered a handful of university teachers, both older and younger, in Wilno, near the Lithuanian border. There was much give and take, question and answer, all of it as among friends; but for the most part I was the inquirer, and my host and his colleagues were trying to quiet my curiosity. One of the toughest matters broached was national unity, a vital matter since the Poles had been separated for generations by the partitions.

I asked these men what signs were to be seen still of the thing called 'orientations' in seventeenth and eighteenth century Poland – of looking for support from Austria, Russia, or even Prussia in national policy; or at least what evidence of sectionalism. Much comment was made on this first by the older men, but then came a shrewd and telling dismissal of the whole thing by a younger man in his thirties: 'For us, who have grown up since liberation came in 1918, this kind of thing has no meaning at all. We are Poles, and that's the end of it. Our younger brothers and sisters were born into a free country, and this alone is what really matters.'

My second study tour in 1938 was full of incident but the major part was spent in Warsaw libraries, chiefly with the pages of bound periodicals. I did, however, make a complete circuit of the country, spending many hours talking with old friends and new acquaintances about prospects for the future. Hitler had seized Austria in April and was threatening the Czechs. On my way home through Berlin, I found myself walking in the afternoon when news came that Chamberlain had offered to go and see Hitler in person about the hope of peace. This news was broadcast on the street near the Tiergarten, and I confess to throwing up my hat in satisfaction. Of course my hope was that the PM would tell Hitler what needed to be said, but, alas, he did nothing of the kind. We know how sorry the consequences were. I was relieved when I got safely across the German-Belgian frontier the next day.

In May 1939 I received a note from the War Office asking me to attend a small meeting of a private nature in the room of Col. x. Of course I went along to Whitehall two days later, and found myself in a group of half-a-dozen officers and two or three civilians. The colonel, as I soon discovered, spoke Polish fluently. The business of the meeting was simple: Poland. There was more than a chance that war would come before the summer was over and the army specialists were looking for help in military intelligence. The prime requisite was, of course, proficiency in languages. They knew that I was fairly competent in German and Polish, and I was asked in the case of need whether I could be available. This was a poser, quite unexpected, but I knew the answer from the outset. After a little reflection I put it this way: 'There are two reasons, gentlemen, why I think not: First, as you know I was a civilian prisoner during the former war and so was never in uniform. I should find it hard to get used to one now. Second, I am already in my fifty-fifth year, which is the usual limit for military service, and in my view I can be of more use to the cause if I stay in mufti. Nevertheless, if you find that you need me, just say so!' That answer seemed to me to make sense and it was accepted. I was invited to other meetings, but as a civilian; and the time came when the wisdom of this decision was made clear. I was never to wear the king's uniform.

WAR YEARS 1939-45

Throughout World War II, Rose found himself fully occupied as an expert on Polish affairs. He continued to direct the School of Slavonic Studies, but his activity was channelled into other areas as well. The Royal Institute of International Affairs (Chatham House), directed by Arnold Toynbee, employed him and the British government sent him on two minor foreign missions: to Roumania in 1939 to meet refugees from Poland, and to Palestine in 1944. Rose also played an active role in British-Polish relations. The Polish government-in-exile had its headquarters in London, but Rose's attention was drawn primarily towards unofficial committees and societies. He appeared frequently before Polish gatherings, sponsored luncheons, concerts, and public lectures. The most noteworthy cultural affair was the series of three lectures delivered to the Scottish-Polish Friendship Society by Rose's former doctoral adviser, Stanisław Kot, at this time minister of information in the Polish government-in-exile. Oxford University played host to these lectures on 'Five Centuries of Polish Learning' and granted Kot an honourary degree. The lectures were also published.

Despite his busy schedule, these years allowed Rose to bring forth some of his own work. He published his Rise of Polish Democracy *in 1944 as well as a series of lectures on 'Poland's Place in Europe.'* From Serfdom to Self-Government, *the diary of Jan Słomka, a village mayor under the Austrian regime, also appeared with a foreword by Stanisław Kot. Rose had translated the work ten years before.* [DS]

Things happened all at once. On the morning of 1 September Hitler's armies attacked Poland without a declaration of war. On that Friday I became director of the school, and I was moving into my new office when officials of the Ministry of Works came in to say that the whole university building was being taken over by the government, and that our section of it would be occupied by the Ministry of Information. Everything had to be left. I forgot to bring away my MA gown, an old one it is true, and I never saw it again. But all this did not happen without much preparation. We already knew that in the event of war the whole university (some forty institutions) would be scattered to the provinces. Knowing this, Pares had asked whether our school could be put in Oxford where the half-finished Regent's Park Theological College (Baptist) was available. This request was granted and for a particular reason. A special service was to be set up, under Professor Arnold Toynbee, director of studies of Chatham House, to become the eyes, ears, and nose of the Foreign Office. The rich accumulation of press cuttings that Chatham House had made during twenty years would be moved for safety and Balliol College was designated for its home. Pares, Seton-Watson, and myself were transferred to the senior staff of this Foreign Press Service – for the duration. Each of us had received notice that, within three day's outbreak of war, we should try to proceed to Oxford and report for duty.

The business of Toynbee's organization was to report to interested government offices any and every scrap of news that was relevant, culled from the press of the world that came to us through official channels direct from every continent. We were, therefore, divided up along the whole west side of Balliol College into sections, some with two or even more workers because of their size and importance, but others with a single specialist who had to be competent both in languages and affairs. I should add that there were times when I felt that very little of the work we did had any tangible value for the war effort. Of course no one could ever know when some scrap of information, gleaned from a column in a newspaper, might be of use to the specialists higher up who knew the whole picture better than we did. Some of our inner circle were men who belonged to the Secret Intelligence Service, so that they formed a link between those at the top and our more general fact-finding company. Some of our work was tedious, and it was always a pleasure when, in addition to our exchange of news at our noon meeting, we welcomed some guest from outside, even overseas, who brought a fresh point of view or even the latest news.

Suddenly, out of the blue, there came in mid-October 1939 the rumour that I was wanted in Roumania. Seton-Watson had heard it in London and it was soon explained. My old YMCA chief, Paul Super, had with his wife escaped by road from Warsaw on a terrible journey to Roumania, along with many of the diplomatic corps. He was now organizing 'relief' for thousands of mostly stranded refugees, both military and civilian. With his usual drive he had gone to the British minister there and asked for two things: help with getting supplies, especially drugs and medical supplies; and Bill Rose. The minister was surprised but promptly forwarded this request to London, and a plan was soon on foot to send two people to find out what was going on in that far-away corner of Europe. As it happened, I went alone.

By the fall of 1940, we sensed a rising protest because London, which had survived Hitler's fury, had no university work of any kind going on, and even the Extension Programme was small. Again on the initiative of our secretary, the school got permission to reopen our work in rented quarters, first in Russell Square and then, from May 1941, after this house had been set on fire by an incendiary bomb, in a fine temporary home nearby in Gordon Square. This house backed up onto quarters owned by University College, among which was a sizeable hall that could be used for all larger gatherings. We now had two establishments, with something going on in both, until in the winter of 1942-3 the services called forcibly for something that should have been set from the start – organizing extensive language courses for the army and the air forces in Eastern European languages.

With the need for concentrating on this task, and perhaps helping with the teaching, I decided in February 1943 to resign from the Foreign Press Service and return to London. Three-and-a-half years away from home was long enough, and my usefulness in Balliol was over.

POST-WAR WORK AND RETIREMENT

The end of hostilities permitted Rose to resume scholarly pursuits while watching developments in Poland. He took up once more the editorship of the Slavonic and East European Review *as the journal returned to London after wartime publication in the United States, wrote* Poland Old and New, *a book which expanded the optimistic portrait drawn in previous studies, and contributed numerous shorter pieces. As before, teaching occupied much of his time.* [DS]

As this is not a general history, I must limit myself to domestic affairs. For our school the first shock came when, before leaving for summer school, we learned that University College wanted back the quarters we had been using, and we had no choice but to move. This meant getting temporary quarters until the Ministry of Information was disbanded. Miss Galton found a 'stop gap' miles away in Bayswater, a flat of four storeys in filthy condition just evacuated by the army.

Here she and I and our seventy-five-year-old 'doorman' toiled for days to clean things up and we moved in on 25 September.

Then came the blessed news that our part of the university building was to become vacant first, and that we could hope to get back home soon. We actually returned to Bloomsbury on 2 November. Of course we were glad, but there were many moments of doubt in the next six months. The shell of the building was intact, but scarcely a pane of glass was left on the west side which suffered most on the night a German blockbuster wrecked the Women's Residence across Malet Street. Various devices of paper and cardboard filled the window spaces, for no glass could be bought anywhere. The winter was one of discomfort in many ways.

The most impressive thing of this time was the enormous expansion of our student body by contrast with what we had known in prewar times. From the services came upwards of two hundred mature and eager people, some of them beginners, but many with a record of studies done in wartime, whose needs were to claim all the strength we had.

Despite added teaching, Rose found the energy to take up personnel matters. He was deeply concerned with the fate of Poles who had finished the war outside of Poland. Should they return to their homeland in which the Communists were clearly gaining power? [DS]

No one could be other than sorry that the Allies did not make a serious effort to have their country handed back to the Poles after its liberation from Nazi tyranny, just as France was handed back to the French. Since this was not done, and since the governmental system in Warsaw was now dictated solely by Moscow, what was one to think, or say? The 'line' I took was to enquire, wherever I did not know, whether there were kith and kin waiting for them; reminded them of the sad futilities faced a century earlier by what is still called 'the Great Emigration,' chiefly in France: a sense of helplessness that grew from year to year. Finally, I did not fail to stress the fact that, for the most part, men and women have a single *patria*, which to the normal person is the most precious thing on earth. For over two years I held to this tactic; but when the Soviet-trained Marshal Konstantin Rokossovsky was put in charge on the Vistula, still more after what happened in Prague in March 1948, I reversed my piece.[4] I should add that, while in Poland in March 1947, I did see some who had taken counsel with me, and none of them regretted his decision, tough as conditions were.

4 Konstantin Rokossovsky (Rokossowski), Polish-born marshal of the Soviet army, supreme commander of Soviet occupation troops in Poland, later appointed Polish minister of war and commander-in-chief of the Polish army. In March 1948 the Communists took over the government of the Czechoslovak Republic.

Rose did his utmost to help those who decided to stay in the West, however. He assisted as best he could in finding academic positions for Polish scholars in Britain and, if necessary, in North America. He mentioned particularly Jerzy Peterkiewicz, who succeeded him at London, and Wiktor Weintraub, who went to Harvard. Despite his interest in Poles, Rose did not neglect English-speaking scholars. He expressed special pleasure in the encouragement and assistance which he gave to two productive scholars, R.R. Betts, who also went to the University of London, and Peter Brock, who like Rose, went to Poland after World War II with the Friends' Service Committee and took his doctorate at Cracow before returning to England. Professor Brock now teaches at Toronto. Another protégé was James St Clair-Sobell, an Australian, whom Rose placed as first head of the Department of Slavonic Studies at the University of British Columbia. Strong differences of scholarly opinion caused Rose to have second thoughts about the aid given to another British scholar, R.F. Leslie, early in his career.

As Rose approached his sixty-fifth birthday, he became 'conscious ... of the need to take things easier [but] was still able to work, and should have been unhappy doing nothing.' He considered moving to the country in the south of England as the likelihood of succeeding Dr George Gooch as chairman of the Stapley Trust would have provided the finances needed to allow him to continue working with Polish societies in Britain. A resumption of original scholarship was another possibility. Rose thought of writing 'a survey of the history of education in Poland, with the University of Cracow getting special attention ... But the Bierut regime certainly had been made even worse under Rokossovky and it was to be doubted whether I should have had any freedom of movement.'[5] Otherwise, Rose would have been willing to go to Poland and 'live there for a year, even though hardship was the order of the day.' Travel, too, had its charms. He reflected upon taking 'the best part of a year free from all duties and spend[ing] at least half of it in Central Italy ... Somewhere along the way a matter of four weeks was needed to have a look at Athens and some of the ageless wonders of Greece.'

While the Roses were discussing these possibilities, an invitation to return to Canada as visiting professor at the University of British Columbia determined the issue. National feeling had much to do with the decision. [DS]

It was not easy to make the final decision. The fact was, however, that both E and myself found the ties binding us to Western Canada stronger than we had thought, and the prospect of a further adventure in pioneering was attractive. We had managed to get together (for such as us) a considerable sum of savings, but

5 Bolesław Bierut, first president of the Polish People's Republic.

no one could take a sovereign out of the UK without special permission from the governors of the Bank of England. Of course an application was made, and it might have succeeded; but the course of things was assuredly made easier by the fact that Sir Ernest Peacock, a Canadian whom I knew as a trustee of the Rhodes Trust, was one of the governors. I secured a few minutes audience with him, and he promised to do what he could. The transaction took some time, but the sequel was for us a happy one. When we needed to buy a home in Vancouver the next summer we had almost enough to pay for it.

Thus ended half a lifetime of banishment from our native land, and I cannot refrain from adding a few reflections on it all.

1 Every man who looks back down a long vista of busy years is bound to be faced with the question: 'Was I in the driver's seat, or was I being driven?' If the latter be conceded, then by what, or whom? And a second question follows hard on the heels of this one: 'Have I, on looking back, to face a series of scenes dominated by regrets, or one sparkling with satisfaction?' Put another way: 'If the chance were given me of doing over again the things I have done, would I have acted differently?' If so, why?

2 The first thing that must be said is that I was fortunate in my life-mate. Not once did she vote a *ceterum censeo*, though there must have been times when she wondered where the way was to lead us. In retrospect I can see that she paid more than her share of the price both of our 'wanderings' and of any successes achieved.

3 But enough on personal matters. I come back to the general question raised above, as to whether we chose our path, or rather it was thrust on us. On reflection, it comes to me that the second is nearer the truth. It is a fact that I did make a decision in 1926-7, which was to return to the teaching profession. To Dr Mott and those around him this looked like running away, and they were disturbed by it. They could point to reasons why I should have stayed in Poland, notably my competence in the language and knowledge of Polish history and traditions, but the kind of work they wanted me to do was something for which I had neither training nor inclination, and I could not face it. My heart had been with teaching, and was to remain there. I am still toying with it in one way or another almost forty years later. My moving from UBC to the Leadership Training School in Naramata in 1956 was not a step downward, though my work here has been mostly of an elementary kind. In addition I have probably learned more here since that date than in any equal period of my life – the Dartmouth years excepted.

4 In conclusion, I must bare my heart and mind on one other matter. Not a few of my Polish friends, on both sides of the Atlantic, men and women of distinction, have felt in their hearts that by coming home in 1950 I 'deserted the

ship.' This may be only a conceit on my part, for no one ever said so in plain speech, but after being for over two decades one of the best-known spokesmen in the English-speaking world for the rights and merits of a gallant and sorely tried nation, I abruptly ceased to 'function' or to 'witness.' Of course this is not quite the case, for as many know I have done some writing, and a little speaking - but not about the great issue. To all intents and purposes I have become a 'has-been.'

Let it be said at once that undoubtedly the greatest experience of my life was the privilege of a ring-side seat when the long imprisoned peoples of Central Europe won back their freedom of action in the last weeks of 1918. Oh, I know that the victory was won in France and not on the Danube or the Vistula, but the fruits of it were seen chiefly elsewhere. I was also not far away in the following years when those peoples were showing that they deserved this freedom. Of course I was nearest to what was going on in Poland, and I have recounted elsewhere many impressions of it all. Both those who had fought and those who came along to bear the burden of citizenship revealed a faith that amazed me, reminding me often of Browning:

Never doubted clouds would break,
Never felt though right could falter, wrong would triumph
Held we fall to rise, are baffled to fight better,
    Sleep to wake.

To those Poles who have missed me from the ranks in the still unsettled struggle for the soul of the nation I am grateful. They are always, and the whole nation, in my thoughts. In 'defecting,' if that is the word, let me say that E and I never quite forgot that we were born and bred western Canadians; that our parents belonged to the first pioneers on the prairies, long before the railway came; and that many Canadians felt about us at times as some Poles do today.[6] Suddenly recalling the famous aphorism, 'Blessed are the homesick, for they shall find their way home!' I realize now that, in all probability, there was a hidden sense of 'homesick' deep in both our hearts as we got older. The decision to come home, taken in 1949, was another of the blind experiences I can record, in retrospect, with *gratitude*. In any case, we were not idle, and we regarded the cause of peace and freedom as one the world over.

6 Rose published a lengthy article about his retirement which quotes some of the words used in the memoir. 'Pro Domo Sua,' *Wiadomości* (London), XX, 36, 1014, 6 Sept. 1965. The next three lines in this edition of the memoirs were added in Rose's own hand at the bottom of the final page of his original manuscript.

Today I take a little comfort from the fact that all the books I wrote (and I wrote too much) are out of print and almost unobtainable. I still get from time to time, and from the most unexpected quarters, an enquiry as to whether this or that is to be had, 'it still could be that you have a copy yourself to spare!' This is flattering to an old man, a sign that he is 'not forgotten.'

Index

ARA *see* American Relief Administration
Abel, Theodore 123, 128, 183
Adriatic Sea 67, 204
Adventists 151
Albania 23
Allen, Richard xivn
Alliance College 198
Allied Commission (Teschen) 94-6
Allied Expeditionary Force 135
Allies (*see also* Entente) 58, 63, 65, 67, 78, 84, 86, 90, 93, 228
Alps, 5, 84
Alsatian Dialect 212
Althammer 41
America(n) *see* United States
American Relief Administration [ARA] 92, 96, 100, 112, 115, 119, 162
Antwerp 10, 108
Arabs 88
Arctowski, Henryk 96n, 97, 118
Aristotle 28

Armistice Day xii
Arnold 162
Askenazy, Szymon xxiii
Asquith, Herbert Henry 24
Astor, Lady (Nancy Witcher Langhorn, Viscountess Astor) 50
Athenagoras, Metropolitan Archbishop of Greece 175
Athens 229
Austria (*see also* Austro-Hungarian empire, Dual Monarchy, Habsburgs) 27, 42, 45, 66, 77, 90, 95, 116, 157, 184, 224
Australia 29
Austro-Hungarian empire (*see also* Dual Monarchy, Habsburgs, Hungary) xv, 3, 4, 63, 74, 94, 202, 208, 217, 225; armies 29, 52, 58, 60, 64, 65, 70, 84; civil service 25, 52, 59, 131; Germans 39, 62; international affairs xi, xx, 23, 25, 27, 58, 224
Axis 222-3

The index was prepared by Ms Gerry Morin.

234 Index

Bach, Johann Sebastian 212-13
Baliński-Jundziłł, Jan 132
Balkans 25, 59
Balliol College 226
Baltic 76, 105n
Baptists 7, 13, 151
Barbeau, Marius 214
Baroque 5, 98
Bass, Lieutenant 96
Bavaria 211
Bayon 83
Bayswater 227
Beard, Captain 91-2
Beard, Charles xviii
Beatenberg 123
Beck, Józef xxiii
Becket, Thomas à 184
Będziń 135
Belgium 26, 81, 176, 203, 224
Belgrade 23, 46, 204, 215
Bell, Lady 207
Belorussia xxiii, 139
Beneš, Edvard xv, xxiii, 9, 15, 17, 87, 104, 211
Berezina River 139, 141
Berlin 6, 26, 30, 32, 56, 108, 109, 131, 177, 203, 205, 209-10, 224
Berne 27, 90-1, 103
Berry, W.M. 139, 164
Beskid Mountains 23
Bethesda 51
Betts, Reginald R. 229
Beuthen (Bytom) 204-6, 210
Belvedere 195
Bible 4, 8, 14, 15, 18, 45, 55, 132, 144
Bickefeld 50
Bielsko [Bielitz] 61, 95
Bierut, Bolesław 229
Biskupin 191
Bismark, Otto von 109, 149, 208, 223

Black Forest 212
Bland, Salem xiv
Bloomsbury 228
Bocca di Cattaro 43
Bodelschwingh 50
Boháč, Karel 8, 15
Bohemia (*see also* Czechoslovakia) xii, 3, 5-7, 12n, 16, 17n, 18, 52, 59, 67, 70, 111, 205, 221
Bohumín *see* Oderberg
Bolsheviks 65, 78, 83-4, 86n, 88n, 90, 102, 108, 111, 123, 178, 189
Bolshevism (*see also* Communism) 72, 82, 140, 171; threat of xiii, xvi, 71, 112, 139, 193
Bolshevist *see* Bolsheviks
Borden, Sir Robert 86
Borowy, Wacław 214
Borysław 141
Bosnia 20
Boston 67, 215
Botha, Louis 86
Boulogne 72
Boyanus, S. 218n
Bracq, Jean 214
Bradenburg 17n
Brattleboro 213
Břeclav 32
Breslau [Wrocław] 184, 201, 210
Brest-Litovsk [Brześć-Litewski] 70, 135, 138, 189
Bristol 48, 131
Bristol Hotel (Warsaw) 195
Britain (*see also* England, United Kingdom) 74, 76, 78, 81, 106, 116, 132, 219, 229; international affairs (*see also* Paris Peace Conference) 24-5, 88
Brno [Brünn] 14-15
Brock, Peter vi, 229

Brodziński, Kazimierz xviii
Bronowice 85
Brooklyn 8
Brooks, G.S. 207
Brother Albert 160
Browning, Robert 231
Brzczany 135
Buchs 91
Buckle, Henry Thomas 53
Budapest 19, 32, 40-1, 70, 104
Bug River 189
Bulgaria 138
Bullitt, William 88-90
Bülow, Bernard von 109, 195
Bułowski, Lieutenant B. 64-6
Bulwer-Lytton, Edward 196

California 92
Calonder, Felix L. 206
Calvin, John 54
Cambridge, England 218, 221
Cambridge University Press 223
Canada ix-x, 25-6, 48n, 61, 68, 75, 83, 101, 107-8, 110, 139, 186, 197, 210, 214-16, 229-31
Canadian Association of Slavists xiv
Canadian National Railway 197
Canadian Peace Mission 81
Canterbury 184
Carinthia 30
Carpathians xi, 19, 21, 23, 31, 33, 40-2, 121, 124, 158, 223
Carter, E.C. 69, 71
Cartier, Jacques 215
Catholic *see* Roman Catholic
Cecil, Lord Robert 88-9
Central Europe (*see also* Eastern Europe, Slavs) 9, 13, 28, 54-5, 57, 62, 69, 71-83, 86-90, 104, 112, 114, 121, 183, 187, 191, 193, 195-6, 218, 221, 231; anti-semitism 15, 45; international affairs (*see* Paris Peace Conference)
Chamberlain, Neville ix, 222, 224
Chambers, Edmund 48n, 118
Charles XII, King of Sweden 32
Charles University 3, 12n
Charles, Habsburg emperor 58
Chatham House *see* Royal Institute of International Affairs
Chicago 8-9
China ix, xiv-xv, 165
Chirol, Sir Valentine 81
Chisholm, Jean 118
Chopin, Fryderyk x, 99, 195-6
Chotek, Sophie 20
'Christocratic' 14
Christocratic Student Movement 16
Chrzanowski, Bernard 109
Chrzanowski, Ignacy xviii, xixn, 56, 127, 144, 184
Ciemniewski, Jan 132
Cieszkowski, August xi, xv-xvi, xxi, 56-7, 83, 94, 108, 122, 153, 172, 194
Cieszkowski, August (the younger) 56
Cieszyń *see* Teschen
Clark, Elizabeth 23, 27, 46, 71
Cleveland 181
Cockin, Frederick Arthur ('George'), Bishop of Bristol 131
Cologne 108
Colton, E.T. 196
Columbia University xviii, 128, 157, 219
Comenius (Komenský), Jan Amos 12
Communism (*see also* Bolsheviks, Bolshevism) xxiv, 219, 228
Conference of Relief Workers 120
Congo 82

Congress of Delegates of the Slav
    Peoples (1848) 5, 32
Conrad, Joseph 40, 191
Constance 12
Constantinople 86n, 89, 190
Connor, Ralph (Charles William
    Gordon) x, xin
Coolidge, Archibald Cary 92
Co-operative Commonwealth
    Federation [CCF] xiv, 107
Cornwall, Colonel 105
Copenhagen 209
Copernicus, Nicholas x, 185
Corbridge-Patkaniawska, M. 219n
Corfu 46
Council of the Provisional Government
    of Slovenia 64
Counter-Reformation 54
Czech Renaissance 3
Czechoslovak Republic 228n
Czechoslovakia 3, 8n, 10, 19, 76, 89,
    90, 95, 205, 209, 222; international
    affairs 52, 86-7, 105-6, 211n, 224;
    Teschen question *see* Teschen
Czechs 6, 7, 12, 15, 31-3, 40, 59-60,
    62, 70, 79, 81-2, 87, 89, 92-4, 96,
    97, 102-4, 106, 110, 173, 223;
    national character xv, xxii, 5, 7,
    16-7, 25, 29
Czekanowski, Jan 85, 90
Częstochowa 135, 152, 179, 190
Czikiel, General 154

Dąbrowa 135
Dafoe, J.W. 81
Dalhousie University 178n
Dalmatia 43
Dandurand, Raoul 214
Danish-Polish Society 209
Dante 45

Danube 42, 59, 71, 113, 218, 231
Danzig (Gdańsk) xii, 70, 78, 82, 105,
    108, 164, 184, 189, 198, 201
Dardenelles 32
Dartmouth College xiii, xviii, 119,
    188, 197-8, 199n, 202, 213, 216,
    230
Davis, A.D. 153, 182
Dłuski, Dr 84
Dmowski, Roman xii-xiii, xxi, 74-8,
    84, 90-1, 195
Dniester River 189
Dominicans 185
Dostoevsky, Feodor 11, 54
Drtina, František 10
Dual Monarchy (*see also* Austro-
    Hungarian empire, Habsburgs) 7, 8,
    20, 33
Dubois 94
Dubrovnik [Ragusa] 204
Dunajec River 29
Dvořák, Antonín 3
Dyboski, Roman 132, 156
Dziewicki, Michał 159, 192

ESR *see* European Student Relief
Eastern Europe (*see also* Central
    Europe, Slavs) 4, 72, 81, 87
East Prussia 86
Eberle, Josef 47
Ebersole, A.A. 179-80
Edinburgh 48, 118
England (*see also* Britain, United
    Kingdom) 40, 48, 50, 72, 74-5, 78,
    80, 83, 85, 183, 212-13; international
    affairs (*see also* Paris Peace Confer-
    ence) 26, 30, 59n
Enlightenment 187
Entente (*see also* Allies) 61, 69, 74, 79,
    80, 84

Eötvös, József 53
Erickson, Pastor 23
Erlangen 47
Esthonia 175
Estreicher, Stanisław 119
Europe 46, 86, 104, 165-6, 187
European Student Relief [ESR] 11, 114-20
Evangelical religion 87, 128
Évian-les-Bains 103
Eyman, Frank 172

Fanger, Captain 96
Faust 209
Fenn, S.P. 181
Filipowicz, Tytus 63-4, 85
Finland 8, 81, 175
Fischer, Pastor 131
Fitzgibbon Young 103
Fletcher Argue, R. 80
Florence 185
Foerster, Friedrich W. 13-14, 54, 71
Foley, Alan 214
Ford, A.R. x
Ford, Henry 46
Fordham, Major 95
France 5, 40, 59, 61, 66, 68, 70, 72, 74-5, 79, 81-8, 102-3, 110-11, 115, 117, 123, 135-7, 171, 173, 188, 212, 215, 219, 228, 231; international affairs *see* Paris Peace Conference
Franciscans 185
Franz Ferdinand, Archduke of Austria 20
Franz Josef, Habsburg emperor 20, 58
Frederick, Archduke of Austria 33
Frederick II, King of Prussia 31, 199
Free Masonry 149-50, 171, 195
Frenssen, Gustav 54
Freytag, Gustav 53

Friends' Service Mission 115, 120, 229
Frinta, Anton 8, 11
Froustka, Jan 10
Frydek 31-2, 42, 60

Galicia 31, 59, 61, 72n, 73, 95
Galton 227
Gardiner, A.G. 108
Gardner, Monica 141
Garesch, Father 151
Gaspé Peninsula 215
Gdańsk *see* Danzig
Geneva xiii, 46, 89-90, 53, 175, 198, 214
Geneva Convention 206, 208
George Muller Orphanages 48
Germans 3, 6-8, 15-16, 18, 27, 32, 33, 40, 60, 78, 80, 92, 95, 99, 120, 132-3, 140, 173, 177, 178, 200-1, 212, 221; national character 14, 111, 175, 191, 202
Germany (*see also* Prussia) xv, xx, 5, 55, 74, 76, 82, 105n, 109n, 201, 203, 204, 208; armies 59, 69; international affairs (*see also* Paris Peace Conference) xx, 25, 26, 40, 100, 114, 176, 189, 198, 221-2
German Reich 29, 59, 106, 109, 176, 202, 205, 208
Gibson, Hugh 69, 72-3
Gilchrist, Colonel 113
Glasgow 123
Gnojnik 26, 51, 55, 92-4
God 11, 149*passim*.
Goethe, Johann Wolfgang von 45, 201, 209, 213
Goleszów 124, 126-8, 131
Gooch, George P. 106, 229
Górniak 58-9
Gospels *see* Bible

Gothic 98
Grace Church xiv
Graz 131
Grazyński, M. 206
Greece 4, 166n, 168, 229
Greek Orthodox 14
Green Guards 70
Grey Samaritans 115, 141
Griffin, A.K. 178-9
Grohman, Alfred 179, 181
Grundtvig, Baron Nikolai 129
Guggenheim Foundation 198
Gunsbach 212

Haberl, Hans 15, 23, 30
Habsburgs (*see also* Austro-Hungarian empire, Dual Monarchy) xviii, 3, 5, 12, 16, 17, 20, 32, 38, 39, 52, 73, 76n, 105, 114, 139, 217
Haig 120
Halifax, Lord (Edward Frederick Lindley, First Earl of Halifax) 222
Halle 201
Haller, General Józef xii, 70, 79, 84, 105, 171
'Haller's Army' 67, 83, 90, 101, 103, 108-9, 135, 180
Hanover 214-15
Harley, J.H. 78
Hartshorne, Richard 200
Harvard x, 87n, 118, 229
Hastings 150
Hauptmann, Gerhard 54
Headlam-Morley, James W. 72-3, 85, 87, 103, 105
Hegel, Georg W.F. xvi, 50
Helsinki 174-5
Hempel, Lieutenant 85
Henlein, Konrad 221-2
Henriod, H.L. 131

Hitler, Adolf 105n, 202-4, 210, 217, 221-2, 224, 226-7
Hlinka, Andrej 210-11
Hlond, Cardinal August 152
Hofstadter, Richard xviii n
Hohenzollern 114
Holland 15, 117
Holy Alliance 80
Holy Roman empire 5
Holy See *see* Vatican
Home for the Aged Poor 96, 99
Hoover, Herbert (*see also* American Relief Administration) 92, 112, 115, 143
Hopkins, Louis Bertram 215
Horodyski 140
Hosenpud 100
House, Colonel Edward 67, 69, 80
Howard, Sir Esme 85-7, 95, 97-8
Hradčany 5, 10
Hubay, Jenö 40
Hugo, Victor 53
Hungary (*see also* Austro-Hungarian empire) 15, 23, 29, 31, 59, 65, 71; national character 20, 22
Hus, Jan 5, 7, 12, 104, 217

Illinois 165
Imka [YMCA] 162
Independent Workers of the World [IWW] 108
India 89, 118
Innsbruck 92
Institute of Sociology (London) 212
Islam (*see also* Muslim) 89
Italy xii, 12, 27, 39, 40, 52, 58, 63, 65-7, 70, 84, 92, 116, 136, 148, 229
Ivens, William 107
Izabella, Princess (Izabella z Lubomirskich Czartoryska) 190

Jablunkov Pass 21, 32, 59, 106
Jacob, E.O. 165-7, 172, 190
Jagiellonian University (Cracow)
  xiii, xviii, xix, 122-3, 185, 191, 199, 229
Janos, Victor 23
Janowski, Aleksander 156, 158
Jasna Góra 191
Jesuits 144, 145, 149, 151-2, 159
Jews xiii, 7, 14-15, 18, 22, 32, 38, 45, 89, 96, 99, 100, 121, 128, 132, 141, 171, 175, 178, 200
Joint Distribution Committee (Jewish-American) 115
Jopson, N.B. 218, 220-1
Joseph, Father 133

Kaekenbeck, Georges 206
Kakowski, Cardinal Aleksander 152
Kallenbach, Józef 140
Kaltenbach, Frederick W. xx
Kamieniec Podolski 189
Karafiat, Jan 18
Karl Gustav, King of Sweden 190
Kaschau [Košice] 32
Kasprowicz, Jan 118
Katowice, 199-202, 205-6, 211
Kaye, V.J. ix n
Kazimierz 189
Keiler, Fritz 54
Kelly, Eric P. 119, 188
Kentucky 92
Kerr, Phillip 73
Kiczera 38
Kielce 154
Kiev 32, 78, 143
King family 24
King's College 217-18
Kirkconnell, Watson x n

Kisch, Colonel 72
Kitchener, Lord Horatio H. 27
Klagenfurt 30
Kleiner, Juliusz 183
Kollmar 212
Konstancin 193
Konarski, Stanisław xiii, xix, 186-7, 209
Konopczyński, Władysław 186
Kopiec Kościuszkowski 185n
Kordecki, Prior 190
Korfanty, Wojciech xx
Korniłłowicz, Władysław 126-8, 132, 156, 195
Kościuszko, Tadeusz 76, 198
Kościuszko Foundation 199n
Kot, Stanisław xiii, xix, 186-8, 225
Kozdon, Józef 95
Kraków see Cracow
Kremnitz 21
Kryński, Adam 183
Krzyzanowski, Julian 167
Krzyzanowski, Wacław 214
Kubisz, Jan 55
Kuehnemann, Eugen 202
Kulisz, Pastor Karol xi, xv, 23, 27, 31, 33, 35, 41, 47-52, 54-5, 60, 62, 71, 75, 82, 85, 87, 93, 110, 124, 132
Kun, Béla 71, 104
Kuśnowicz, Father 159-60
Kutno 135

Lake Gopło 191
Lambaréné 212
Lambeth, Bishop 87
Lanctôt, Gustave 214
Lansing, Robert 86
Laslowski, Ernst 204-5
Latin 186
Latinik, Colonel 95

Latvia 175
Lawrence, T.E. xiii, 88-9
League of Nations, xx, 104, 105n
Leipzig 5, 8, 53, 133
Lenaugasse 13
Lenin, Vladimir Ilich 112
Leo XIII, Pope xiv
Lepszy, Leonard 184n
Leslie, R.F. xx, 229
Leszczyński, Stanisław 86
Ligotka xi, 14, 16, 17n, 19, 22, 27, 30, 32-3, 36, 43-9, 56, 58, 62, 75, 81, 87, 92, 94, 103, 126, 193; description 23
Limanowa 29
Limanowski, Bolesław 192
Lindley, Sir Henry 177
Lithuania 139-40, 224
Ljubljana (Laibach) xii, 63-6, 70
Lloyd George, David ix, 31, 73
Łódź xiii, 114, 169, 172, 175-82
Lombardy 67
London v, xxiv, 10, 15, 26, 27, 37, 57, 58, 64, 72-8, 81-4, 90, 100, 108, 131, 187-8, 191, 197-9, 207, 209n, 211, 213-18, 222-3, 225-9
London School of Slavonic Studies *see* School of Slavonic Studies
Londziń, Father Józef 61
Long, H.W. 159
Lord, Robert H. xiii, 87, 95-6
Lorraine 83-4, 135
Losonc [Lučenec] 19-20
Loyola, Ignatius 54
Lublin xxiv, 39, 119, 135, 180
Lublin (Catholic) University 115, 119
Ludwiczak, Father 129
Lukl, Adolf 8
Luther, Martin 5, 7, 51, 54
Lutheran xv, 16, 22, 27, 31-2, 36, 45, 47, 56, 100, 111, 128, 200, 204

Lutosławski, Wincenty 140, 151, 192-4
Luxemburg 17n
Lwów 27, 29, 62, 70, 72, 85, 96, 104, 118, 124, 132, 135
Lwów University 96n, 115

Mackensen, General Augustus 59
Magdeburg 63
Magyars (*see also* Hungary) 18, 20
Maiski, Ivan 222
Mamica, Pastor 51
Manitoba xi, 80, 91, 97, 141, 215
Manitoba Free Press 81
Marchlewski, Leon 122, 166, 190
Maria Theresa, Habsburg empress 31
Marne 46
Marseilles 127
Mary, J.C. 118
Mary Macdowell Settlement 8
Masaryk, Alice 8-9
Masaryk, Jan 9, 222
Masaryk, Tomaš G. xiii, 8-11, 53, 81, 93, 104, 217
Massachusetts 138
Materialism xiv, xxi
Max-Muller, Sir William 219
Mazurians 86
Mazzini, Giuseppe 194
McBride 120
McNaught, Kenneth xvn
Mediterranean Sea 88
Melle, Pastor 91
Messianism xvi, xvii, xxi, 56, 194
Methodist 87, 151
Metternich, Prince Klemens von 80
Meurthe 83
Michalik, Tadeusz 159, 162-3
Michejda, Franciszek 59, 61
Michejda, Jan 86
Michelet, Karol Ludwig 56
Mickiewicz, Adam xvi, 56, 140, 192

Index 241

Mickiewicz, Władysław 192, 194
Middle East 88
Middlebury College (Vermont) 197
Milan 67-8
Milanówek 180
Minnedosa xi, 3
Mińsk 139, 141, 143
Mitana, Tadeusz 123, 127-8, 156
Modane 67-8
Modlin 135, 153, 160
Montenegro 204
Montreal 39, 215
Moravia (*see also* Czechoslovakia) 7, 16, 29, 31, 41-2, 52, 59, 70, 95, 111
Morawski, Father 144, 149-50, 153
Morel, E.D. 82
Morrow, Ian D. 198, 199n
Morse, Richard 157
Mościce 224
Mościcki, Michał 85
Moscow 32, 108, 141, 222, 228
Moselle 83
Mott, John R. (*see also* Young Men's Christian Association) 6, 14, 26-8, 46, 83, 86, 104-5, 110, 117, 122-3, 127-8, 136, 143-4, 156, 159, 165-6, 182, 184, 196, 230
Motz, Bronisław 88, 96
Munich, 13n, 222
Monroe, Paul 157
Münster 212
Murray, Gilbert xvii, xviii n
Muslim (*see also* Islam) 14, 89
Mussolini, Benito 222
Mysłowice 208

Nałkowska, Zofia 192
Namier, Sir Lewis (Bernstein-Namierowski) xiii, 72-3
Nancy 66, 83, 85
Napoleon 7, 26, 193

Naramata Christian Leadership Training School xiv, 230
Narutowicz, Gabrial 170n
National Democrats 78
Nazi 56, 106, 181, 204-5, 211n, 222-3, 228
Near East 88, 165
Němcová, Božena 53
Nero 55
New England 23, 119, 159, 197, 214, 217
New Europe, The 77, 218
New Hampshire 119, 197
New Statesman, The 77
New York v, 39, 46, 65, 104, 128, 155, 157, 165, 166, 192, 197, 213, 219
Nicholas I, Emperor of Russia 139
Nicolay, Baron Paul 15, 17
Nicholson, Harold 103-4
Niemen River 140
Niesse River 205
Nihilism 11, 54
Nobel Prize 192
Non-Aggression Pact (1934) xxiii, 208, 223
North Africa 88
North America 229
Norwich 185
Noulens, Joseph 86, 92
Nova Scotia 178n
Nowicki, E. 158
Nowy Targ 121

Oberholzer, E.J. 119, 154, 159, 161-2
Oder River 31, 202
Oderberg [Bohumín] 32, 59, 62, 92, 106
Oderland 199
Odessa 32
Ojców 132, 154, 157

Ołkusz 154
Olsa River 42, 58, 106
One Big Union 108
Oppeln [Opole] 211
Oraczewski, Father 117n, 184n
Orkan, Władysław 159
Orr, William 138, 155, 156, 158
Orthodox 99, 101, 111, 125, 128, 131, 143
Osada 154-6, 164, 166, 170, 180, 185, 187; description 157-8
Oświęcim 135
Ostrava 38, 59, 61, 62, 77, 93
Ottawa 214-15
Oxford ix, xi, xvii, 3, 10, 76, 80, 88, 168, 178, 183, 214, 218, 225-6

Paderewski, Helena 100-1, 116, 192
Paderewski, Jan 74-5, 77, 82, 90, 98, 183, 195
Padua 67
Palacký, František 12
Palestine 225
Palmer, US Attorney-General A.M. 108
Pares, Sir Bernard x, xiii, 214-15, 218-22, 226
Paris xii, 30, 58, 59, 64, 67-8, 72-9, 82-90, 93-4, 96, 98, 102-3, 105, 108, 110, 112, 118, 119, 137, 195, 209, 219
Paris Peace Conference xii-xiii, xvi, xvii, xxiv, 17n, 67n, 74, 79-80, 84-5, 88, 103, 105n, 209
Parkin, George 37, 76
Patek, Stanisław 104
Peacock, Ernest 230
Peking 127
Pennsylvania 198
People's University (Dalki) 129
Peterkiewicz, Jerzy 229

Peters 209
Petlura, Semon 143
Petrazycki, Leon 183
Petrick, Herbert 13
Philadelphia 189
Phildius, Eberhard 9, 13, 16, 23-4, 26, 30, 46, 48, 53, 90-1
Piaskowa Skala 157
Piave River 52, 60, 65
Pietist 48
Piłsudski, Józef xii, xiii, xvi, xx, 63, 74-6, 78-9, 82-4, 88, 90-1, 98, 186n, 195, 207; Rose's opinion of xxi-xxii; interview with 101-3
Pindor, Karol 94
Plato 71
Płock 135, 189
Podoleński, Father 151
Pol, Wincenty 140
Poland (*see also* Poles) xiii, xiv-xv, xviii, xxii, xxiv, 8, 14, 15, 28, 31-3, 40, 45, 47, 52, 56-61, 64, 70, 74-8, 80-5, 88, 91, 96, 101-2, 105, 106, 108-10, 115, 117, 120, 123, 126, 130, 131, 133, 135-8, 150, 153, 154, 156, 158, 166-7, 173, 179, 184, 188-9, 192, 194, 197, 203, 205, 206, 209, 216, 223, 230; anti-semitism 132; army xxiii-xxiv, 59n, 113n, 143, 171; culture xv, 56, 139, 149, 183, 187; description 191; economic conditions xxii, 111-14, 130; history xx, 83, 111-12, 187; international affairs (*see also* Teschen) xii, xx, xxiii, 40, 56, 106, 112, 117, 143, 223, 226; nationalism xv, 132, 224; political organization xii, xvi, xix-xxii, 16, 59, 79, 86, 106, 113, 138, 195, 225, 228; religion 32, 87, 190
Poland 197

Index

Poles (*see also* Poland) 17, 25, 65, 70, 83, 89-90, 92, 94, 103, 111, 175, 200-2, 223; national character x, xvii, xx-xxii, xxv, 16, 95, 113, 137
Polish National Committee 74, 78, 83-5
Polish National Council (Teschen) 58, 59, 61, 94-5
Polish People's Republic 229n
Polish Review 78
Pomerania 164
Popiel, King 191
Porter 7
Portland 144
Positivist 192 n
Poznań xii, 57, 70, 82, 109, 119, 123, 129-30, 133, 149, 194, 202, 223
Poznań University 115
Poznania 55, 118, 149, 195
Pragmatism 10
Přerov 62
Prague xi, xiii, xv, 3-8, 11-13, 15, 17-18, 23, 25, 27, 29-30, 32, 44, 58, 62, 63, 70, 81-2, 87, 89, 93, 103, 105, 117, 122, 209-11, 215, 217, 221, 228
Prinkipo Island 86n, 90
Prinkipo Plan 86
Pripet River 143
Protestant 14, 18, 32, 48, 60, 86, 99-101, 110, 117, 125, 165
Prussia (*see also* Germany) 128, 149, 177, 198, 203, 204, 223-4
Przemysl 27
Puławy 190
Putnam, George Palmer 192

Quebec 118
Queen's University 214

Raczyński, Countess Róza 153, 223
Radhost 41-2

Radość 131
Raffi, A. 218n
Rajewski, Zdzisław 191n
Raphael 102
Red Cross xii, 25, 27, 37, 67, 70, 91, 115, 163, 218
Red Triangle *see* Young Men's Christian Association
Reddaway, W.F. xix
Reformation 188
Reformed Church of Hungary 48
Regedziński 182
Reiter, Marjan 96
Rej, Mikołaj 100
Rembartów 135, 143
Reut-Nicolussi 222
Reymont, Władysław 54, 159, 175, 191-3
Rhine River 50, 211-12
Rhodes Scholarship xi, 178
Rio Grande 214
Robinson, James Harvey xviii
Roche, W.J. 215
Rokossovsky (Rokossowski) Konstantin 228-9
Roman Catholic (*see also* Jesuits, YMCA) xiv, 5, 12, 14-15, 18, 32, 56, 87, 99-101, 111, 125, 127-8, 132, 143, 149, 151-2, 165, 169, 171, 193, 199, 200, 204, 210, 215, 223
Romanov 114
Romantic Movement 56
Rome 4, 144, 151
Romer Eugeniusz 85, 104, 118
Rose, Arthur v, xv, 48n
Rose, Emily Cuthbert [E] xi, 6, 8*passim*
Rose, William John born 1885 xi; died 1968 xi; family 23, 86, 95, 107; university education ix, xi, xiii, xiv, xv, xvii, xviii, xix, 3, 182-8; goes to

Prague xi, 4; trapped in Silesia xi, 25; diplomatic mission xi-xiii, 58, 63-72, 89-90, 93-103, 225; returns to Poland xiii, 117, 141-2, 144, 159-67, 175-82, 184-8; teaches at Dartmouth xiii, 197-8; research in Silesia 198-213; teaches in London xiii-xiv, 217-20; World War II 225-7; returns to Canada xiv, 227-30
- Language proficiency: Czech xi, 53; French 197; German 198; Polish xi, 54, 101, 118, 183, 198
- Opinions on history xvi-xxi, 53, 200
- Publications: 'Behind the Scenes in Silesia' 77, 'The Building of the Social Order' xvii; *Cambridge History of Poland* 223; 'Czech-Polish Understanding: The Teschen Question' 106n; *The Drama of Upper Silesia* xiii, xix, 202, 213, 220; 'Facts for Friends in America' 172; 'The Heart of Poland' 97n; 'In Darkest Europe and the Way Out' 81; 'My Mission from Silesia' xvii; 'National Minorities in Europe' xxii; 'A New Idealism in Central Europe' xvi, 77; 'Old Wine in New Bottles' 197n; 'The New Warsaw' 97n; *Poland* xix; *Poland Old and New* xix, 227; 'Poland's Place in Europe' 225; 'Realism in Polish History' xx-xxi; *Stanisław Konarski* xix, 187-8; 'Turmoil and Confusion in Central Europe Graphically Portrayed' 81n; as translator: *The Desire of All Nations* xv, 51, 108; *From Serfdom to Self-Government* 225; *A Visitor from Poland* 117n
- Social Services (*see also* SCM, YMCA): in Winnipeg xi, xv; in Prague xi, 10-13*passim*; during World War I 25-7, 36-8, 44-7; after World War I 80-8; student relief 110, 114-21
- Speeches: untitled 76; 'Frontier Problems of Central Europe' 211; 'The New Poland' 221n; 'Progress in Poland' 221n; 'The Polish Tradition' 219; 'The Spirit and Work of the Y.M.C.A. in America' 123; 'A Talk on the Polish-German Non-Aggression Treaty of 1934' 221n; 'Y.M.C.A.-America' 194
- Summer travels 19-24, 40-4, 208-9, 211-13
- Teaching ix, xi, xiii-xiv, xviii, xix, 213; of social work 155-6; as examiner 219
Roumania 59, 225-6
Rouse, Ruth 117, 121n, 122
Royal Institute of International Affairs (Chatham House) xiv, 198, 212, 221-6
Rubczyński 124
Russia xxii, 4, 8, 11, 14, 15, 23, 28, 30, 39-40, 55, 70, 74, 78-80, 86, 86n, 88, 90, 98n, 99, 102, 112-16, 123, 128, 131, 138, 145, 154-5, 157, 162, 173, 175-7, 183, 193, 198, 202, 208, 218-19, 224; international affairs xx, 25-9, 113n, 117, 133, 143n, 178, 222-3
Ruszczyc, Ferdynand 140
Ruzomberok 210
Rydel, Lucjan 160
Rydź-Śmigły xxii

SCM *see* Student Christian Movement
Salonika 158
Salzburg 204
Samborski, Michał 211
San Domingo 193

Index 245

San River 27
Sand, George 53
Sandomierz 127, 129-32
Sapieha, Cardinal Adam 151-2
Sarajevo xii, 20, 22, 45, 70, 204
Sarnek, Lieutenant 66-7, 79
Saskatoon 197
Savery, Frank 103
Saxony 176-7
Scandinavia 117
Scharley 207
School of Slavonic Studies (*see also* University of London) v, ix, xiii, xiv, 214, 217-20, 225
Schweitzer, Albert 212-13
Serafinowicz 96
Serbia 20, 29, 46, 81, 102, 218; international affairs 23, 25
Serejski, Marian Henryk xixn
Seton, Walter 27
Seton-Watson, R.W. x, xiv, 76, 78, 214, 218, 220-2, 226
Seym 113
Shotwell, James T. 198, 200, 204-6, 213
Siberia 156, 222
Siedlecki, Michał 85, 119
Siegmund-Schultze, Pastor 131
Sienkiewicz, Henryk x-xi, xvi, 55, 195-6
Sikorski, General Władysław 154
Silesia xi, xiii, xv, xviii, xxiv, 8, 11, 15, 17, 17n, 21-2, 29, 31, 41, 47, 58, 67-70, 74, 81-2, 86, 87, 90, 94, 97, 104, 110, 112, 114, 133, 180, 190-3, 197, 200-9, 211, 214, 223; international affairs xx, 205
Simpson, J.Y. 76
Skelton, O.D. 214
Skłodowska-Curie, Maria x

Skoczów 95
Skrach, Basil 10
Słomka, Jan 225
Slosson, Preston William 108
Slavs (*see also* Central Europe, Eastern Europe) x, 4, 13, 14, 18, 20, 25, 29, 45, 51, 59, 61, 66, 76, 105-6
Slavic Studies ix-xi, xiv, xxiv, 14n, 183, 217-18, 220, 225, 229-30
Slavonic and East European Review 220-1, 227
Slovakia xii, 22, 32, 41, 45, 65-6, 70, 81, 196, 208, 210-11
Słowacki, Juliusz 194
Smith, A.L. 76
Smith, Wilson xviii n
Smoleński, Władysław 183, 187
Smyrna [Izmir] 165, 166n
Snowden 82
Sobieski, Jan 76
Social Christianity 8
Social Gospel xiv-xv
Social Science Research Council (Canada) vi
Social Science Research Council (US) 198, 199n
Sokolnicki, Michał xiii, 84-5, 209
Solarz, Ignacy 158
Sonntagsberg 126
Sosnowiec 135
South Africa 86
South Slav State *see* Yugoslavia
South Tyrol 222
Southeast Europe 12
Southampton 72
Soviet Union *see* Russia
Spain 193, 214
Spett map 82
Split [Spalato] 204
St Andrew's College (Saskatoon) 197

St Clair-Sobell, James 229
St Petersburg 166, 183, 218
St Stanisław 184
Stalin, Joseph 219
Stanisławów 135
Stanstead College 214
Stanisławski, Jan 172
Steed, Henry Wickham x, xiii, 53, 77, 104, 195
Stephen Daye Press 213
Sterczyński, M. 78, 82
Strasbourg 211-12
Stresemann, Gustav 208
Struve, G. 218n
Student Christian Movement [SCM] xi, 3, 6n, 8, 9, 17, 20, 30, 46, 57, 111, 122, 126, 129, 133, 151, 156, 172; Bohemia 13-19ff; Canada 129; France 123, 127; Hungary 19; Poland 47, 124-5, 126, 131, 132, 134; Russia 8, 15; social services xiii, xv, 10, 15, 117, 121-34
Student Christian Movement Press xvi, 108
Styka 88
Subotić, D. 218n
Sudeten Germans 221
Sujkowski 84
Šum, Anton 8
Super, Paul xvii n, 135n, 156, 165, 168, 173-5, 179-80, 182, 226
Sweden 28, 190
Świętochowski, Aleksander 192
Świętochowski, George 82
Świrski, Lieutenant 88, 101
Switzerland 15, 23, 24, 26, 28, 79, 84, 95, 123, 131, 195, 203, 217
Szarota 64
Szczawnica 120
Szczepanowski, Stanisław xvi, 56

Szczurek 59
Szeptycki, Stanisław 139
Szeruda, Jan 47

Tarno-Góry 208-9
Tartar 185
Tatlaw, Tissington 57
Tatra Mountains 21, 41, 131, 154, 191
Taylor, A.S. 138-43, 153, 156, 161, 193
Teschen (Cieszyń) ix, xi, xii, 15, 21, 22, 25-8, 30-6, 40, 46, 47, 110, 123, 124, 155, 195, 205; Teschen question 70, 86, 87, 89, 97-8, 103-6
Teschen, duchy of xii, xv, 8, 31, 59, 61, 65, 76, 89, 95, 97-8, 104, 199
Teschen Commission *see* Allied Commission
Teslar, J.A. 219
Tetmayer, Bronisław 85
Thirty Years War 5
Thugutt, Stanisław 183
Times, The 81
Tiso, Jozef 211
Tissi, Colonel 95
Tokyo 105
Tolstoy, Leo 11
Tomkiewicz, Stanisław 184n
Toronto 178, 229
Toruń [Thorn] 184
Tosio 96
Total Abstinence Society 18
Toynbee, Arnold iv, 225-6
Treaty of Brest-Litovsk 189
Treaty of Versailles 206, 222
Trenčin 196, 210
Trinity College 178
Troppau, duchy of 31
Trotsky, Leon 112, 189
Truxal, Andrew 213

Index 247

Turčansky St Martin 210
Turek, Victor ixn, 81n, 117n
Turgenev, Ivan 54
Turkey 166n
Turks 20, 76n, 140, 204

USSR *see* Russia
Ukrainians xxiii, 14, 40, 143
Ukraine 35, 115, 190
Ujejski, Józef 127-8, 183
Ulrich 38-9
Ulster 138
Union of Christian Youth (*see also* YMCA-Poland) 170
United College *see* Wesley College
United Kingdom (*see also* Britain, England) 218, 222
United States [USA] 9, 25, 61, 63, 69-70, 74, 76-7, 81, 83, 105, 107, 116-7, 126, 136, 151, 156, 159, 160, 167, 181, 190, 196, 202, 227
University of British Columbia v, xiv, 141n, 229-30
University of California x
University of Cracow *see* Jagiellonian University
University (Dalki) *see* People's University
University of Liverpool 218
University of London xiii, xix, 4, 76n, 194, 213-15, 218, 229
University of Manitoba 61
University of Munich 14
University of Poznań 180
University of Toronto vi, 229
University of Warsaw *see* Warsaw University
University of Wilno 130
University of Winnipeg *see* Wesley College

Upper Silesia (*see also* Silesia) 198-9
Ural Mountains 118
Urban, Father 145, 151, 153
Urbanek, Pastor 23
Ustron 42

Vaihinger 10
Vancouver 230
Vatican 28, 145; Letter of November 1920 145-8
Venice 204
Vermont 197
Versailles 202
Victor, Janos 21
Vienna (*see also* Austro-Hungarian empire) xii, 3, 6, 7, 9n, 13-16, 18, 19, 23-6, 28, 30, 32, 35, 39, 41, 44-7, 50, 53, 58-9, 61-4, 66-7, 70-1, 76n, 85, 91-2, 117, 126, 139, 155, 209
Vistula River 42, 111, 113, 117, 127, 143, 184, 189-91, 228, 231
Vltava (Moldau) River 6

Waggoner 141
Wagner, Richard 54
Wambaugh, Sarah 202
Warsaw xii, 32, 35, 61, 63, 69-70, 74, 78-80, 82, 84-91, 94-101, 103, 104, 106, 109-10, 113, 116-20, 122, 123, 127-8, 130-3, 135, 138, 143n, 144, 150-2, 154, 156, 158, 161, 164, 168-70, 172, 175-6, 179-81, 192-5, 202, 205, 215, 219, 223-4, 226, 228
Warsaw University 47, 115, 133, 183-4
Warta River 191
Washington, DC 64
Wawel 96
Weber, Otto 53
Weimar 209

Weintraub, Wiktor 229
Wesley College v, vi, xi, xiv-xv, 3, 61n
Western Allies (*see also* Allies, Entente) xii
Wernigerode 89
White Cross 115
White Russians 86n, 112
Whitehall 224
Whitsuntide 205
Wiadomości 172-3n
Wiktor, Jan 118
Wilder, Robert 8, 13, 15, 26, 45, 91, 122
Wilejka River 140
Williams and Norgate Publishing Company 213
Wilno 119, 132, 135, 139-40, 163-4, 190, 193, 224
Wilno University 115
Winnipeg ix, x, xi, xiii-xv, 3, 48, 95, 107
Winnipeg General Strike 107
Winnipeg Free Press 117
Wilson, J.O. 118
Wilson, Woodrow 52, 58, 60, 67n, 69, 84, 86, 88, 90, 108
Witos, Wincenty 143, 195
Wittenberg 5
Włocławek 135, 189
Wójciechowski, Stanisław 170n
Woodsworth, J.S. xiv-xv, 107, 215
World Student Christian Federation (*see also* SCM) 48, 85
World War I x, xi, xiv, xv, xviii, xix, xxi, xxiii, 3, 13, 23, 36, 66-7, 217
World War II xiv, 105n, 109, 124, 138, 186n, 194, 220, 225-7, 229
Wrocław *see* Breslau
Wrong, Margaret 114n
Wujek 132

YMCA *see* Young Men's Christian Association
YWCA *see* Young Women's Christian Association
Yakobson, S. 218n
Young Men's Christian Association [YMCA] xvii, xxiv, 6n, 21, 193-4, 221, 226; criticism of 143-51; during World War I 67-71, 80-4, 90-3, 101, 105; during Russo-Polish War 139-43, 159-61, 178; in Cracow 122-3, 129, 159-67; in Łódź 175-82; in Warsaw 168-75; World Conference (1925) 174
– Polish Association xiii, 108-11, 115-19, 135-53, 202; constitution 124-5; organization 136-8, 155-6, 169-71; philosophy 151, 169; social services 135-6; training centre (*see* Osada)
Young Women's Christian Association [YWCA] 115, 144
Yugoslavia 64, 204, 218

Zabkowice 135
Zagreb xii, 70
Zakopane 118, 130-1
Zaleski, August 78, 82, 90, 91, 101
Zamość 189
Zdziechowski, Marian 15, 140, 192-3
Żeromski, Stefan 192-3
Zieliński, Tadeusz 183
Zimmern, Alfred 72
Zionism (*see also* Jews) 15
Znaniecki, Florian 156, 202, 207
Żółtowski, Adam 109
Żuk-Skarzewski, Tadeusz 96, 166
Zurich 13n, 91
Zwemer, Samuel M. 89

www.ingramcontent.com/pod-product-compliance
Lightning Source LLC
Chambersburg PA
CBHW071152070526
44584CB00019B/2765